The Vintage Motor Car

The Vintage
Motor Car

CECIL CLUTTON AND JOHN STANFORD

B. T. BATSFORD LTD LONDON

Dedicated to
The Members of the
Vintage Sports-Car
Club

First Published 1954
Fifth Impression 1959
Paperback edition 1961

Revised Edition © *Cecil Clutton and John Stanford, 1961*

PRINTED AND BOUND IN THE NETHERLANDS BY
THE HOOIBERG PRINTING COMPANY, EPE, FOR THE PUBLISHERS
B. T. BATSFORD LTD
4 FITZHARDINGE STREET, PORTMAN SQUARE, LONDON W. I

Preface

THE Vintage Car got its name just twenty years ago.

Appalled at the current trends of automobile design, a small band of enthusiastic people formed a club for real sports cars—by which they meant cars made not later than 1930. They proposed to call themselves the "Veteran" (they were all very young at the time) "Sports-Car Club". But the Veteran Car Club of Great Britain very properly objecting that this would cause confusion, they compromised with the "Vintage Sports-Car Club".

In the course of twenty years, this Club has multiplied exceedingly until it numbers over two thousand members, and the "Vintage Car" has become almost as much a household word, and almost as widely misapplied, as an "old crock"—that deplorable epithet against which the Veteran Car Club wages a valiant but somewhat forlorn battle.

The Vintage Car is reckoned to have been born with the recommencement of motor manufacture after the first world war, so that its history covers a little more than one decade.

The Veteran Car, by the equally arbitrary definition of the Veteran Car Club, means one made not later than 1904. Between the veterans and the vintage were many cars of an unnamed period; and nobody seemed to care for them. Shortly, however, the Vintage Sports-Car Club took them under its wing and, with a fine sense of fitness (and an equally cavalier disregard of historical accuracy), called them the "Edwardians".

So we have the three great eras of motoring history:

    the Veterans up to 1904;

    the Edwardians from 1905 to 1916; and

    the Vintage from 1919 to 1930.

It is with the latter that this book is particularly concerned.

Summer, 1954

                           CECIL CLUTTON
                           JOHN STANFORD

Acknowledgment

THIS book could not have been written without the help of many friends, mostly members of the Vintage Sports-Car Club. They are too numerous to mention by name, but for outstanding help and advice we are indebted to Messrs. A. Jeddere-Fisher, Peter Hampton, W. R. Matthews, and Brian Morgan. In addition we have, of course ransacked the files of *The Autocar*, *The Motor*, and *Motor Sport*. Our indebtedness to certain invaluable reference works is mentioned in the text. Most of all are we beholden to Mr. Anthony Harding, of the Publishers, whose patience, encouragement, and advice have been a tower of strength at all times.

C.C. & J.S.

The Authors and the Publishers are indebted to the following for permission to reproduce the Plates, and the drawings which appear on the pages listed after their names:

A. C. Cars Ltd., page 139; Alvis Ltd., page 133; Austin Motor Co. Ltd., Plate 38; page 115; Editor of *The Autocar*, Plates 24, 25, 28 and 31; Mr. J. Barron and Squad. Ldr. A. C. M. Millar, Plate 44; Lt. Col. J. R. Buckley, Plate 27; Mr. W. J. Brunell, Plates 22 and 57; Character Cars, Plate 15; Conservatoire Nationale des Arts et Métiers, Paris, Plate 49; Daimler-Benz A. G., Plates 3 and 26; pages 21 and 182; Mr. D. Denne, Plate 9; Mr. C. Dunn, Plate 58; Mr. J. Dunscombe, Plate 42; Mr. C. J. Edwards, Plate 16; F. I. A. T. (England) Ltd., page 112; Mr. D. Fitzpatrick, Plate 8; Ford Motor Co. Ltd., Plate 56; page 118; Mr. G. Griffiths, Plates 7, 35, 37 and 40; Mr. C. W. P. Hampton, Plates 45, 51, 54 and 55; Mr. A. S. Heal, Plates 20 and 34; Mr. J. M. Hill, Plate 43; Hooper and Co. (Coachbuilders) Ltd., Plate 47; Mr. F. Hutton-Stott, Plate 50; Mr. D. B. Jocelyn, Plate 14; Lea-Francis Cars Ltd., page 69; Leyland Motors Ltd., Plate 52; Mr. P. A. Mann, Plate 21; Lt. Col. L. S. Michael, O. B. E., Plate 39; Monde et Caméra, Paris, Plate 6; Editor of *The Motor*, Plates 12, 33, 36, 48 and 53; D. Napier and Son Ltd., Plate 46; Mr. R. Norton, Plate 41; Nuffield Organisation, Plates 18 and 19; pages 71, 73 and 128; Mr. G. A. Oliver, Plates 17 and 23; pages 45 and 49; Packard Motor Co., page 187; Radio Times Hulton Picture Library, Plate 10; Renault Ltd., Plate 30; Rolls-Royce Ltd., Plates 1, 4 and 11; Rootes Motors Ltd., Plate 32; page 149; Topical Press Agency Ltd., Plate 2; Mr. D. Thirlby, Plate 13; Vauxhall Motors Ltd., Plate 5; page 156; Mr. R. K. Wright, Plate 29. The quotation from *The Green Hat*, by Michael Arlen, is made by permission of the author and Messrs. William Collins Sons and Co. Ltd.

Contents

List of Illustrations

Between pages 136 and 137

Between pages 184 and 185

The photograph on the cover of this book, showing Mr. Harry Rose's 1928 4½-litre supercharged Bentley, was taken by Mr. J. B. Mason of Fact Photography

1

Antecedents

NEVER mind who invented the motor-car. On the whole, complicated things like motor-cars do not get invented, they are developed, and among the pioneers no single one can be saddled with the responsibility of having invented the motor-car. On the other hand, there is seldom much difficulty in deciding who first made a thing *in practicable shape and proceeded to do so on a commercial scale.* In the case of the motor-car, this was un-questionably Carl Benz.

Benz made his first car in 1885 and it worked, and he went on making basically similar machines for over fifteen years. This is a long run for a model even today, when progress has inevitably slowed down; in the nineteenth century it was astounding. To begin with, it showed the remarkable soundness of Benz's invention; latterly it merely showed his remarkable obstinacy in refusing to admit that it was capable of improvement. He first sold a car (to Emile Roger) in 1887, and this was the be-ginning of the motor industry; in 1888 he had fifty men working under him making motor-cars.

Gottlieb Daimler also made his first car in 1885–6, from which time, unlike the complacent Benz, he constantly improved upon it. But he was certainly after Benz in establishing an industry. As against this, his influence was more far-reaching than that of Benz, whose car was essentially a horseless carriage operated by one of his stationary gas engines, adapted to run on liquid fuel ignited by an electric spark.

Benz's engine operated at 250–300 r.pm., but as early as 1883 Daimler had made an engine running at 900 r.p.m., and in 1889 his third car was fitted with a two-cylinder narrow-V engine. He saw from the first that the future lay with the light, high-speed engine; Benz continued to pin his faith to the slow, heavy, low-efficiency engine of stationary type.

It is therefore strange that Daimler always used the grotesque system of hot-tube ignition,[1] while the conservative Benz always used electric ignition, troublesome as it often then was.

The next step forward was taken by the French firm of Panhard and Levassor, who began making motor-cars in 1890, at first using Daimler's V-twin engine. Their contribution was to fix the component parts of the motor-car in the positions they have continued to occupy ever since. They also standardised the gearbox with sliding pinions, such as is still almost universal in European cars, refined only by the addition of the synchromesh mechanism. Having established this excellent foundation Panhards concentrated for the last decade of the century upon making it reliable, and in this they succeeded to a remarkable extent, especially having regard to the then low level of metallurgical knowledge. The reputation for unreliability possessed by the early cars was largely due to the unmitigated ignorance of their drivers and mechanics.

Motor racing started in 1895 with a race from Paris to Bordeaux and back, a total distance of 732 miles. Panhards came to the line with the new vertical twin Phénix engine, of $1\frac{1}{4}$ litres capacity, giving 4 b.h.p.[2] at 800 r.p.m., with tube ignition, while one experimental machine had a four-cylinder engine. The compression ratio was about 3 to 1. The race was won by Levassor, who drove the entire distance single-handed at an average speed of 15 m.p.h., and this must be accounted one of the very great drives in motoring history. His car (an ordinary two-cylinder) had three speeds giving $5\frac{1}{2}$, $12\frac{1}{2}$, and $18\frac{1}{2}$ m.p.h. respectively at the governed engine speed of 800 r.p.m.

At this time little or nothing was known about carburation, and although the primitive surface carburettor had a throttle it

[1] A hollow metal tube was inserted through the cylinder head in the same position as a sparking plug. It was maintained at red heat by an external blow-lamp. The red-hot element in the cylinder head fired the gas as it was compressed.

[2] B.h.p. stands for "brake horsepower". An engine is connected to a dynamometer, or "brake". The brake is applied until the engine, at full throttle, will just maintain a desired crankshaft speed. The brake has a calibrated dial, which indicates the load being imposed on the engine in terms of horsepower. This is the "brake horsepower" of the engine at that speed.

was practically useless, and it generally served only to stop the engine. The speed of the engines with electric ignition could be controlled over a considerable range by advancing and retarding the spark, but the engine with hot-tube ignition had no such facility and was, in fact, a constant-speed machine controlled by a governor. The driver was, however, provided with a lever which defeated the governor, thus (in the sinister words of the instruction book) "permitting the engine to run to its *terminal velocity*" (1200 r.p.m.). Nevertheless, the need for a means of controlling engine speed was acute, and one of the 1895 Panhards had a float-and-jet carburettor, with which Daimler had also for some time been experimenting.

Veteran tourer: a 1902 Humber

The Paris-Bordeaux race finally signed the death-warrant of the steam car for racing. The petrol cars had shown their overwhelming superiority.

Steam design, though achieving some degree of popularity in the United States, had no influence on petrol practice in the long run, and remains a dead limb on the tree of motoring history. The theoretical advantages and undoubted beauties of a steam car in tractable mood are outweighed in effect by its complexity and unreliability in the hands of the average owner-driver, nor will it stand lack of maintenance in the manner of the petrol car. Although the Stanleys were still producing quite advanced steam cars well into the 1920s, they were scarcely an important part of the contemporary scene.

Thus did Panhards continue to dominate the great town-to-town races of the nineties, always getting the necessary extra speed to keep abreast of competition, yet without jeopardising reliability. Only after the turn of the century did they begin to lose ground, when the mere increase of engine *size* was no longer sufficient, and improvements in engine *design* began to produce greater volumetric efficiency.

Daimler died in 1900 but the firm was carried on by his partner Wilhelm Maybach, who in 1901 made the next great advance in design, which was, in fact, as great a step forward as the Panhard and Levassor had been a decade earlier.

The Panhard had always had a wooden chassis, strengthened where necessary with metal plates; Maybach used a pressed-steel chassis such as we still employ.

The selection of ratios in the Panhard gearbox was effected by a lever moving in a quadrant, so that every gear must be gone through in succession; it was impossible to go direct from top to bottom. Also, there was a neutral at some undefined point between each pair of gears. Those with experience of the quadrant change know that it is a difficult and temperamental device to operate successfully. Maybach used a gate-change such as we still find in cars of high quality.

Maybach's engine was a four-cylinder 35-h.p. unit with low-tension magneto ignition. However, he still did not care to rely on the throttle for controlling engine speed, but incorporated a variable-lift device in his valve gear for this purpose. The mere fact of using mechanically operated inlet valves was in itself revolutionary at a time when the automatic inlet valve was almost universal As a result, Maybach's engine was more silent and flexible than anything then known.

The Panhard was cooled by water circulating through a long coil of piping which was finned to secure improved radiation; it was a cumbersome and unsightly arrangement. Maybach used

14

a honeycomb radiator such as remained current as long as radiators were exposed to the public gaze.

In fact, Maybach had, at one sweep, produced the first modern motor-car.

This remarkable machine had been bespoken by one Emile Jellinek, a wealthy and influential person. Jellinek represented to Maybach that there was considerable sales-resistance in France to the German-sounding Daimler, and accordingly the new car was called, not "Daimler", but "Mercedes", which was the name of Jellinek's daughter. And thereafter all the products of the German Daimler factory continued to be so called.

In the meantime, Benz continued with Teutonic obstinacy to produce his horseless carriage, although no one wanted them very much any more. And if it seems strange that any of these slow and ponderous dogcarts could still be sold at all, it should be remembered that such a simple and reliable car must have had a considerable appeal to the uninstructed private owner of the time; no less than a thousand Benz cars were in use in England in 1901. Not until 1903 could he be persuaded to have them replaced by a more modern design, for which he was not responsible.

Before leaving the Veteran class, mention should be made of the work of the Comte de Dion and M. Bouton, who in the closing years of the century not only saw the merits of the high-speed engine but had the temerity and skill to make and offer for sale motors – admittedly single-cylindered – which would run at the alarming speed of 1800 r.p.m. Contrary to expectation these were completely reliable, and although the firm never officially supported racing in the fanatical manner of their competitors, they were always willing to supply these small engines to other manufacturers for building into light racing cars and tricycles, where they were extremely successful.

The last decade of the old century had seen the search for reliability; the first decade of the new saw the quest for refinement, and the 1901 Mercedes set the pace.

In 1904 Frederick Royce, a Manchester electrical engineer, made his first car and in 1906 (by then in partnership with the Hon. C. S. Rolls) he produced the "Silver Ghost" Rolls-Royce

This car attained a level of silence and refinement which has not been and never can be surpassed, because there is no improving upon perfection. The first "Ghost" had a six-cylinder, 7-litre "square" engine of $4\frac{1}{2}$ in. $\times$ $4\frac{1}{2}$ in. It produced 48 b.h.p. and had a top-gear range of $3\frac{1}{2}$–53 m.p.h. Particularly viewed in the context of its time, this car must have been really astounding for it was by no means as costly as the majority of cars in its class; and it is an extraordinary tribute to its excellence that it continued for nearly twenty years in basically the same form, and for no less than fifteen years it was the only model to be produced by the firm.

The emphasis next shifts to increased efficiency, in the shape of greater power per litre of engine capacity, and the period 1908–14 saw remarkable advances.

Until 1908, improvements in power were fairly meagre, and it is doubtful if any racing machine even approached a specific output of as much as 10 b.h.p. per litre. This was largely due to the maximum weight formula, imposed for the major races, of 1000 kilogrammes (roughly one ton). Under this formula manufacturers apparently found it more rewarding to increase engine size rather than engine efficiency, and they succeeded in racing cars of up to 17 litres capacity within the ton weight, frequently by disastrous economies in chassis design. Probably the outstanding car of the weight formula was the 1905 F.I.A.T., which produced 135 b.h.p. from 16 litres of engine, turning at 1300 r.p.m. These huge machines, capable of 90 m.p.h., must soon have torn themselves to pieces and it is hardly surprising that no specimen is known to have survived. Controlling them, too, must have called for heroic qualities, with their exiguous chassis, high centre of gravity, inflexible engines, negligible brakes, inadequate and unreliable tyres and modest damping arrangements (Mors had first worn shock-absorbers in 1902). It seems likely that the 1000 kg. formula called for greater driving skill than under any subsequent formula until the next weight formula, of 750 kg., was introduced in 1934. Curiously enough, under the latter formula manufacturers again found a large light, relatively low-efficiency engine more rewarding than the quest for high specific output.

After a fuel-consumption formula in 1907 the formula for the 1908 Grand Prix demanded a minimum (instead of a maximum) weight of 1100 kg, and a maximum bore (for four-cylinder engines) of 155 mm. At once the criterion became, not b.h.p. per ton overall weight, but b.h.p. per square inch of piston area, and both stroke and crankshaft speeds were drastically increased. As a result, although power output was generally still only about 10 b.h.p. per litre, power per square inch of piston area exceeded unity for the first time (as a rough guide, the piston area of any engine in square inches is about twice its Treasury Rating). Even so, the Grand Prix machines had little relationship with real life, and two of the three 1908 machines which have survived (the Itala in England, and the winning Mercedes in America) seem so fabulous as to be hardly true. The third, a six-cylinder Austin of 7 litres, can scarcely be regarded as a serious competition car, being a fairly standard 58.6-h.p. production chassis. The team's showing was not particularly brilliant, though the cars seem to have been very reliable, and in a way this rather amateurish approach to the problems of a *grande épreuve* remains typical of British practice even today. It seems that our designers were generally not keen to try their products against the fierce competition of the Continental factories, and surprisingly few firms here actively supported early racing. This was to some extent because timid authorities never permitted racing upon public roads in England, such as was encouraged abroad. The enterprising firm of Napier had been alive to the possibilities from the first, and, in fact, built a team of advanced cars for the 1908 Grand Prix, which were disqualified at the last minute by the alarmed organisers of the meeting because they were fitted with detachable wheels.

It was in a seemingly unlikely sphere that the next great advance in design took place. In 1908 the Royal Automobile Club organised a reliability trial over an extremely stiff course of 2000 miles in England and Scotland, concluding with a 200-mile race at Brooklands. This was won by a Vauxhall. The directors having decided (rather late, as usual) to enter a team for this event, it happened that their chief designer (a man of conservative views) was away ill at the time.

However, his twenty-six-year-old assistant had no qualms in undertaking to design a machine to win the competition and the directors had the good sense to give him a free hand. He quickly made an innocent-looking side-valve monobloc engine which produced the surprising output of 40 b.h.p. from a capacity of only 3 litres (soon improved to no less than 52, equal to 17 b.h.p. per litre). This he did by using the then remarkably high crankshaft speed of 2500 r.p.m. with a stroke of 120 mm.

The designer's name was Laurence Pomeroy, father of a hardly less famous son, and the car was the direct parent of the 30/98 Vauxhall, one of the greatest cars of all time.

Talbots entered a somewhat similar and hardly less successful machine for the 1908 trial, and it may really be said that this historic event, in which other excellent performances were put up by Cadillac, Singer, Ariel, and Rolls-Royce, gave birth to the sports car. Previously, high road speed meant large engine capacity; thereafter, at some expense of smoothness and silence, a keen motorist could go pretty well as fast as he wished with an engine no larger than the most humdrum tourer.

After the 1908 Grand Prix everyone decided that Grand Prix racing was no longer worth the candle and in 1909 there was no race. In 1911 there was a rather desultory *formule libre* affair which was tremendously significant for one reason only. The winner conformed to precedent by being a large car, albeit of distinctly advanced design. It was a F.I.A.T., basically a production model, of 10½ litres capacity, with an overhead camshaft and four (vertical) valves per cylinder. But running it into second place was a mere toy of 1327 c.c., a Bugatti.

This was Ettore Bugatti's first production model in his own right. At one leap the light car had grown from a panting monocylinder to a luxury car in miniature, capable of 60 m.p.h. The impression created by what Charles Faroux called "cette boîte de vitesse lilliputienne" was nothing short of a furore.

Fortunately specimens similar both to the winning F.I.A.T. and the Bugatti (the "type 13" as it came to be catalogued) both survive in England, in excellent order. Two more dissimilar cars could hardly be found. The F.I.A.T. is in direct line of descent from the slightly earlier giants. Chain-driven, and geared to do

60 m.p.h. at 1000 r.p.m., every beat is separately felt. The car can certainly be made to corner very fast indeed, but it must be taken firmly in both hands; if the driver does not show he is master, the car will quickly do so.

What a contrast is the tiny Bugatti.

Both steering and gear lever work with watch-like precision and delicacy; the car is driven with the finger-tips more than with the hands. Double-declutching is unnecessary for changing either up or down. The lever can be sliced from notch to notch without a sound, while the engine runs like a turbine up to about 3000 r.p.m. The 1910 Bugatti type 13 was one of the most – perhaps the most – epoch-making cars of all time. The sports voiturette had arrived overnight, and up to the outbreak of war in 1914 the Bugatti was in a class alone.

There was another *formule libre* race in 1912 which was widely supported. Most manufacturers again doggedly pinned their faith to huge engines; the fastest was the 15-litre four-cylinder Lorraine-Dietrich, of which an example ran for many years at Brooklands and still survives. But it was the final struggle of the giants, for the winning car was a Peugeot of revolutionary design, exactly half the capacity of the Lorraine. Its designer, a Swiss named Ernest Henry, was to dominate racing-car design for almost a decade and his influence was permanent, for he first produced the twin overhead-camshaft layout with inclined valves which has remained the standard pattern for practically all successful racing cars ever since.

By 1914 all makers had followed the lead given by Henry, although, as yet, for racing machines only; it was not until the middle twenties that any production machine was offered to the public with two overhead camshafts.

The 1913–14 Grand Prix and Tourist Trophy machines are among the most attractive ever made and at least half a dozen survive. Power output reached 30 b.h.p. per litre and crankshaft speeds went to 3500 r.p.m., facilitated by the new lightweight steel pistons. This gave piston speeds of 3500 feet per minute. To make the most of such engines the speed must be kept up, and Henry's engines produce very little below 2500 r.p.m., at which they suddenly seem to gather themselves together and start

19

working. This calls for close-ratio gearboxes and a much freer use of the gearbox than had previously been necessary. A low centre of gravity and close attention to weight distribution and damping produced a very high standard of roadholding, while for the 1914 Grand Prix, Peugeots came to the line with front-wheel brakes. Unfortunately they did not stay the course and the race was won convincingly by Mercedes.

Not until the French light-car races of 1910–14 did British cars show their paces abroad to any extent; and these were often constructed by such seemingly unlikely firms as Singer, Arrol-Johnston, and Calthorpe. Even so, these "racers" were as a rule lightened and slightly tuned standard models, and this was, of course, reflected in their modest success. Our prestige was quite suddenly established following the appointment of one of the most famous designers of all time to the Sunbeam Motor Company of Wolverhampton. Louis Coatalen, who had designed cars for William Hillman of Coventry, joined the Sunbeam staff in 1909, and by the excellence of his cars transformed them from a little known and conservative firm to a *grande marque* almost at once. For the next twenty years Sunbeams enjoyed enormous success, being not only in the forefront of racing but also of touring-car design. This double achievement rested on the appreciation of the value of publicity gained by racing for their domestic products, which later bore little relation to the competition models In 1912 a team of basically standard side-valve 12/16 car won 1st, 2nd, and 3rd places in the Coupe de l'Auto race at Dieppe for 3-litre cars, at speeds above sixty miles an hour for nearly a thousand miles. In 1914 Sunbeam won the Tourist Trophy race with a machine which was generally recognised as being virtually a replica of the 1913 racing Peugeot, and this was not the last occasion on which Coatalen was to flatter by imitation.

But the specialised demands of formula racing had been producing machines which were not typical of contemporary practice, although they were to have a great influence on the post-war "Vintage" decade. The fascination of these early competition cars must not obscure the gradual acceptance of the motor-car as part of everyday life, and its extension to a wider and wider public, for whose hands it developed from an eccentric and generally rather messy and profitless hobby into an efficient and reliable means of transport for commercial and pleasure use. Certainly by 1910 it had established itself, and most manufacturers, whether or not they indulged in racing, were producing thoroughly sound touring cars of medium size which could safely be bought by the unskilled, and satisfactorily used for many thousands of miles with little attention. Racing had hastened the development of efficient systems of lubrication and ignition and its demands for haste were reflected in the popularity of detachable wheels, for instance; but by this time it was no longer necessary to race one's products to achieve commercial success. Nor were the family cars of the period as crude or noisy as the complacent motorist of today probably thinks, but refined to a surprising degree and capable, so far as the very poor roads would permit, of a creditable performance.

The excellence of such cars of 1910–14 provided a firm basis for the Vintage years which we are to discuss, and a great many of them went on being produced in improved but essentially similar form until the middle 1920s. In England the side-valve four-cylinder cars of 2 to 3 litres made by Rover, Sunbeam, Talbot, and Wolseley set a very high standard indeed, and were produced in large numbers; and while they were probably not as technically adventurous as their Continental counterparts they are likely to have been better made. This type of car was capable of about 50 m.p.h. upon the open road, and high gear ratios gave

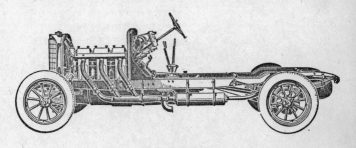

Late Edwardian chassis: the 1914 Mercedes 28/95

a very fair economy of petrol; but the greatest tribute to their soundness is seen in their considerable capacity for development.

We have already seen how Coatalen's 12/16 Sunbeams, perhaps one of the most typical of such designs, maintained their reliability in a foreign race against much more advanced Continental cars; and it was just such an English machine which was the first to achieve one hundred miles in an hour. In February 1913 Percy Lambert drove from the Clement-Talbot factory in Kensington to Brooklands track in a lightened version of the 25-h.p. production Talbot of the period. He then proceeded to drive no less than 103·84 miles in sixty minutes, the first time that this had ever been done, and a very notable feat indeed. Brooklands was the scene of many such record drives, of which the first had been S. F. Edge's definitive opening gesture when he had taken a stripped 60-h.p. Napier chassis round and round for twenty-four hours at an average speed of more than 65 m.p.h. in June 1907; and in subsequent years quite ordinary specimens of English design were to show really phenomenal speeds in races there.

The first fourteen years of the century saw tremendous strides.

The Edwardian era produced the prototypes for all that was to become current practice during the Vintage years. There is no more fascinating chapter in the history of the motor-car.

The V-eight 200-h.p. racing Darracq,
which achieved 122.45 m.p.h. in 1906

2

The Vintage Car

TO some extent the Vintage motor-car was a product of post-war conditions, but its roots go back much further. Up to 1914 the average car had a slow-turning, low-efficiency, side-valve engine, usually held, together with the separate gearbox, in a sub-frame. Braking was on the rear wheels only and shock-absorbers were seldom found on anything but a racing car. Although the emphasis in coachwork lines had moved steadily from the vertical to the horizontal, the straight line from radiator cap to scuttle was a rarity, even in 1914. Luxury or high performance meant a large engine, and an engine of 3 litres capacity or less was considered small. There were a few well-designed light cars built for economy, but the cycle-car, which began to appear in about 1912, was capable of the most squalid mechanical crudity.

But the 2000 Mile Trial of 1908 from which emerged the A-type Vauxhall; the Voiturette class of the 1908 Grand Prix from which came the type 13 Bugatti of 1910; the Coupe de l'Auto races of 1910–13 for 3-litre cars, culminating in the amazing machines of the 1914 Grand Prix; were all part of an undercurrent which was steadily flowing towards the Vintage car. To this, wartime aero-engine technique also contributed notably, and when the production of private cars recommenced in 1919 the stage was set for the dawn of a new era.

The 1914 war had also provided a splendid proving ground for touring cars which were pressed into use at the front. These varied from the tiny Bugatti-designed Bébé Peugeot (which was, improbably enough, used for despatch riding) to the solid 4½-litre 25/30 Crossley, of which many thousands saw active service as staff cars, tenders, or ambulances. Sunbeams and Talbots were also built in large numbers for such purposes, and the performance of the overloaded 40/50 Rolls-Royce armoured chassis in the Near East has become almost a legend. Such searching tests cannot have failed to show up any defects in design; but more important still they must have justified the motor-car's reliability and usefulness to hundreds of people, who were thus likely to spend their gratuity on the purchase of one of the fearsome light cars of the early post-war period.

Before the war, taxation was on a basis of roughly a guinea per 4 horsepower and, in addition, a petrol tax of 3d. per gallon. In 1920 (with effect from January 21st, 1921) followed the iniquitous Motor Taxation Act, which taxed private cars at £1 per horsepower calculated under the R.A.C. formula (which, in round figures, reckoned one horsepower for every two square inches of piston area). This was known as the "Treasury Rating".

All of this encouraged the design of small and efficient engines. The R.A.C. formula has been much blamed for forcing designers to use narrow-bore, long-stroke engines, but although this was to a considerable extent true of the thirties, it is very doubtful if it was a conscious factor in the mind of the Vintage designer. The Coupe de l'Auto races produced such freaks (and successful freaks) as the "Alfonso" Hispano-Suiza of 80 × 180 mm., while the 3-litre Bentley, when it first appeared in 1919, simply copied a popular Coupe de l'Auto cylinder dimension.

Nor is the long-stroke engine without practical advantages. It enables a reasonably high compression ratio to be attained without recourse to combustion chambers of peculiar shape, although, as against this, the small bore makes it difficult to obtain adequate valve areas. Bugatti and Bentley followed the lead of Henry in using four valves per cylinder to obtain the largest valve area possible. On the other hand, small valves secure a brisk gas-flow at moderate revolutions, giving good pulling power at low speeds.

The wartime development of aluminium pistons created entirely new potentialities in engine output. With cast-iron pistons a piston speed of 2000 feet per minute was seldom exceeded. Lightweight steel pistons were used for racing before the war, and in one or two production models, such as the D-type ("Prince Henry") Vauxhall; but they had an exceedingly short life and were entirely superseded by aluminium. With these, 3000 feet per minute was a commonplace and Bentley used as much as 3500 feet per minute – a speed rarely exceeded today. The Grand Prix cars of 1908, with their iron pistons, developed about one b.h.p. per square inch of piston area; the first post-war 30/98 Vauxhall, with its aluminium pistons, but still with side valves, doubled this figure, while the 1921 Grand Prix cars were giving over $2\frac{1}{2}$ h.p. per inch. Indeed, for a time, piston-speed almost ceased to be a limiting factor, and bearings and valve gear became the major problem, few designers caring to exceed 4000 r.p.m. at most.

Aircraft practice had developed the use of aluminium in engines and various manufacturers introduced it extensively in their post-war car engines. Some of them – including Napier – had considerable trouble with porous castings, but undoubtedly the most successful was the six-cylinder A.C. engine, using an aluminium block and wet liners, which was introduced in 1921 and is still in active production today with doubled power output.

In contrast with such advanced designs as A.C., Napier, or Hispano-Suiza, it is a mistake to suppose, on looking at the crude side valve engines of so many cars of the early 1920s, that their constructors were incapable of producing anything better. For many firms had been engaged during the war on the construction of advanced, powerful and reliable aero-engines with quite complex valve gear, usually a shaft-driven single overhead camshaft, and the knowledge thereby gained undoubtedly advanced the power which they could obtain from their touring engines. None the less it comes as a surprise to learn that so pedestrian a *marque* as Swift of Coventry had been busy making Hispano-Suiza aero-engines, and, in this case at least, no good seems to have come of it. Many manufacturers quickly put engines on the market which showed very clearly their aerial antecedents, and some of these, such as the Napier 40/50, Lanchester 40 and Hispano-Suiza, must count as among the most pleasing ever installed into luxury chassis. On the smaller touring chassis, where perhaps makers could not afford to work to such fine limits, valves operated by an overhead camshaft did not become so popular and at least two firms (Wolseley and Arrol-Johnston) withdrew such post-war designs in favour of earlier side valve types. But gradually popular prejudice decreased,

25

or manufacturing skill increased, and by the end of the period overhead valves, even although operated by pushrods, were commonplace. It is rather surprising that the technique of air-cooling was not more generally applied to car manufacture, and although various schemes for air-cooled cars of medium size were put forward it was only in the lightest class that they achieved any success.

The double sleeve-valve had a remarkable innings during the Vintage period. This rather cumbersome device had been invented by an American, C. Y. Knight, and adopted by Daimlers, for reasons of silence, late in 1908. Soon Minerva, Mercedes, and Panhard all took it up, and were followed after the war by Peugeot and Voisin. It is an arrangement which does not lend itself to cheap manufacture, and backed by two of the oldest, and perhaps the most progressive of the youngest, French factories, it was developed in France to a far greater extent than in England. The capacity which it presents for fairly high compressions and a well-shaped combustion chamber was used, especially by Voisin, to produce some extremely attractive and fast sporting cars, and Peugeot sleeve-valve engines gained a great reputation for their economy of fuel in the touring Grand Prix.

A very decided improvement in braking took place during the Vintage period. From the very earliest days of motoring this had been on the rear wheels only, often with a powerful contracting brake on the propeller-shaft; and the inefficiency of these methods of stopping adds enormously to the excitement of driving an Edwardian car in modern traffic. So long as there was little traffic on the roads, and while cruising speeds remained as low as they were from 1910 to 1914, there was little need for effective brakes on all four wheels, and a really well laid out two-brake system, as on a post-war "Silver Ghost" Rolls-Royce, is undoubtedly preferable to a poor four-wheel brake layout. However, the incessant demands of the motorist for speed caused the almost universal adoption of front-wheel brakes in England in 1924–5. For although these had been adopted with enthusiasm by a number of British firms in 1910 they had almost at once been abandoned owing to their unpredictable effects,

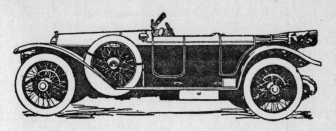

French fast tourer: the 1919 Hotchkiss 18/22, with four-wheel brakes

which notably included applying themselves automatically on
full lock and not freeing until after the accident. This unfortunate
prelude was doubtless remembered even when they had become
a necessity, and formed a useful excuse for the manufacturer
whose cars were not equipped with them and who could therefore safely denounce them as dangerous. The French manufacturer, on the other hand, was less inhibited by early failure
and could in fact point to the respectable performance of front-
braked Peugeot and Delage racing cars which had given a good
account of themselves before the war. It is also a fact that
French cars from quite early days have been designed to be
driven as hard as possible without falling apart; so that even if a
medium sized French family car of the early twenties had a
maximum of only 45 m.p.h. it was absolutely certain that it
could be driven at this speed indefinitely. Although its English
counterpart is likely to have had a higher maximum, it was
probably happier at 35 m.p.h. Allowing a certain measure of
progress in thirty years, this remains just as true today. It is
therefore not surprising that front brakes were adopted much
earlier abroad, so that by 1922 a rear-braked French car outside
the utility class was rather the exception. The lead in the luxury
class had been taken by the post-war Hispano-Suiza shown at
the 1919 Paris Salon, with its powerful servo brakes, and following
such an illustrious example few makes could afford not to fit
them from then on. Certain of our own makers left this adoption
dangerously late, and they were not standard on all Rolls-Royce
until 1925. Sunbeam, probably as a result of their racing experi-

ence, fitted them on all but their smallest models in 1923, and it is a great tribute to the prescience of the late Lord Austin that they appeared from the first on the Austin Seven, even though their small size rendered their benefit more apparent than real. Perhaps he, like Bugatti, really always intended his cars to go rather than to stop.

Electrical equipment first came into general use in the Vintage period. Cadillac had marketed an electric starter as early as 1912, and electric lighting and starting was found on the majority of American cars by 1916. In Europe, however, even electric lighting remained an "optional extra" until the war, and starters were almost unknown.

The typical Edwardian tourer, with its very flat power curve, called for very little use of the gearbox. The gearbox was for climbing hills; prior to 1914 probably very few drivers ever thought of using it for accelerative purposes. Accordingly there was little need for close ratios, and in the average four-speed box the relationship of each pair of gears was as $1\frac{1}{2}$ to 1. Three-speed boxes naturally had much wider ratios; there is no satisfactory way of spacing the ratios when there are only three of them. Changing down on an Edwardian car is generally the height of simplicity; the heavy flywheel prevents the engine from speeding up unduly quickly, and the whole double declutching operation can be carried out quite leisurely with the throttle held fully open, from start to finish. It is doubtful when double-declutching became fashionable; right up to 1914 writers were still talking about "slipping the clutch and sliding the gears through". Double-declutching is actually possible with a quadrant change; but silent change of speed on a quadrant is always a matter for self congratulation (assuming the passengers are so unresponsive as not to comment upon the achievement). But to old-time drivers it seems that such tricks were regarded as slightly decadent.

As against this ancient tradition of widely spaced ratios, the type 13 Bugatti had ratios as beautifully spaced as any modern sports car could covet, and the inflexible engines of Henry, with their narrow effective power-band, also called for very close ratios.

All this was reflected in the more advanced early Vintage sports cars, such as the Brescia Bugatti and 3-litre Bentley, and the new generation of drivers took the new technique of driving in their stride. As long as the gearbox remained a separate unit, so that the gear lever grew vertically out of the floor, gear-changing remained a pleasure. As soon as the box got joined up with the engine, and the gear lever presented itself to the driver at an angle varying from 45 degrees to the nearly horizontal, most of the fun went out of it. It is natural to the human arm to push and pull, but lifting from the shoulder is an unnatural and uncomfortable operation. In a Bentley or Frazer-Nash the hand drops naturally on to the stiff vertical lever, and with complete control over what he is doing the driver effects a pleasurably perfect gear-change. In his M- or D-type M.G. he places his hand, palm upwards, under the knob on the end of a long piece of bent wire, to which he imparts a convulsive twitch. Sometimes he lands in neutral, but he is as likely to hole out in one into the next gear with a nasty crunch or (in the words of one Edwardian author) "prolonged side-grubbing of the teeth". The same difficulty is not unknown with modern steering-column gear levers. If the late Vintage motorist was so (relatively) fortunate as to possess an early Riley 9, he found, indeed, a nicely made, rigid lever, albeit at an angle of 45 degrees, which merely pinched his fingers between it and the dash. Later, M.G. largely overcame this deficiency by a remote control lever to their unit-construction gearbox, and whatever other shortcomings the J2 Midget may have had, the use of its stiff, stubby gear lever was always a pleasure.

The steering apparatus is another great merit of the better sorts of Vintage and Edwardian car, in which it is rivalled by very few modern makers. The steering may, in some, be rather heavy, but this is more than offset by its positive action. The steering box nearly always comprised a worm and wheel, or rack and pinion. If properly made, even thirty years of hard use may produce no more than 5 or 10 degrees of play at the steering wheel – in a Frazer-Nash or Bugatti usually none at all. The action is completely positive; the driver can feel the front wheels change direction, and he can tell at all times what sort of grip they have got on the road surface. On the average Edwardian or early Vintage sports car, one revolution of the steering wheel suffices to turn the road wheels from lock to lock, so that the driver can use the full steering range to control a skid, without removing his hands from the wheel. In later or luxury Vintage cars as many as three complete turns of the steering wheel may be needed to go from one lock to the other, but even this is sufficient for control in most circumstances, especially with really positive gearing.

Most Vintage steering gears allow a certain amount of road shock to reach the steering wheel; that is to say, the gearing is to some extent reversible. With such Continental cars as Lancia and Alfa Romeo, the play-back is so considerable that the steering wheel constantly flicks to and fro and must not be tightly held. Even this, however, is considered by the connoisseur to be a cheap price to pay for sensitive, positive action.

What, then, has happened to make the steering gear of most modern cars such unspeakable anathema to the connoisseur?

It is spongy in feel and indefinite in action.

It is utterly insensitive.

It is grotesquely low-geared.

Even assuming it is free from play when new (which is by no means always the case, as can be proved by a visit to the Earls Court Motor Show) it rapidly develops an unsafe amount of backlash; often as much as 30 degrees.

There are several reasons for this sad state of affairs.

When beaded-edged tyres gave way to low-pressure tyres of larger section they made the steering wheel disagreeably heavy to turn when travelling at low speeds. Finger-light steering was found to be a selling point and the cheapest way of attaining it was to lower the steering ratio, until 4½ or 5 turns of the steering wheel is now usual in American cars. In such a car it is impossible to correct a skid.

The spongy "feel" is partly a direct result of low gearing but it is also attributable to general whippiness, and to the large amount of indiarubber introduced into steering joints for the purpose of masking the geometrical errors which are inherent in many independent suspension systems. The worm-and-wheel

30

steering box is expensive to make and it has generally been supplanted by a variety of cheaper proprietary devices. It is difficult to allocate the blame between them and the bad geometry, but it is noteworthy that such modern cars as still employ worm and wheel, or rack and pinion steering are comparable to the best Vintage cars. Possibly these are the only makes whose steering is sufficiently well laid out geometrically to permit the use of these rewarding but unforgiving systems.

As steering became lower geared so also did it become increasingly irreversible, and in a way this was just as well, because the geometrical imperfections of so many independent suspensions would otherwise produce so much "fight" at the steering wheel as to be intolerable. Designers made a virtue of necessity by claiming that they had eliminated road-shock. But when one reads that "the steering is completely free from road shocks" this really means that "the steering is completely dead".

The indefinite action is due to all the flexible joints, which have to be wound up before much steering-wheel movement reaches the road wheels. It is this which makes many modern steering gears feel like stirring a bowl of treacle.

A famous motoring journalist once said that every designer should be forced to drive a Bugatti once a year so that he should be reminded just how good steering can be, and it does indeed seem that a fitting sense of shame is at present provoking a general improvement.

In the Edwardian era engines and gearboxes were generally carried in a sub-frame which had the merits that it insulated the passengers from engine vibration and the engine from being twisted by the very flexible chassis of those times.

Conversely, the chassis was thereby denied any bracing from the radiator to behind the gearbox, where the sub-frame terminated; and this was not conducive to good road-holding. A car with a subframe is, in fact, no better braced than one with a flexibly mounted engine. This was not a very serious disadvantage so long as unsprung weight remained low, but when brakes became heavier, and attached themselves to the front as well as the back wheels, and wheels became heavier with the advent of large-section tyres, the situation was no longer a happy one.

At least from the time of the 1908 Grand Prix, some designers had faced up to the fact that really good road-holding can only be achieved if the front half of the chassis is thoroughly rigid, and this can only be secured by a rigid four- or six-point engine mounting. Bugatti thorughly understood this and it is the main reason for the fine road-holding abilities of most of his products.

In modern design means have been found of making the chassis extremely rigid without assistance from the engine, but this desirable state of affairs had not been attained in the Vintage decade, throughout which designers fought a steadily losing battle against ever-increasing unsprung weight. To keep the movement of a heavy axle within manageable limits, and to resist the torque of ever-improving brakes, road springs became progressively shorter and stiffer, and shock-absorbers became more and more unyielding. This was not so noticeable in large cars, but in smaller ones, especially as they became capable of speeds in the neighbourhood of 80 m.p.h., the high ratio of unsprung to sprung weight reached such alarming proportions that the unsprung tail had a distinct tendency to wag the dog.

In the end this was a main factor contributing to the death of the Vintage tradition, but it did not become a mortal ill as long as the weight was concentrated as far as possible towards the middle of the car. But when the sales demand for increased passenger space on reduced wheelbases pushed the engine further and further forward, with counteracting weight-concentration at the back-end, so much dead weight immediately above the axles produced an impossible state of affairs and in the early thirties few small cars were even moderately safe.

Citroën and B.M.W. showed the way to circumvent these difficulties as early as 1934, but it is only twenty years later that a general improvement in chassis design is becoming manifest. In the meantime this concentration of weight at the two ends has turned the modern car into a sort of dumb-bell and entirely altered its handling characteristics. So long as weight was concentrated in the middle of the car its moment of polar inertia remained low; that is to say, it readily changed direction or, put another way, responded quickly to the steering. The modern car has a high moment of polar inertia and answers reluctantly to the steering (another contributory factor to its apparent sluggishness), while once it has started a movement it is reluctant to give it up. It therefore becomes a matter of importance whether a modern car over- or under-steers. A car which under-steers tends to go straight on at a corner and a car which over-steers tends to go round corners on the straights, both of which can become a source of embarrassment. Cars with an excess of weight at the front end usually under-steer and vice versa.

In the Vintage era nothing was heard about over- and under-steer, and indeed, so nicely balanced is a good Vintage car that it is often quite difficult to decide which it does. In any case, so lively is its cornering behaviour that in the course of a corner it may change from one to the other, but always remaining so thoroughly under control as not to matter. Vintage cars have, in fact, a marked tendency to change from under- to over-steer as a corner winds up This is because the front springs are placed fairly close together (to allow for the steering movement of the wheels) and the back springs are as far apart as possible (to prevent the car from rolling on corners). As a result, on a corner there is a greater transference of weight from the inside to the outside wheel at the back than at the front, with the result that when the degree of weight-transference reaches a certain point the back-end will break away. In rather narrow cars with tall saloon bodies this "roll over-steer" tendency can become unmanageable. On the other hand, in the case of racing cars, where the centre of gravity is low and there is little roll-tendency to be kept in check, designers generally tended to bring the back springs almost as close together as the front, with resulting equality of weight-transference. This, coupled with a low moment of polar inertia, resulted in cornering characteristics which cannot be improved upon, provided the road surface is smooth. On a rough surface a Vintage car will tend to bounce its way off the road, and the scientifically independently sprung car will have an advantage.

Increasing overall weight was another menace which the Vintage car had to withstand – and failed. Heavier brakes and axles called for heavier chassis; electrical equipment increased in complexity and weight; coachwork became wider, more luxurious, more rigid, heavier. To counteract all this engines were called upon to produce more and more power. In the process they became more obtrusive and less flexible, so that by 1930 the stage was set for the flexible engine mountings and lowering of gear ratios which brought design to that pit of beastliness in the middle thirties out of which it is still only laboriously climbing.

At its height the Vintage car was a superb achievement. In its later manifestations, although the sharp edge of creative enthusiasm had departed from design and the war against weight was reaching a crisis, it remained a sound, controllable working proposition, a source of pride, and a pleasure to drive. Not until after 1930 did the salesman oust the designer as the ruling factor in motor manufacture.

What follows is no exhaustive analysis of all Vintage cars, but only of those which achieved greatness, or notably influenced the course of history.

3

Sports Cars

NO ONE has satisfactorily defined a sports car, but it is seldom difficult to decide whether or not any particular vehicle is a sports car.

At no time have the tastes of the sporting motorist been catered for so widely as in the Vintage decade. Up to 1914 motoring was an expensive business at any time; fast motoring was beyond the reach of all but a very few. The very high cost and short life of tyres alone made it prohibitive.

The financial depression of the early thirties, which killed the Vintage tradition of design, disposed of the sports car even more conclusively. Frazer-Nash and Aston Martin continued in modest production in this country, and Bugatti and Alfa Romeo abroad. In the later thirties the type 328 B.M.W. became all-triumphant, and there were a few others. But the sporting motorist of modest means and discriminating taste was pretty well forced into the second-hand Vintage market – not that this was much of a hardship in that depressing decade; and it was for him that the Vintage Sports-Car Club was founded in the autumn of 1934.

After the Second World War fast motoring again became the monopoly of the very rich, and even Vintage sports cars commanded astronomical prices despite their already considerable age. Now, at last, the ever-growing enthusiasm for motoring is once more making it economic to produce real sports cars within the reach of the moderately well-off.

But in the 1920s the enthusiastic motorist had a very wide choice indeed: a choice of size and price, and of types to suit every shade of mechanical temperament. As in the latest post-war era, this happy state of affairs did not follow immediately upon the cessation of hostilities. It was not until about 1924 that the Vintage sports car entered upon its heyday.

Undoubtedly the car which set the standard for the Vintage

decade was the 37·2-h.p. Hispano-Suiza which appeared in 1919 with an overhead-camshaft engine and powerful four-wheel brakes, operated by a mechanical servo engine. The performance and appearance alike were something quite new, and the car quickly attained that almost legendary reputation which it still enjoys. With its 6½ (later 8) litre engine the Hispano-Suiza belongs more to the luxury class, where it will be more fully considered; but it set up a worthy target for the sports car to aim at.

Hardly less legendary is the Vauxhall "Velox", more affectionately known as the "30/98". Constructed very rapidly indeed to capture the Shelsley Walsh hill-climb record in 1913, which it did most conclusively in the hands of J. Higginson, it was essentially a 4-litre, D-type, "Prince Henry" Vauxhall distended to 4½ litres capacity. Pomeroy redesigned it with better brakes and electrical equipment and it was put into production during 1919. In production form and full touring trim it was capable of 85 m.p.h. and thus even faster than the Hispano-Suiza; stripped for racing, every car was guaranteed to be capable of 100 m.p.h. This, moreover, it achieved on a side-valve engine with a standard compression ratio of 5 to 1, and so flexible that it would accelerate briskly in top gear from less than 6 or 7 m.p.h. Sleek and tense in appearance, the 30/98 did not carry an ounce of superfluous metal; it is immensely handsome. Yet it remained essentially an Edwardian car, the great link between the Edwardian and Vintage decades, nor was it ever listed as a sports car. The Vauxhall "Velox" was in a class by itself, immortal. To have revived the name for another model in recent times was hardly in good taste.

If the Hispano-Suiza set the standard for Vintage design, the 30/98, or "Velox", set the pace for Vintage performance, and it was a long time before anything could be bought that was able to live with it. Its sole and grave shortcoming lay in its characteristically Edwardian brakes, and even when it achieved front-wheel brakes, in 1923, they were of a decidedly tentative nature.

People are much inclined to wordy arguments as to the respective merits of the 30/98 and the 4½-litre Bentley; in doing so they seem to forget that when the first "4½" was sold, the 30/98 was already on the verge of going out of production.

In the meantime two other makes in all ways poles apart were establishing themselves as the prototypes of the true Vintage sports car, although neither of them could rival the performance of the 30/98. They were the 3-litre Bentley and the "16-valve" type 13 Bugatti. The Bugatti had actually been put on the market in 1914; the first Bentley did not run until 1919, and entered into limited production two or three years later.

The Bugatti was pre-eminent as the super-sports car of the early twenties, but it really only maintained the position which the 8-valve type 13 had made for itself in 1910. Prior to 1924 few people regarded the 1½-litre car as a serious means of transport, let alone high performance, although remarkable speeds were attained by very ordinary side-valve units in extremely sketchy chassis with the most exiguous coachwork. Among these, Bugatti stood alone with his temperamental, high-efficiency, overhead-camshaft, 16-valve engine. Efficiency and supreme road-holding were the qualities which Bugatti sought to the exclusion of all else; and he was a man absolutely incapable of compromise. In 1912 Bugatti had experimented with a straight-eight by the homely expedient of joining two type 13 engines end to end, and in 1919 he showed a 3-litre straight-eight at the Paris Salon, of which no more was subsequently heard, and not even its type number is known. However, in 1923 he produced the first small multi cylinder sports car in the shape of his 2-litre straight-eight, type 30. It was, as it happened, a fairly bad car, but it has its place in history as a pioneer effort and it was followed by other straight-eights of complete excellence. During the second half of the Vintage decade, Bugatti enjoyed the same pre-eminence with his eight-cylinder cars as he had in the first half with his 1½-litre four-cylinder cars.

In a way, however, the 3-litre Bentley was even more significant in that it was the first car available to the public which incorporated most of the features of the Henry school of racing design which dominated the years 1912–14. In point of fact, the Bentley had more in common with the 1914 Grand Prix Mercedes than with the Henry technique. One of these Mercedes racing cars was in this country at the outbreak of war and it is by no means unlikely that W. O. Bentley had an opportunity of examining it. With its plain-bearing crankshaft and single overhead camshaft (operating four valves per cylinder) the Mercedes was certainly much better adapted for general consumption than the noisy, oil-throwing, ball-bearing Henry engine with its precarious and complicated system of lubrication.

Although the 3-litre Bentley is now looked upon as quite a large car, it was thought of in 1920 as the smallest sort of machine from which real performance could be obtained in conjunction with tolerably comfortable four-seater coachwork. Thus, although no 3-litre Bentley could live with a 30/98, it nevertheless represented a very real advance towards the typical Vintage sports car, with its well designed electrical equipment, high-speed, high-efficiency engine, and close-ratio gearbox, which had to be used to the full to extract from the engine the best performance of which the car was capable. Bentley only claimed a 75 m.p.h. maximum for his 3-litre, but a sustained cruising speed of 65 m.p.h. from a 3-litre production car in 1920 was an entirely novel proposition. Long mileages between overhauls and low petrol consumption (30 m.p.g. at 30 m.p.h.) were other features justly claimed for the Bentley, which did so much to put England on the map by its Le Mans successes and thus greatly enhanced the prestige of English cars on the Continent.

In 1923 Alvis produced the first "12/50", of which innumerable variants remained in production for the next eight years. In this car something approaching Brescia Bugatti standards of performance were made available in a 1½-litre car, in conjuction with Bentley standards of reliability and comfort. Nor is there much to choose in performance between the 3-litre Bentley and a 12/50 Alvis. The achievement was therefore notable and it met with instant and widespread popularity.

Although the 12/50 Alvis has never attracted the fanatical loyalties of the Bugatti, its great combination of virtues endeared it to its owners, so that its survival-rate among Vintage cars must be among the highest.

From about 1922 a wide variety of tiny French sporting cars

became available on the British market, and these little Amilcars, Salmsons, and Senechals were very much a part of the contemporary scene, being cheap to buy and with a fairly lively performance. Although called by different names, they were virtually identical to the naked eye, and prolonged application is necessary to distinguish, say, a Lombard from a B.N.C. They mostly had 1100-c.c., overhead valve engines (but the popular Amilcar was side-valve) set in the most improbably frail chassis, negligible brakes, and quarter-elliptic suspension; all were capable of 55–60 m.p.h. on a long straight road, while their very low weight gave them quite smart acceleration. Their coachwork was distinctly scanty, consisting of a staggered two-seater body shell with a pointed tail, and comfort was never one of their virtues. The tentative nature of the early examples gradually declined until they became quite fast and even fairly roadworthy little cars, some of them, such as the late Salmsons, having really well-made and potent twin overhead-camshaft engines. But, in general, they are the ephemerals of the Vintage period and it is too much to expect consistent performance from them after nearly thirty years of hard use. In their day, though, they provided tolerably rapid motoring at a lower cost than almost anything else on four wheels, as did the Singers and M.G.s of the next decade, and remain a most amusing memory.

Most stark of all was the G.N.

The cycle-car fashion, which started in about 1912 and survived into the early twenties, produced a crop of mechanical improbabilities which testified more to the optimism than to the engineering abilities of their creators. Among them, the G.N. alone has stood the test of time and joined the immortals. It had a V-twin, air-cooled engine and a separate chain for each gear, engaged by dog clutches.

Although it was designed as a utility car, the sporting propensities of its makers, H. R. Godfrey and A. Frazer-Nash, soon led them to seek high performance, which they did to such effect that the G.N. became a serious rival to the Brescia Bugatti as the pre-eminent sprint car of the early twenties, especially when handled by Frazer-Nash himself. The production "Vitesse" made high performance available to the ultra-enthusiast. In

1914 it sold for £155 and had a guaranteed maximum of 62 m.p.h.

When the G.N. firm stopped manufacture in 1924, it was supplanted by the Frazer-Nash, although Frazer-Nash himself did not long retain his interest and sold out to the Aldington Brothers, in whose hands the firm still prospers. The basic principle of the G.N. transmission remained in active production up to 1935 in these cars and was made to special order until the outbreak of war. At least one historic G.N. (the "Spider") remains in active and successful sprint use today.

During the second half of the Vintage decade the Frazer-Nash was one of the most popular and successful sports cars. Powered at first by the side-valve Anzani engine, it achieved a brisk performance (although not a high maximum) by very low weight and excellent handling quatilies, while its solid back axle made it almost unbeatable in reliability trials. Moreover, the extreme simplicity of both engine and transmission made it a most suitable machine for the amateur who did his own maintenance with minimum resources and equipment. Towards the end of the twenties came the more powerful push-rod Meadows engine, four speeds instead of three, and an overall weight soon reaching 15 cwt., despite which a maximum of over 85 m.p.h. was attained by the fastest production models. The "chain-gang" had an enthusiasm equalled only by their rivals the Bugattisti, and the Frazer-Nash section of the Vintage Sports-Car Club keeps that tradition alive today.

The Frazer-Nash transmission is most attractive to handle, affording gear changes as instantaneous as a motor-cycle and, of course, each gear is completely silent. Moreover, by a simple change of sprocket sizes, an owner could alter his ratios to suit his individual whim or any particular course.

Having traced the pioneer basic of types Vintage sports car in diminishing order of size – the 30/98, 3-litre Bentley, 12/50 Alvis, Brescia Bugatti, Frazer-Nash, and G.N., there were latecomers which had a great effect: the 3-litre Sunbeam, introduced in 1925, the 4½-litre Bentley in 1927, and the type 43 Bugatti in the same year. The six-cylinder, 3-litre Sunbeam was the first serious production car to be sold with the twin overhead camshafts pioneered by Henry. Although it was never given as good a chassis as it deserved, nor was it seriously raced, the Sunbeam could always see off a 3-litre Bentley (as indeed it should, being introduced a good five years later) and coupled a 90 m.p.h. maximum with characteristic Sunbeam mechanical refinement.

The 3-litre Bentley had always been rather difficult to sell in competition with the 30/98, despite its superior design, and the 4½-litre car provided more body-space and more performance with greater mechanical refinement and flexibility. Although, to the 30/98 addict, the Bentley seems rather a "lump", its success is undeniable and a very large number survive in regular use, providing the backbone of the Bentley Drivers Club. Moreover, while a 30/98 is generally spoilt by seeking increased performance a "4½" reacts most favourably to tuning and modification. The 30/98 is a top-gear car and its fairly wide-ratio gearbox is very little use above 50 m.p.h. To make the most of a 4½ the gears must be used freely, although not to the same extent as on a 3-litre. In fact, the 30/98 is essentially a very fast Edwardian touring car; the 4½ a true Vintage sports car. It is therefore not at all remarkable that the 4½ generally beats the 30/98 in current Vintage competition; the remarkable thing is that the archaic 30/98 ever could compete on level terms, and it sometimes still does so with success.

The joint authors have no hesitation in expressing their preference for the 30/98, which does not mean that they necessarily think it is the better car. Not all good cars are nice. But whichever is preferred, a large, high-geared, four-cylinder engine has an appeal quite its own. Such cars, with long loping stride, put up surprisingly high average speeds without any apparent effort by the driver. The multicylinder, high-speed engine may be potentially faster, but because of its fussiness it tends not to be driven so hard, nor to last so well.

Concurrent with the introduction of the 4½ came the type 43 Bugatti, which for the first time made an easy 100 m.p.h. available to the general public. Its 2·3-litre, straight-eight, overhead-camshaft, roller-bearing, supercharged engine was closely related to the type 35B, perhaps the most successful racing car of all time. It was the first production Bugatti available with powerful brakes and its Grand Prix type chassis gave it Bugatti cornering and steering at its best. The model was essentially reliable and its only serious drawback was a slow gearbox, which is a strange failing in a Bugatti. Instantaneous upward and downward changes, with a bare easing of the clutch, are the rule with most Bugatti types. Also in 1927 came the type 44, plain-bearing 3-litre, great coupling flexibility and considerable silence with an 80 m.p.h. maximum. Were it not that this model has had considerable competition success it would more properly be considered as a touring car, and it often carried saloon coachwork. It is, perhaps, the best plain-bearing model Bugatti ever made and was immensely durable and reliable.

Alfa Romeo made little impression in the Vintage years, nor did the Continent in general produce the variety of makes and types of sports car available in England. In Germany, Mercedes produced a series of thunderous supercharged six-cylinders, the 33/180, 36/220, and 38/250, which have always had a following peculiarly their own.

But Bentley and Bugatti represent the extreme opposites of motoring; they appeal to people of entirely opposite temperament and arouse equally fierce partisanship in defending their great respective merits. It is such widely differing styles which make the Vintage sports car such a fascinating study. They continue to attract many discriminating and wealthy enthusiasts even when the majority of Vintage sports cars are, after twenty-five or thirty-five years, outpaced by the latest models.

ALFA ROMEO

The Alfa Romeo firm was founded shortly before the 1914 war. Its first production of sporting quality was the RLSS 22/90, produced in 1924, which was a development of the touring RLT 21/70, and had nothing to do with the current Grand Prix car. The engine was a six-cylinder, 76 × 110 mm., having a capacity of 3 litres. The overhead valves were pushrod-operated and safe maximum speed was 3500 r.p.m. This makes it extremely difficult to believe that the output of power even distantly approached the 90 horsepower indicated by the name. The normal maximum was about 80 m.p.h., although 90 was claimed.

Like several Continental cars, the 22/90 was spoilt for English use by gear ratios which seem to have been plotted on the assumption that you were always either sweeping along a straight, unobstructed highway at terminal velocity, or clawing your way up an Alp. Accordingly, top was so high that peak revs could never be obtained on it, and the other gears were all so low as to be of little use for accelerative purposes. The actual ratios were 3·75, 6·85, 9·8, and 13·2 to 1, which gave a theoretical 90 m.p.h. in top and an actual 50 in third. For English roads, therefore, the considerable potential performance could never be fully realised, and the engine had nothing like the slogging power of, say, a 30/98 Vauxhall. The brakes were of exceedingly ingenious layout and, as often happens in brake layout, the ingenuity resulted in so much lost motion that it was almost impossible to make them work. A complicated compensation system allegedly operated the brakes via short lengths of chain and cable sprouting somewhat unexpectedly out of the tops of the king-pins. The steering, however, as on all Italian cars, was excellent.

The 22/90 continued in production until 1929, when it was replaced by the 17/95. This splendid car had a capacity of 1750 c.c. and was an enlarged edition of a basically similar 1½-litre produced in 1927. This, in turn, showed evident signs of having drawn its inspiration from the successful 1924 Grand Prix "P.2", which was a twin overhead camshaft straight-eight. The 1½-litre had a six-cylinder engine and was offered blown or unblown, with one or two overhead camshafts. The model, while satisfactory, was not a great success, and in 1929 was enlarged to 65 × 88 mm., giving a capacity of 1750 c.c. with two overhead camshafts. This, too, was available either blown or unblown. In either case it was an immensely successful and reliable car, and in supercharged form had a maximum over 90 m.p.h.; later models with open coachwork could reach 100 m.p.h. With a permitted maximum of 4400 r.p.m. the short stroke of 88 mm. ensured so moderate a piston speed that the car could be driven to capacity with no ill effects, and even with the lowest available axle ratio of 4 to 1, the maximum was 90 m.p.h. The engine was so smooth and relatively silent that saloon coachwork was quite acceptable, and was frequently fitted. Unlike the 22/90, the 17/95 had a gearbox with splendidly chosen ratios which were a delight to use; the steering and cornering were first-rate (although the steering was so light that it needed knowing) and the brakes were powerfully effective.

The 17/95 Alfa Romeo is certainly one of the finest products of the late twenties. In 1930 a team of these cars took the first three places in the Tourist Trophy race.

ALVIS

The Alvis Car and Engineering Co. was formed in 1919 by T. G. John, who had previously been chief engineer of Siddeley-Deasy, to market a light car of conventional design but very much better performance than usual. (The name had been invented by another founder of the company, G. P. H. de Freville, as a trademark for a special sort of aluminium piston which he had designed). In the early twenties many manufactures were producing special sporting versions of their 1½-litre side-valve cars, and these little Calthorpes, Singers, and Hillmans, although only of indifferent performance, represented something quite new on the motoring scene. It was also soon obvious that the 10/30 Alvis, although costly, was quite the best of them for appearance and speed; and this design continued to be developed as a first-rate sports car until shortly after the end of our period. This first Alvis had an outwardly ordinary long-stroke side-valve engine of 65 × 110 mm., giving 30 b.h.p., a four-speed gearbox of close ratios, and was capable of about 60 m.p.h. It remained in production until 1923. In all about two hundred side-valve cars were made.

By 1922 nearly twenty Alvis's were leaving the works each week; and in this year the bore of the 10/30 was enlarged to 68 mm. and the engine made to give 40 b.h.p.; this appeared as the 11/40 sporting model, which in turn became the 12/40 later in the same year. Pushrod overhead valves in a detachable head were added in 1923 and the Alvis 12/50 was born, one of the most famed and durable of all Vintage cars. This continued to be produced until 1932 and could be bought in many forms, from the elegant "duck's-back" twoseaters with pointed tail to the very homely-looking artillery wheeled family tourers. In performance the 12/50 was outstanding for a British 1½-litre car, and even early examples were capable of 60 m.p.h. on third gear and over 75 m.p.h. on top in "super-sports" form, and recorded astonishingly good fuel consumptions. The manner in which they delivered this performance was most pleasant, with a characteristically crisp exhaust note and an all-round lightness of handling. Few changes in the basic specification were made over the years, the cone clutch being replaced by a single-plate with stop in 1926 and a cylinder head with better porting introduced in 1927; front brakes of ample size had been added late in 1924. A touring version with a stroke of 110 mm. against the 12/50's 103 mm. and a capacity of over 1½ litres was always available in the same chassis.

The basic soundness of Alvis design and the excellent workmanship of these cars caused them to have a consistently distinguished competition career throughout the Vintage period and they were quite as successful in their class as were the Bentleys in theirs. Even the little 10/30 had scored at hill-climbs and speed trials and had been persuaded to lap Brooklands at 93 m.p.h. in 1921; but the firm's most notable success in the early days was

Front-drive pioneer: the 1928 Alvis fabric-bodied two-seater.
The front brakes are mounted inboard

scored by a special 12/50 in 1923, when Harvey won the Brooklands 200-Mile Race at 93 m.p.h. after the retirement of the supercharged F.I.A.T.s. His car had a higher axle ratio than standard but the engine still gave only 53 b.h.p. at 4000 r.p.m. and its overall fuel consumption for the race was 24 m.p.g. The designer to the company, Captain G. T. Smith-Clark, was alive to the value of such performances for publicity and late in 1924 Harvey and Cushman took a large number of class records at Brooklands, including the Twelve Hours at over 86 m.p.h. and several others which still stand to this day. Another admirable feat came in 1927 when 12/50s, led by S. C. H. Davis, finished first, second, and third in their class in the Essex Six-Hour Race.

Nor was the firm averse to experiment, and in 1925 introduced a supercharged 1½-litre car with front-wheel drive. As this gave nearly 100 b.h.p. and the total weight was only 9½ cwt. the performance was first-rate. On its first appearance at the Shelsley Walsh Hill-climb the car climbed in 54·2 seconds, gaining a class win; 30/98 Vauxhall addicts will, however, note that this was only one second faster than Higginson's 1913 climb. In 1926 a supercharged 1½-litre straight-eight appeared, still with front-drive, but having horizontal valves and supposed to give 125 h.p. This model was introduced to comply with the 1926–7 1½-litre Grand Prix formula, but the cars were never very successful and do not appear to have been put into serious production. The front-drive four-cylinder was, however, sold in appreciable quantities from 1928–30, and was the first of its type to be made on a serious basis in the world; and to produce a successful front-drive car at that time must be considered a tolerably clever feat. The engine differed from the normal 12/50 in having a gear-driven overhead camshaft and a Cozette blower delivering through a large Solex carburettor; front suspension was by transverse quarter-elliptics and the front brake-drums were inboard beside the differential casing. Rear suspension was by reversed quarter-elliptics as on a Bugatti, but independent. The two-seater was capable of about 85 m.p.h., but the long wheelbase and low centre of gravity of the car rendered it rather difficult to hold; and this, combined with a high fuel consumption and the complexity of the front suspension/drive unit prevented it from becoming a very popular car[1]. In 1928 a team of these was entered at Le Mans, winning first and second places in their class; and Cushman was second to the victorious Lea-Francis in the Ulster T.T. later that year. So great was the manufacturer's confidence in the front-drive model that for a time they concentrated on it to the neglect of their well-tried models. Normal production was resumed after this policy had nearly brought them to ruin.

The 12/50 for all its excellence had a fairly rough power unit, and the 6-cylinder 14/75 and "Silver Eagle" models of 1928 onwards were supposed to give a similar performance with greater smoothness and flexibility. They are certainly refined cars with reasonable performance, the short-chassis "Silver Eagle" tourer of 1928 having been tested by *The Autocar* at 85 m.p.h. This model eventually grew into the highly attractive and potent "Speed Twenty" and "Speed Twenty-five" of a few years later. But the typical Alvis of the Vintage period remains the 12/50; we cannot but consider it one of the classic designs of the time, and it remains of all Vintage sports cars the one which needs least apology.

ASTON MARTIN

Shortly before the first war Lionel Martin, who was well known as a driver of Singer cars in competition, installed a specially built side-valve Coventry Simplex engine into a small Isotta Fraschini chassis. This Edwardian "Special" was quite successful in competitions and was christened the Aston Martin from the then popular hill-climb at Aston Clinton, near Aylesbury. A company named Bamford and Martin was formed to make similar cars, but the war intervened and production of any kind was halted until 1920, when there began to be made in very small quantities an exceptionally refined and attractive 1½-litre side-valve car. Beautifully constructed along quite conventional lines, and still with a very special Coventry Simplex engine, the Aston Martin, although exceedingly expensive for its modest size, began to attract the discerning customers for whom it was design-

---

[1] Though its tendency to remain on full lock during a corner has probably been exaggerated.

ed, and production started in earnest in 1923. From then until 1926 it seems that only about sixty were made, one at a time, in workshops round a tiny courtyard in Kensington. This was pretty small-scale production for the period, when even Sunbeams and Arrol-Johnstons were leaving their respective works at the rate of fifty a week, and it is rather surprising that from such modest beginnings so respected a name should survive at all. The customer who cared to pay nearly £800 for a 12-h.p. light car was, however, rewarded for his taste by the exquisite quality of that car, which generally, although the engine produced a mere 35 b.h.p. at 4000 r.p.m., combined a fuel consumption of 35 m.p.g. with a maximum of over 70 m.p.h., and offered exceptional road-holding for a small British car. Perrot-type front brakes were added early in 1923, and the refinement of all detail work rendered it almost the native equivalent of a Bugatti; it was, in fact, in spite of its rather homely design, capable of giving the Brescia a good run and frequently beat it in speed trials and hill-climbs.

The association with the firm of such well-known enthusiasts as Count Zborowski and Clive Gallop ensured that the cars took part in all appropriate competitions, and it must be agreed that they put up a highly creditable showing for so small a concern. Consistent entries were put in for the 200 Miles Race at Brooklands and the voiturette class of the French Grand Prix from 1920 to 1924; it is very unfortunate that their limited resources did not permit them to develop their special competition engines to any extent, but they were always prepared to enter standard cars against far more advanced competition, often with remarkable results. In 1921, for instance, the famous experimental side-valve car "Bunny" finished sixth to the invincible Talbot-Darracqs in the 1500-c.c. class of the Le Mans Grand Prix, and in the 1922 200 Miles Race this same car (already referred to by the Press as "that ancient vehicle") achieved second place to one of these at 86 m.p.h. after the failure of two of the special twin-camshaft Astons. These were designed by Marcel Gremillon of Peugeot on Henry lines, but suffered from an unreliable mounting of the magneto; nevertheless they were fairly successful. Earlier in 1922 "Bunny" had taken twenty-five class and sev-

1   "40/50" – the aristocrat of Vintage touring

2   The ancestor: an 1891 Panhard, photographed in Paris in 1929

3   The prototype of the modern car: the 1901 Mercedes

4   First perfection – a 1907 Rolls-Royce "40/50" or "Silver Ghost"

5   The quest for efficiency – a 1914 "Prince Henry" Vauxhall. Developed from the successful 2000 Mile Trials car of 1908, it was in turn the ancestor of the "30/98". Mr. Laurence Pomeroy, son of the Vauxhall designer, is at the wheel

6 A luxury car in miniature. The 1910 type 13, 1.3-litre Bugatti was the ancestor of all high-efficiency voiturettes. Ernest Friderich at the start of the 1911 Grand Prix, in which he finished second to a 10-litre F.I.A.T.

7 Giant racer – Cecil Clutton driving his 60-h.p. 1908 Grand Prix Itala in the Brighton Speed Trials

8   Early Edwardian tourer: a 1906 Wolseley-Siddeley

9   Late Edwardian tourer: a 1913 Sunbeam 12/16

10 Mr. Raymond Mays at the wheel of his Bugatti "Brescia", a type 13, with which he scored many of his early successes

11 Edwardian magnificence – a 1912 Rolls-Royce "Silver Ghost" with coachwork by Hooper. The owner, Mr. Stanley Sears, is at the wheel

12 The most successful of the cycle-cars – a G.N. with bearded French owner

13 Alastair Pugh's 1928 Anzani-engined Frazer Nash at the twenty first birthday party of the Vintage Sports-Car Club at Goodwood in 1955, with Captain "Archie" Frazer-Nash at the wheel

eral world records at Brooklands, and in 1923, though with the Gremillon engine installed, finished fourth in the 200 Miles Race, in which sixth and seventh places were taken by normal side-valve cars. A day or so before the same race in 1924 Lionel Martin was towing the Hon. John Benson (the late Lord Charnwood) in one of the special 16-valve cars. He found the temptation to race with a passing Alvis quite irresistible and as a result the remains of the special car had to complete the journey on the back of a lorry. So a standard three-seater tourer prepared at very short notice took sixteenth place in the race after the retirement of two of the 16-valve cars; the driver, H. S. Eaton, took the car on his honeymoon the next week.

1922 Grand Prix Aston Martin: four-cylinder 1½-litre engine with twin overhead camshafts and four valves per cylinder. The example illustrated belonged to the Count Zborowski

The firm of Bamford and Martin was not financially successful, and in 1926 Renwick and Bertelli acquired the name for the production of a car to their own specification; but until 1930 under twenty were made. Although several hundred pounds cheaper it was altogether more advanced than the previous cars, with a chain-driven overhead camshaft and a shorter stroke, though, curiously, with worm final drive, in the interests of low build. It was capable of rather more than 80 m.p.h. At the close of our period this model had achieved a certain popularity and its development when production had seriously begun in the new works at Feltham in 1930 as the "International" and "Ulster" models is well known.

A typical late Vintage cockpit: 1930 Aston Martin

The name of Aston Martin certainly deserves to have survived and is worthily borne today. In the early Vintage period it stood for a pioneer attempt to give a simple light car an exceptional performance for the discerning few, and must be considered as one of the most attractive cars of this type ever made.

BENTLEY

The 1914 Tourist Trophy had been extremely hard on the competing cars and only six finished the two-day race at all, out of twenty-two starters. The sixth car was remarkable in that it had an engine capacity of 2 litres only against the permitted 3 litres, and was a tuned-up touring 12/15 D.F.P. driven by Mr. W. O. Bentley, a partner in the London agency for these French cars. During the war this talented designer developed two highly successful rotary aero-engines and these were built by Humber (among others), who had on their design staff F. T. Burgess, who had built the 1914 T. T. Humber. It was announced in 1919 that Bentley and Burgess were engaged on the design of a truly sporting car; a company was formed and the first Bentley took the road late in that year. This period saw the production of hundreds of schemes to produce cars of all types, but few met with such immediate and lasting success as this one. Basically, the Bentley design was a development for road use of the light racing cars of eight years earlier, and with its high speed mono-bloc engine of very long stroke, with an overhead camshaft operating four valves per cylinder, and high, close gear ratios, it was a distinctly unorthodox specification for a road car in the period. These early 3-litres were capable of speed and acceleration particularly in the intermediate gears, which had been totally unknown to the drivers of touring cars of 15·9 h.p. before that time. These factors, coupled with its tremendous robustness and solidity, caused it to be received with great enthusiasm by seekers after high performance.

The first production model left the factory in September 1921, but relatively few cars were produced in the first twelve months and indeed, until about 1926, lack of capital handicapped production, and the cars had to be assembled from parts made or machined by sub-contractors, which partly accounted for their high cost. This, and the undeniably superior performance of the contemporary 30/98, with its $4\frac{1}{2}$-litre engine, seems always to have made the selling of 3-litre Bentleys an uphill job, despite the enthusiasm of their owners.

The cylinder dimensions of the 3-litre were 80 × 149 mm., thus reproducing a favourite Coupe de l'Auto shape which happened also to give a soothingly low Treasury Rating under the iniquitous new road tax of £1 per h.p. But a rather awkwardly shaped cylinder head resulted, which made it possible to do much less tuning than was possible with the later, shorter stroke $4\frac{1}{2}$-litre. The first cars produced about 65 b.h.p. at 3500 r.p.m. but this was gradually increased until in 1926 the standard cars gave 86 to 88 b.h.p. at the same speed, and the Le Mans cars as much as 92 b.h.p.

A Tourist Trophy replica was produced in 1922, which was the forerunner of the 100 m.p.h. chassis brought out in 1925. These cars had a wheelbase of only 9 ft., as against the standard short chassis of 9 ft. $9\frac{1}{2}$ in., and a tapering radiator, narrower at the bottom than the top. Fifteen of the 100 m.p.h. chassis were made.

In 1926 the engine was considerably modified, with a new camshaft, integral sump (in the earlier cars the sump is recognisable as an almost separate container, below the crankcase proper), and other improvements.

51

In typically English contrast to its otherwise advanced design, the Bentley did not acquire front brakes until 1924, in which year the 3-litre had its first win at Le Mans, and in 1927 this was followed by one of the most dramatic wins in racing history. A multiple crash at the White House Corner eliminated the new 4½-litre car, but a 3-litre, driven by S. C. H. Davis and Dr. Benjafield, extricated itself and, although grievously damaged, limped on to win. This great car become known as "Old Number Seven '. In all, 1620 3-litre cars were made, of which about 300 survive at the date of publication.

By 1927 the 3-litre was clearly at the end of its tether, and it was completely outclassed by such multicylinder 3-litre cars as the twin overhead camshaft Sunbeam and type 44 Bugatti. There was, therefore, a pressing demand among Bentley enthusiasts for something at once faster, smoother, more flexible, and more roomy. The answer was the 100 × 140 mm. 4½-litre, which certainly complied with all these requirements, although it looked a heavy, ponderous machine beside the light and comely lines of the standard Vanden-Plas-bodied 3-litre. The standard model had a 10 ft. 10 in. wheelbase and with a 3·53 to 1 back-axle ratio, a power output of 110 b.h.p. at 3500 r.p.m. gave a maximum speed of 92 m.p.h. The 4½-litre was altered surprisingly little during its period in production, one of the most important modifications being the substitution, in 1928, of a remarkably heavy and cumbersome plate clutch for the previous cone clutch.

A 4½-litre car won at Le Mans in 1928.

In 1930 a Roots-blown edition of the 4½-litre became available, which had a clear 100 m.p.h. maximum coupled with remarkable smoothness and flexibility and a quite uncontrollable thirst for petrol. Late in 1930 the very heavy blower-type crankshaft was fitted to the ordinary 4½-litre, which, however, proved quite unequal to the task of rotating this enormous mass of metal.

In fact, the day of the large four-cylinder was passing and no mere palliative could ensure its survival. The last 4½ was made in late 1931, although about six more were assembled during the thirties, from old stock taken over when the company went into liquidation. Apart from these, 662 unblown and 50 blown 4½-litre cars made were.

Unlike the 3-litre, the $4\frac{1}{2}$ engine can be tuned to a remarkable extent, and it is certain that some have been developed to give at least 160 b.h.p.

Although the $6\frac{1}{2}$- and 8-litre cars belong to another chapter they may also be mentioned briefly here because of their racing successes. In 1925 was produced a six-cylinder 100 × 140 mm. $6\frac{1}{2}$-litre car, primarily as a luxury vehicle, capable of moving heavy saloon coachwork along at 75 m.p.h. The engine layout very closely followed that of the four-cylinder cars. These early sixes had tapering radiators very much like the 100-m.p.h. 3-litre chassis. In 1929 came the "Speed Six", with a tall edition of a $4\frac{1}{2}$-litre radiator, twin carburettors, higher compression, and some 180 b.h.p. at 3500 r.p.m. The very first "Speed Six" won the Le Mans race in 1929, which was the peak year of Bentley racing success. It was followed by $4\frac{1}{2}$-litre cars into second, third, and fourth places. Never in the history of motor-racing had there been such an overwhelming British victory, and the $6\frac{1}{2}$ again won in 1930, the last racing season of an official Bentley team.

The "Speed Six" coupled American standards of smoothness and flexibility with a nearly 100 m.p.h. performance and it was in many ways the most successful production of the whole Bentley range. In 1930 the $6\frac{1}{2}$-litre was joined by the 8-litre, 110 × 140 mm., with an entirely new chassis available with 12 ft. or 13 ft. wheelbase. This engine, in standard form, developed 220 b.h.p. at its peak of 3500 r.p.m. It was a remarkably successful attempt to produce Rolls-Royce standards of luxury and mechanical refinement with immense performance and a 100 m.p.h. maximum. But it came out at a most unpropitious moment, at the depth of a great financial slump, and merely served to accelerate the already impending insolvency of the company. About 100 8-litre cars in all were made, of which undoubtedly the most famous is the much modified example which belonged to the late Forrest Lycett, with its maximum speed in the neighbourhood of 140 m.p.h., acceleration from 0 to 100 m.p.h. in the order of eighteen seconds, and yet a tractable and pleasant touring car.

One other model came from the old firm, although, fortunately after the Vintage decade had ended. This was the disastrous 4-litre six-cylinder of 1931, a car combining great weight with negligible performance and a low-geared, rough, and fussy engine. A famous authority once guardedly remarked that it was a "very good engine for marine purposes".

Two aspects of Bentley lore are much discussed and merit some separate explanation. One is gearbox types; the other radiator badges.

The gearbox types most commonly found are the A, B, C, D, and F.

The A and D are those most sought after, and most commonly found on red label 3-litres and open 4½-litre cars. They have very close ratios with the unusual distinction that second and third are closer than third and top. There is, by contrast, a yawning gap between second and bottom, involving a very slow change which almost completely precludes a rapid getaway from rest. The D is a stronger edition of the A and was developed for the 4½-litre model.

The B-type is a wide-ratio box found on blue label 3-litres. The standard six had a box known as BS, which was, in effect, a C with a high-ratio third.

The C-type box is in many ways the best of all, having reasonably close ratios coupled with great ersilence than the A or D. It is, however, a more difficult box to operate. It appeared on the first 4½-litres, and after being supplanted by the D, was reinstated in 1928 for use with saloon coachwork. It was also the standard box for the "Speed Six" cars. An E-type box was made but not put into production.

The F-type box was standard for the 4- and 8-litre cars and there was a variant known as G which is hardly distinguishable.

The ratios of the various types are as follows:

type	top	3rd	2nd	1st
A and D	1	1·33	1·63	2·64
B	1	1·453	2·073	3·826
C	1	1·357	1·823	3·364
F and G	1	1·357	1·79	3·24

Although the designation was never official, the 3-litre cars are generally known by the colour of the enamel filling in the famous

"Winged B" radiator badge. The different colours used for the different models are as follows:

3-litre long chassis and all cars up to 1924	Blue
3-litre short chassis speed models from 1924	Red
3-litre 100 m.p.h. chassis (mostly)	Green
4½-litre and supercharged	Black
Standard Six, 6½-litre	Blue
Speed Six, 6½-litre	Green (or to choice)
4-litre	Blue
8-litre	Blue

Few vintage marques enjoy such a devoted following today as the Bentley. Not only is a substantial proportion of the cars in the Vintage Sports-Car Club composed of Bentleys but there is in addition the prosperous Bentley Drivers Club. Bentleys did for British prestige in sports car racing in the late twenties what Sunbeams had done in the late pre-war and early post-war years. Right up to the outbreak of the Second World War, the memory of the great Bentley successes at Le Mans remained green in France and there was always a warm welcome for "le beau Bentelée" . . . or, as Ettore Bugatti less elegantly put it, "le camion le plus vite".

BUGATTI

Among many famous names in motoring history, two stand out from the rest because of their dominating personalities, innate engineering instinct, and unyielding integrity of purpose. Frederick Royce is, of course, one; Ettore Bugatti is the other.

Ettore Bugatti was born in 1881: he died in 1947.

After working for various other concerns, notably De Dietrich, he set up on his own in 1909.

Bugatti type numbers are deeply mysterious, since experimental models each had their own number and the identity of many of them is now completely unknown. Thus, the first car bearing the actual name "Bugatti" started life with the unpromising type number 13, but it easily lived this down by showing itself to be one of the half-dozen outstanding designs in the first thirty years of motor manufacture. More than that, it is, indeed, the undoubted parent of all high-efficiency light cars (i.e. of 1½-litres capacity or less). The type 13 secured early fame for Bugatti by finishing second to a 10½-litre F.I.A.T., in the *formule libre* Grand Prix of 1911.

The engine had four cylinders of 65 × 100 mm., giving a cubic capacity of 1327 c.c. The shaft-driven overhead camshaft operated two valves per cylinder and ran safely up to about 3000 r.p.m., with a cruising speed of 2300 r.p.m., equal to 55 m.p.h. The gear ratios were the perfectly spaced ones of 3·43, 4·5, 6·25, and 11 to 1. The clutch was the famous semi-centrifugal, wet multi-plate pattern used by Bugatti on all his Vintage types; final drive was by shaft. The all-up weight in touring trim was rather less than half a ton. These cars possess all the handling qualities which have characterised every Bugatti, making them at once the delight and despair of their devoted owners. For Bugatti ownership is in itself a cult; it can hardly be defended on logical grounds. But for a motorist of refined sensibilities the operation of Bugatti steering, clutch, or gearbox is a source of epicurean pleasure which no other car can provide.

Bugatti steering is like cutting butter with a hot knife; play in the steering of a Bugatti is practically unknown. The steering box is worm and wheel.

As already stated, a Bugatti clutch is semi-centrifugal in operation. With the engine idling it can be pushed out with one finger. At full engine speed it can only with considerable exertion be moved at all. This is achieved by toggle arms which may be adjusted for varying conditions, from all-in or all-out for racing, to near-fluid-flywheel for use in traffic. Bugatti clutches are accused of never freeing, but this is always due to one maladjustment or another – too fast a tickover; engine and gearbox mis-aligned; buckled plates; sticky oil in the clutch; worn and ridged clutch shaft.

At high speeds they never do disengage fully and this enables very rapid, single-declutch downward changes to be made on most models. The procedure is as follows: the throttle is held fairly wide open and the hand exerts pressure on the gear lever. As the clutch is depressed the lever, under the pressure of the driver's hand, instantly moves into the next lower gear, while the revs fly up (unimpeded by any flywheel). In so doing, they speed up the layshaft, since the clutch only partially disengages. The whole operation is instantaneous and completely silent.

Most engines run unsteadily when cold, and slow down gradually when switched off. A Bugatti, if it starts at all, does so on a single pull up (it cannot be swung) and instantly runs at whatever speed the hand throttle is set for. When switched off it stops absolutely instantaneously. No Bugatti engine is silent, but they are nearly always very refined and the peculiar sewing-machine noises they make are rather pleasing.

Bugatti made four- and eight-cylinder in-line engines (and a few two-row sixteens); never a six. He adopted various rather odd firing orders which produce peculiar effects of balance in some engines.

Bugattis are said to be unreliable, but this is absolutely untrue. A Bugatti properly maintained, in standard form, is outstandingly reliable and (except for some type 57s) an unfailing starter. On the other hand, when a Bugatti has been raced, and probably modified, and finally sold "detuned for road-work" almost anything may happen, and will.

Worn valve-guides will promote persistent plug-oiling, while a Bugatti is immensely sensitive to ignition, and the most trivial faults will produce quite alarming results. It is therefore true to say that, although a Bugatti is inherently reliable, it may well be temperamental. One of the authors (C.C.) ran a type 49 Bugatti for ten years for business use. Although it had 750,000 miles to its credit, it only once failed to reach its destination (through a dead battery short), but it did manifest some unusual whims of temperament from time to time.

The first type 13 cars had a single shaft-driven overhead camshaft and two valves per cylinder, but in 1914 a sixteen-valve engine was fitted, having four vertical valves per cylinder operated from the single camshaft by very unusual curved tappets, working in guides, and popularly known as the "banana-shaped tappets". These sixteen-valve cars were the only Bugattis to have their carburettor on the near-side of the engine and the exhaust manifold on the off-side.

The types 13, 22, and 23 are closely related, being, in fact, only distinguished by length of wheelbase: short, medium, and long respectively. Apart from the early eight-valve engine, all had the single overhead camshaft sixteen-valve engine. Apparently the first sixteen-valve engine in 1914 was 66 × 100 mm. The 69 × 100 mm. engine did not really appear until 1923–4. It was a team of sixteen-valve type 13 cars (with 6 ft. 5 in. wheelbase) which took the first four places in the Brescia race in 1921, for which reason Bugatti christened them "Brescia", by which name all sixteen-valve cars are now generally but erroneously known. The two longer-chassis models, types 22 and 23, then became known as "Brescia Modifié", but the true "Brescia" is only the short-chassis type 13. Another triumph of the type 13 in 1921 was in an Italian race officially described as the "Grand Prix des Gentlemen".

With a safe maximum of 3800 r.p.m. the sixteen-valve cars could be supplied with various back-axle ratios. An average set gave overall ratios of 3·75, 4·87, 6·9, and 11 to 1, giving a theoretical maximum of just over 80 m.p.h.

There followed a series of racing and touring (at any rate, that was what Bugatti called them) types, and the next avowedly sports model was the type 43 Grand Sport, 2·3-litre, 60 × 100 mm., supercharged eight-cylinder, with roller bearings and single overhead camshaft. It was a production edition of the 35B Grand Prix car, both being produced in 1927. It was, in fact, a Grand Prix car which anyone could buy and it was probably the first car available to the public which would comfortably exceed 100 m.p.h. in touring trim. It is by no means temperamental and can be run in traffic without undue difficulty, having an excellent top-gear performance. A variety of final-drive ratios were available, from 3·6 to 4·66, but the normal set of overall ratios was 3·85, 4·98, 6·95, and 10·37 to 1. The gear change is depressingly slow for a Bugatti, and the type 43 is improved out of all recognition by fitting a Grand Prix type 35 box. As is to be expected with roller bearings, considerable care has to be exercised during warming up, and failure to observe this precaution has resulted in expensive trouble on occasion. With its standard pointed-tail, open body and cast aluminium wheels, the Grand Sport looks almost grimly purposeful and is one of the most outstanding Bugatti types.

Last of all in the Vintage era, in 1930, came the type 50, 4·9-litre, 86 × 107 mm., supercharged eight-cylinder, with plain bearings and twin overhead camshafts. It is one of the most impressively fabulous of all Bugatti types. Developing 200 b.h.p. at 4000 r.p.m. it was capable of 115 m.p.h. or more. The engine was in one integral piece, so that to remove a valve the crankshaft had to be taken out of the engine. Possibly in the interests of weight distribution, the gearbox was integral with the back axle, thus substantially increasing the unsprung weight. Three ratios were considered adequate, these being 3·46, 4·8, and 8·6 to 1, giving 26½ m.p.h. at 1000 r.p.m. in top gear. Cast aluminium wheels were again used, but of a different pattern to the types 35 and 43, with their flat, dished spokes. As with the 35 and 43, the brake drum formed part of the wheel, but the spokes were only short ones, set transversely, between the periphery of the drum and the rim of the wheel. This arrangement was most effective in getting heat away from the brakes, though somewhat at the expense of overheating the tyres. In the year following, the type 50 was developed into a full Grand Prix car, type 54. A more impressive looking and sounding car than the type 50 would be difficult indeed to imagine.

Although some other types, such as the 40 and 44, are now generally thought of as sports models, they were described by Bugatti as touring and will be so treated in this book.

The Bugatti Owners' Club was founded in 1929, and owns the famous Prescott hill-climb course, near Cheltenham.

G.N. AND FRAZER-NASH

Late in 1910 two young engineers named Godfrey and Frazer-Nash formed a partnership for the production of a really simple and inexpensive car with an air-cooled twin-cylinder engine and belt transmission. Unlike so many other people who had the same idea, they did this (in a splendidly light-hearted manner) with considerable success, for the G.N. had an appreciably better performance than the average cycle-car of the period, and quite a number were made until 1915 to the original specification. This included a light wooden frame, quarter-elliptic suspension, and steering by cable and bobbin, and the whole car was considerably less liable to fall off the road than other similar layouts – although there was a fairly marked tendency for the wheels to fall off the motor-car. During the war this design was revised to include a four-chain final drive, but the chassis and engine remained the same, though the latter was now set across the frame instead of along it. The engine had various markedly agricultural features which were accounted for by the homely equipment of the factory. The car was seriously produced from 1919 to 1923 in this form.

At this time motoring of any sort was extremely expensive, and few, if any, cars as cheap as this were capable of performing and handling as well. Although the G.N. was crude and noisy and gave little comfort, th ecombination of a fairly powerful small engine in a two-seater car weighing about 8 cwt. gave excellent acceleration to a maximum of over 50 m.p.h., as well as outstanding economy; many owners claimed up to 70 m.p.g. The price in 1921 was in the region of £250, whereas some orthodox light cars of far inferior performance cost nearly twice as much; but the G.N. appealed to a rather different public who were looking for a small sporting car. As such it was highly successful, and the cars are remembered with affection by many who owned them, though there are extremely few in existence today. Special versions such as "Mowgli" and "Akela" were successful in competition, too, and the 1100 c.c. class of the 1921 200 Miles Race was won by a G.N. driven by Frazer-Nash, after a lap at 77·4 m.p.h. The very light weight of the cars led to outstanding appearances at hill-climbs and speed trials, and in a different sphere they were used by the Paris police as staff vehicles.

In 1922 the policy of the firm unfortunately changed. The intensive development of light and cheap cars by such big concerns as the Rover Company had rendered the limitations of the G.N. design more prominent, and the effort to mitigate them by adding bigger and better coachwork inevitably resulted in loss of performance. A shaft-driven chassis with a little water-cooled engine with an overhead camshaft was introduced for 1923, and the two founders of the firm left. The shaft-driven G.N. proved disappointing and in a year or so G.N.s ceased to be made altogether, in spite of a hasty reversion to the older type of chassis. Godfrey retired from car production until his successful introduction in 1937 of the H.R.G., which even to-day bears faint traces of its G.N. ancestry. Frazer-Nash set up on his own to make an improved car on G.N. lines, which should be a sports car in its own right, rather than an economy car which happened to go better than most in its class.

As such, the Frazer-Nash had much in common with the G.N., and when production started early in 1925 it was apparent that quite an exceptional sports car had been born. The earliest cars had an overhead-valve engine of high compression known as the "Powerplus", but later the tough, light, and surprisingly potent British Anzani 12 h.p. was adopted. This side-valve engine, which was supposed to deliver about 40 b.h.p., was strong but noisy; it was incapable of much development, though, even when a Cozette supercharger was added in 1927 to some models. It was finally superseded by the popular 4ED Meadows engine of the same dimensions in 1929, when a fourth speed was added. This gave an altogether more vivid performance, even with the heavier coachwork ($15\frac{1}{2}$ cwt.) then fitted, and combined a maximum of over 80 m.p.h. with a fuel consumption better than 30 m.p.g. In the Anzani-engined 'Nash, three-speed (four to special order) and reverse chain drive and quarter-elliptic springs were used as on the G.N., and coupled with elegant and very light aluminium coachwork gave an extremely snappy perform-ance. A touring version was tested by the motoring press at 70 m.p.h., in 1925, and gave 40 m.p.g., thanks to an all-up weight of only 13 cwt. It is an interesting reflection that even then it was thought worth mentioning that such a car would "carry on all day at 40 m.p.h." – although in fact such a car would cruise between 60 and 65 m.p.h. Considering its fairly low price of £315, the "Nash", though distinctly crude in places, with almost solid suspension at low speeds, represented very good value for money, for such performance could not be bought elsewhere for the same cost. The chain drive and very smooth plate clutch gave an exceptionally rapid gear change and the solid rear axle made the car stable under the most difficult conditions, although with some tendency on greasy surfaces to go straight on. The steering was always of the highest quality, absolutely accurate and devoid of play, rather heavy, and very high-geared (usually less than one turn from lock to lock).

Undoubtedly what singled out the G.N. from its contemporaries, contributed largely to the great success of the Frazer-Nash, became the foundation of innumerable specials, and survived in limited production until 1939, was the unique system of transmission. The propeller-shaft ended in a bevel-box and cross-shaft under the driver's seat. This shaft carried four loose pinions and four corresponding dog-clutches, sliding on and keyed to the shaft. The back axle also carried four sprocket wheels connected by light chains to the pinions on the cross-shaft. Thus, by engaging any one of the dog-clutches, a silent and direct ratio was obtained. By a special refinement on the Frazer-Nash, which was absent from the G.N., it was made impossible to connect two different ratios at the same time. The resultant gear change is unique and tremendously enjoyable, contributing largely to the outstanding character of this great car – tough, light, simple, fast, and eminently controllable. The Frazer-Nash was always in a class by itself.

INVICTA

The Invicta appeared on the market in 1925, and although never made in large quantities gained quite a following as a large and fast sporting car of very handsome lines. In the Vintage period it came in 3- and 4½-litre forms, having the big pushrod six-cylinder Meadows engines which Lagonda subsequently used with such success, and if these were not notable for their smoothness, they produced, in conjunction with a light chassis, a very fierce performance indeed. The acceleration times recorded for Invictas are amongst the best of their period, and in spite of quite high gearing the cars were outstandingly flexible on top speed. The low-chassis 4½-litre had first-class brakes and was capable of well over 80 m.p.h. in 1928. It was further developed until it appeared as the "100 m.p.h." car. Invictas were particularly well equipped in every way, though rather expensive, and in general carried on the earlier tradition of a large engine, working easily within its capacity, in a light chassis.

Nowadays it is common (and perhaps judicious) for car manufacturers to demonstrate their products by long-distance reliability runs rather than by active support of real competition. Invicta were among the first to see the merits of this, and Miss Violet Cordery put in some very determined driving on these lines. In 1926 she gained a certificate from the R.A.C. for driving 5000 miles at 73 m.p.h. on Brooklands, and in the next year took a 3-litre car through an extremely tough world tour of 10,000 miles, driving relentlessly through Africa, India, Australia, Canada, and the U.S.A. with negligible mechanical trouble, to win the Dewar Trophy. In 1929 she and her sister drove a 4½-litre car 30,000 miles in 30,000 minutes and won it again. In 1930 came the most eccentric proposal of all from this indefatigable lady, who hoped to drive the car from London to Edinburgh and back in bottom gear, London to John o'Groats and back on second, London to Monte Carlo and back on third, and finish off with six laps of Brooklands in reverse. It does not appear that this fatiguing performance was in fact carried out, however.

All this sort of thing perhaps prevented Invictas from taking part to any extent in genuine competitions, and in any case the Bentley opposition would probably have been too much for them if they had. Also, as is usual in very low-built cars with non-independent suspension, the road-holding and cornering characteristics were somewhat treacherous. In 1930 the tremendous appetite of the 4½ for hills caused a creditable class win in the Alpine Trials for Donald Healey, who has of course become well-known as a manufacturer; and the same driver won the Monte Carlo Rally for the firm in 1931.

LAGONDA

Few motor manufacturers can have undergone such a radical change in policy so suddenly as did Lagonda late in 1925. From 1913 until that time they had been strictly a one-model concern, producing the charming if somewhat eccentric light car of 11·9 h.p. which we discuss elsewhere, and which could not be considered a sports car by any stretch of the imagination. In August 1925, however, the 11·9, whose performance had been becoming more and more imperceptible for some time, was supplanted by a car of entirely different calibre which in the next few years was to attain considerable fame. This, the 2-litre Lagonda, seems not to have been designed as a sports car but rather as an extremely refined and smooth touring car of better than average efficiency, and this was a capacity which it fulfilled quite well. For the very reliable engine was of particularly attractive design, and differed from previous Lagonda practice in having chain-driven twin camshafts set high in the sides of the block and a fairly high compression-ratio, although this bid for high efficiency was largely nullified by inlet manifolding of labyrinthine complexity. It was placed in a robust chassis on conventional lines with agreeable steering and sizable brakes. It soon became obvious that all this could do something better than drag heavy saloon or touring coachwork about, even though it would do this at over 60 m.p.h., and various sports four-seaters on lowered chassis became available from 1927 onwards. The smooth running and economy of the car were altogether exceptional for an engine of under 2 litres and only 12·8 R.A.C. rating, and in this respect the Lagonda was one of the earliest truly modern designs. For some reason, however, no attempt was made to reduce the very high chassis weight, and even the fabric-bodied tourers weighed about a ton and a half, whereas, as we have seen, the Vintage Frazer-Nash in its latest and heaviest form weighed only half this. Vivid acceleration was thus never a Lagonda feature, and the guaranteed 80 m.p.h. of the 1928 Speed Model was probably unobtainable on any but the longest and straightest roads. The designers sensibly provided a reasonably close-ratio gearbox which counteracted this to some extent by providing a high speed on third, but one cannot but feel that the car should have had either a bigger engine or a less ponderous chassis to be really successful. At the very end of our period the 2-litre was fitted with a supercharger which helped the mixture to thread its tortuous path through the manifold, but only by reducing the fuel consumption from about 28 to 18 m.p.g. This expedient was alleged to provide a 90 m.p.h. maximum, but it was patently attacking the problem from the wrong end and this model was not made in any quantity. The unblown 2-litre remains a notably pleasant car to drive, the long wheelbase giving great comfort and the engine by

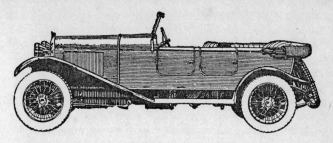

1928 Lagonda sporting four-seater: 2-litre four-cylinder,
twin-overhead-camshaft engine

no means so obtrusive as might be expected from its age and
layout. It well deserves the considerable following which it has.

The firm was obsessed, as were Lea-Francis and Alvis, by
the wish to produce six-cylinder cars of $2\frac{1}{2}$–3 litres, but although
these were fairly fast they seem to have shown few advantages
over the 2-litre. Not until this model was dropped in 1932 did
they really concentrate on high-performance cars of excellent
quality, usually with big Meadows engines, but culminating in
the remarkable Bentley-designed twelve-cylinder of 1937 – a
quite extraordinary contrast to the quaint 12/24 light car of
only eleven years before.

LANCIA

We have already suggested that Continental Vintage cars were
better adapted than their British equivalents for travelling at
relatively high speeds with complete equanimity; this is well
demonstrated by the Lancia "Lambda" model, which by its
considerable merits became very popular as a fairly fast touring
car during the Vintage period. Late in 1922 Lancia showed this
car at the Paris Salon, and when the first examples came to this
country early the next year it was apparent that the design was
quite exceptionally advanced for its time; and in fact several of
its features have been used by the firm with brilliant results to the
present day. The "Lambda" at this time had an ingenious and
compact narrow-angle V-four engine of just over 2 litres with an
overhead camshaft, which gave 48 b.h.p. at 3000 r.p.m. and was

installed in a very rigid chassis-frame of welded steel sheet which also formed the main body structure. From the first the cars had front-wheel brakes of generous size. Most notable of all in the context of 1922 was the extremely successful Lancia independent front suspension, with enclosed coil springs incorporating a hydraulic damper. Independent suspension had occasionally been used before in a very tentative and crude manner, as on the Edwardian Sizaire-Naudin cars, but to Lancia must go the distinction of first marketing on a large scale a principle which is now universal.

As the total weight of the early "Lambda" four-seater was only 15 cwt., the performance and behaviour of the car were most satisfactory for the time. The speed was guaranteed to be in excess of 70 m.p.h., while most 2-litre British tourers were content with 55; and even when other cars of similar size became capable of this speed, the Lancia still scored by its remarkable road-holding qualities and was able to put up high averages. It was not intended by its makers to be a real sports car, and even as the engine grew larger and larger to carry heavier and longer bodies the maximum speed was never much more than 75 m.p.h. The engine too had certain internal limitations of porting arising from the narrow-V layout which prevented its development to give much more than the standard power output. For these reasons the "Lambda" was not seen often in competitions, and even for the classic long-distance trials it was hampered by its low build and great length. But on the road it was, and still is, an enormously entertaining car to drive. The gear change with its central control is very rapid indeed (although the ratios are better adapted to Alpine surroundings than to English roads), and the whole outfit feels unusually taut and responsive, with brakes second to none for their date, and light and accurate steering. The appearance too is entirely distinctive, from the exposed front suspension to the oddly pointed rear boot; while the late fabric saloons of uncompromising angularity, with wickerwork seats, are full of character. It should be put on record that the "Airline" saloon of 1928 was perhaps the ugliest car ever made, until the inception of the Chrysler "Airflow" models of 1934.

The "Lambda" appeared in eight series and, roughly, after a

rapid succession of the first three, they appeared yearly, the last of the eight coming off the line in late 1928.

The first six had cylinder dimensions of 75 × 120 mm. The seventh was bored out to 80 mm. bore and the eighth to 82·5 mm. The seventh and eighth had H-section connecting rods and the remainder tubular.

The first three series had three-speed gearboxes and at any rate some of the fourth had four. All these early series are now rare, but the fifth is still very popular, often having been "cut-and-shut" and tuned, or fitted with a seventh or eighth series engine. The sixth was very similar to the fifth but had Bosch (instead of Marelli) electrical equipment, the first low-pressure (but still beaded-edge) tyres, and was available in long-wheelbase form.

The seventh series had the integral body-cum-chassis, but a few ordinary chassis were also made for special coach-work, and this became standard for the eighth. There was a ninth, which differed only minutely from the eighth, but very few were made. The eighth continued in production until 1932.

In the tale of Vintage Lancias must be included the "Kappa", which was in production in the early post-war years, but differed from the pre-war "Theta" only in having a detachable head to the

1928 Lancia "Lambda" eighth series with Weymann
saloon coachwork

fine 5-litre, four-cylinder, side-valve engine. The "Di-Kappa" was a further development of the "Kappa" and in 1922 came a V-eight "Tri-Kappa". This was probably conceived as a reduced version of a wonderful V-twelve which was shown in 1919, but which apparently never went into production. The V-twelve had a 80 × 100 mm. 6-litre engine, whose particular interest is that it was the first to have the narrow (22°) V arrangement used for the "Lambda". Very few "Tri-Kappas" were made, as the great success of the new "Lambda" soon absorbed the full resources of the factory.

The "Lambda" appeals to many connoisseurs because of its uncompromising individuality. The engine was undoubtedly rough and rather noisy, even by the standards of the time; but to the keen motorist this was far outweighed by its remarkable toughness and stamina, and by the advanced handling qualities of the chassis. It remains one of the most pleasant "honorary sports cars" (with acknowledgments to D. B. Tubbs), and certainly one of the outstanding mechanical achievements, of the Vintage decade.

LEA-FRANCIS

The Coventry firm of Lea and Francis, well known for their high-grade motor-cycles, entered the light-car market late in 1922 with three models of very ordinary design, an air-cooled twin-cylinder and two small fours. These were not at first intended to be anything but fairly pleasing economy cars, and were certainly of quite unsporting appearance with their comfortable coachwork and disc wheels. The side-valve engines were soon dropped, as was the two-cylinder, and the extremely robust 9·8-h.p. Meadows engine with overhead valves adopted. This, although alleged to produce only about 20 b.h.p., for some reason produced a surprisingly lively little car which soon came to be recognised as having qualities of endurance and solidity which were not then associated with economy. The marque performed extremely well in arduous R.A.C. light-car trials of 1924 and was one of the fastest over the flying mile at Brooklands driven by Tatlow, who later became the firm's competition manager. The first really sporting Lea-Francis appeared in 1925 with the celebrated 4ED Meadows engine of 11·9 h.p. as the 12/40, and had a guaranteed speed in touring form of 60 m.p.h. From then onwards until the end of our period these cars flourished exceedingly, bearing little trace of their pedestrian ancestry. Even in 1926 the 12/40 was capable of a good 70 m.p.h., with brakes to match, and in 1927 was provided with a Cozette supercharger vertically mounted behind the sloping radiator as the Hyper-Sports Model. This ultimately proved able to do nearly 90 m.p.h., which was outstanding for a 1½-litre car at that time. The firm sensibly relied on a known proprietary engine for their sports models, but persisted at the same time in trying to produce various small touring six-cylinders, often with engines and transmissions by Vulcan; these were of quite advanced design, with optional free-wheels and the like, but invariably over-bodied and of inferior performance. It is tempting to see in this, and particularly in the ill-fated and complex "Ace of Spades" 2-litre, the main reason for their virtual cessation of production in 1930, when receivers were appointed. However, after a period in abeyance during the thirties this make was revived with considerable success for a short time after the war, and again in 1960.

As a sports car the Lea-Francis deserves to be remembered, particularly from its heyday in 1927–30. The "Hyper" was not without its moments in competition, the most notable of which was the exceedingly narrow victory in the first of the new series of Tourist Trophy races in Ulster in 1928; in this Kaye Don's car finished first at 64·06 m.p.h. to Cushman's front-drive Alvis at 64·02. At Le Mans, too, these cars showed a rather unexpected degree of reliability and speed, and privately entered cars finished

1929 Lea-Francis 12/40: a typical late Vintage medium-sized saloon, mounted on a sporting chassis

eighth in 1928 and sixth in 1930. While certainly never outstanding in any way, they remain thoroughly honest and worthy sporting cars which it is impossible not to respect.

M.G.

One of the most notable features of the Vintage decade was the general and universal increase in the speed of quite ordinary cars, which by 1930 provided a performance which would have been unthinkable in 1920. This progress was to some extent nullified in the decadent years 1930–39, and it is only since the war that any similar tendency towards higher cruising speeds in relation to engine size has been apparent. Looking back, it seems obvious that any manufacturer who could, in 1925, provide cars of rather better than average performance with pleasing lines at low cost was bound to succeed; and this is precisely how the M.G. started life. While these cars in Vintage form do not perhaps fall into the best traditions of beautiful construction and fine handling qualities, they represented even then the toughness and value for money which have given them such great popularity. With the establishment of the firm in its new factory at Abingdon in 1930 began an extremely distinguished competition career, and the road-racing M.G.s of the early 1930s were highly successful and advanced cars.

The first M.G. of all was constructed by Cecil Kimber, the real progenitor of the firm, in the Morris Garages, Holywell Street, Oxford, in 1923. It consisted of an 11·9 h.p. Morris "Cowley" engine converted to pushroad overhead valves, in a very light and simple frame also made up of Morris components; and in fact the cars were entirely based on the production Morris cars of the period. This not only showed the soundness of Morris design, but enabled them to be sold at thoroughly attractive prices; and they really were the earliest determined attempt to produce a cheap sporting car in any quantity. The 1923 car, which still survives, was used experimentally and performed quite well in long-distance trials; but the first production cars did not appear until 1925. They were simply a slightly more elegant version of the round-nosed Morris "Oxford" of 13·9 h.p., with aluminium coachwork and wire wheels. The "Oxford" was capable of about 55 m.p.h. on a side-valve four-cylinder engine and it is doubtful if the speed of the M.G. was at first much higher, as few mechanical alterations were made. It was, however, of quite smart appearance, and continued in modest production, becoming the 14/40 in 1927. The later versions would do about 65 m.p.h., a fair speed then for an engine of 1800 c.c. propelling a cheap car weighing just over a ton. It would have had considerable appeal as an economical sports car had it not used a standard Morris three-speed gearbox having ratios of disastrous ineptitude.

The domestic Morris range widened considerably at the end of the Vintage period, and two of its models became the basis for the production M.G.s for 1929–30, the 847-c.c. Morris "Minor" becoming the M-type "Midget" and the 2½-litre Morris "Isis" becoming the 18/80. The "Minor", with its little overhead-camshaft engine and conventional frame, was a quite advanced specification for a really cheap car, and formed a sound basis for the M.G., which was the first really small sporting car on these lines; the "Midget" had a maximum of about 65 m.p.h. and with a total weight of only 10 cwt. gave nearly 40 m.p.g. In view of its price of £175 this was thoroughly praiseworthy and the car sold very well, and the name has been applied to the smallest of the range ever since. The Morris "Isis" in standard form was a ponderous and dull car with three very ill-chosen gear ratios; but when two carburettors had been added to the overhead-camshaft engine, and various changes effected in the manifolding, it gave (as the 18/80) a much superior performance, with a maximum of well over 75 m.p.h. The dreadful three-speed

1927 M.G. 14/40, closely related to the Morris "Oxford"

71

gearbox was to some extent offset by a really remarkable top gear performance. If these early M.G.s seem uninteresting cars produced at the tail-end of a fascinating decade, they should really be seen as the first of the inexpensive sports cars of the 1930s, and considerably better than the majority of these.

RILEY

Until the first war the pioneer firm of Riley had concentrated production largely on a successful V-twin light car and it was not until 1919 that they showed their first small four-cylinder of 10·8 h.p. This was a fairly homely little car, though always well-made, and its side-valve engine produced 35 b.h.p., which was enough to give it a moderately lively performance. In 1924 the engine was enlarged to form the basis of the celebrated 11/40 "Redwing", a thoroughly pleasing and entirely orthodox 1½-litre car of attractive lines and quite sporting habits. This sold well, but in 1926 the Riley stand at Olympia was graced by a totally new and different car conceived by Victor Riley and of only 1100 c.c.; this was built on lines to which the firm remained faithful for many years, and which soon gained very great popularity. It was in fact a pioneer version of the modern high-efficiency light car, and had an engine with twin high camshafts operating valves at 45 degrees in a hemispherical combustion chamber, a two-bearing crankshaft of great solidity, and a four-speed gearbox with constant-mesh third gear. This engine has been used on all subsequent Rileys, developed by Hugh Rose, who is also responsible for the Lea-Francis engine on the same lines. It proved in 1926 to have quite a capacity for high revolutions, and the low top gear of 5·2 to 1 ensured brisk acceleration although with the high weight of 17 cwt. for the touring version, the acceleration was only attained at the expense of a maximum well under 60 m.p.h. The car was also very cheap for so ingenious a design, the tourer costing £235 in 1927. This admittedly compared unfavourably on a weight-for-money basis with the Swift at £210 or the Clyno at £160, but the Riley was a truly advanced design and the other two cars were totally lacking in subtlety or merit by comparison. With its exceptionally low build, tough chassis, and good brakes it sold very well, no less

1920 Riley 11-h.p. coupé

than 6000 being on the road by 1929; and this ensured considerable success for the firm. The well known fabric saloon "Monaco" version accounted for most of these sales and was certainly of far more agreeable appearance than the majority of the small perpendicular saloons of the time.

Such an engine was patently capable of further development and as such attracted the attention of Parry Thomas. After his death in 1927 Reid Railton took the matter in hand and produced a shortened and lowered version known as the "Brooklands" which gave 50 b.h.p. at 5000 r.p.m. and was able to do about 90 m.p.h., cruising at speeds up to 60 m.p.h. with a reasonable economy, if a complete lack of comfort. This was a surprising performance for a car of 1100 c.c. and essentially touring antecedents, and was the earliest indication of the extremely creditable series of competition successes scored by Rileys in the early thirties, particularly in the Tourist Trophy race. Nor should it be forgotten that the first E.R.A.s were basically developments of the Riley theme. In short, the Riley Nine was less a sports car in itself than a thoroughly distinguished ancestor of worthy higher-performance vehicles.

THE THREE-LITRE SUNBEAM

The Sunbeam Company's production cars of the early Vintage period showed little reflection of their extensive support of Grand Prix racing, being beautifully made along conventional lines and with a performance more refined than lively. A very

73

fine fast light tourer was marketed for a few years called the 24/60, having the prewar six-cylinder 25/30 engine with pushrod overhead valves in a light chassis, but it remains little known and was hardly a true sports car. It must, however, be counted among the prettiest cars ever made, with its long, slender lines. In 1925, however, the firm added to their wide range a very notable car indeed, the famous twin-cam 3-litre, which remained in modest production until the end of our period. Its design closely followed the best contemporary racing practice and differed from all other high-performance cars of the period in having a six-cylinder engine of moderate stroke (75 × 110 mm.) with two overhead camshafts driven by a train of gears at the front of the engine. This exceptionally attractive unit gave 90 b.h.p. at 3800 r.p.m., and was really a rather subtler and modernised version of the Bertarione racing designs, as well as being the first twin-camshaft engine to be offered for sale by any European factory[1]. Set in a fairly light chassis and not unduly burdened with coachwork it gave a substantially better performance than the 3-litre Bentley, as might well have been expected from its more advanced design, and it was capable in standard form of rather more than 90 m.p.h., which was a very creditable speed for a production car at this date.

The Sunbeam shared the smooth transmission and light controls of all its lesser brothers, together with fine steering and servo brakes, and was in many respects the most technically interesting and advanced sports car in production at the time. Unfortunately, few designers in the 1920s seemed to have thought of everything at once and the chassis was not on a par with the mechanical side at all. It had the excessively long wheelbase of 10 ft. 10 in. and a relatively narrow track; but worst of all, presumably to keep in line with design policy on other models, cantilever rear springs, which (despite the theoretical advantage of low unsprung weight) have always been more suited to heavy or luxurious class than light sporting models. Hence the car earned a name for difficulty of control at high speeds; and as by the time of its introduction the Bentley was so

[1] Except for the fifty twin-cam cars made in 1923 by Ballot.

well established in its class, it perhaps never earned the success which it deserved. It is interesting to remark that Sunbeam had announced in 1919 that they had plans for the marketing of a production car on the lines of the 1914 T.T. model; and had they in fact stepped off the mark so early as this, motoring history in our period might have been very different.

The 3-litre was never outstanding in competition, but finished second to a Lorraine-Dietrich at Le Mans in 1925 after the retirement of both Bentleys, and won various races at Brooklands including the Essex Six-Hour in 1927. In 1928 a supercharger was added to the engine, which thus realised its potentialities more fully by giving 138 b.h.p. at 3800 r.p.m., but to some extent at the expense of reliability; the blown 3-litre was never a serious factor in events of the late 1920s and very few indeed were made.

It is particularly difficult after so many years to assess the merits of the twin-cam Sunbeam, for so few were made and their rather complex construction has rendered them so much less durable than the tougher Bentleys and Vauxhalls. Its place in history is certain as an early attempt to produce a tamed and road-equipped racing car with the sweetness of a smallish six-cylinder engine and a performance second to none on the road. To attempt this in 1925 was distinctly daring, for it is only in the last few years that designers have really trusted their customers with similar engines; and to this extent Sunbeams were, as usual, well advanced for their time.

TALBOT

The respected firm of Clement Talbot was not enjoying any great fame or prosperity during the early Vintage period, and except for the astonishing little 8/18 was marketing no very distinguished cars. The glory of the earlier period from 1910 to 1914 had gone; and it was not until the appointment of Georges Roesch as chief engineer in 1925, from another factory of the Sunbeam-Talbot-Darracq combine, that they once more achieved success in the touring and sporting fields. Roesch is a man of exceptional talent whose unorthodox approach to design problems produced extremely good results; and Talbots in the early 1930s under his guidance once more became popular and fast cars. His first move on becoming chief engineer was to discontinue their entire range of cars and concentrate production on one model only, the 14/45; and since he did not have to build it round existing components he created a most unified and distinctive car whose pattern was followed in all subsequent models until the failure of the firm in the late 1930s. The 14/45 was in many ways a novel conception for 1926, and not at all characteristic of contemporary practice, for it had a small pushrod overhead-valve six-cylinder engine of 1665 c.c., with coil ignition. It produced about 48 b.h.p. by reason of its very light moving parts and high compression, and was set in a solidly constructed chassis of fairly standard design. Although the production

Talbot "75" with four-door coachbuilt saloon body, 1930: the final Vintage statement of the famous Georges Roesch design

coachwork was attractive in appearance it was fairly weighty and the performance was not remarkable; but the car soon became popular as an exceedingly comfortable and reliable tourer with particularly low running costs. Routine maintenance was in fact more sympathetically considered and easier to carry out than on any car of moderate price up to that time; but as later owners have discovered to their cost, anything in the nature of complex overhaul or adjustment presents formidable difficulties. Difficult starting was a chronic shortcoming, due to using a dynamotor, which was hardly equal to its work, even when fortified by a 24-volt battery.

The large brakes and rigid chassis of these cars with their willing engines formed an obvious basis for a sporting car and in

1929 the engine was enlarged to 2 litres at the "75" model; this had a creditable performance but was not powerful enough for real competition work. Roesch therefore made several changes in the valve gear and compression ratio in 1930, until the engine gave 93 b.h.p. at 4500 r.p.m.; and this model, the "90", ran with great regularity at Le Mans that year, two cars in fact finishing third and fourth to the winning Bentleys of nearly three times their capacity; this they did in impressive silence, too. The last year of the Vintage period also saw teams of these cars achieve first, second, and third places in their class in the Irish Grand Prix, Ulster Tourist Trophy, and 500 Miles Race at Brooklands, all finishing this last race at over 103 m.p.h. Even this was not enough for Roesch, who enlarged the engine still further to 3 litres as the "105" model, which in competition form gave the prodigious output of 140 b.h.p. on a 10 to 1 compression ratio and was altogether one of the outstanding sports cars of the early thirties. Its numerous successes, however, do not come into our period, which really saw only the beginning of the Talbot revival; but the story of the 14/45 shows more than any other how a basically standard touring design could give power, smoothness, and reliability in 1928 which would have been unthinkable even five years earlier.

The 30/98 Vauxhall

It is a wholesome thought for the designers of motor-cars that the greatest fast touring car of the Vintage period came into being more or less by accident. In 1913 J. Higginson of Stockport, a well known amateur motorist and inventor of the "Autovac", approached the late L. H. Pomeroy and Vauxhall Motors with the request that they would build him a light and very fast car for hill-climbs, and it is highly fortunate that they agreed to do so. This primeval 30/98, as it was known from the first for no really satisfactory reason, consisted of an overbored standard side-valve engine of 98 × 150 mm. in a light chassis, similar to those used for the Coupe de l'Auto racing cars. It was remarkable for its extremely effective power-weight ratio, which gave it all the performance that Higginson had hoped for. A very few similar cars were made for sale before the war, following successful appearances at Shelsley Walsh, including a frightening ascent in 55·2 seconds with four passengers aboard. After the war this so-called E-type car went into catalogue production with modern equipment and better brakes; about two hundred of these were made until late in 1922, when the engine was slightly reduced in size and converted to pushroad overhed valves as the OE-type, of which just over three hunderd were produced. Front brakes of a curious nature were added in September 1923, but basically the 30/98 retained the same chassis, engine layout, transmission, and general appearance from 1913 until 1927, when production ceased. An important alteration in the last few cars was a balanced crankshaft, which rendered the engine incredibly smooth for its size, and enabled it to give 120 b.h.p. at 3500 r.p.m.; and these latest 30/98s shared the gearbox and hydraulic brakes of the contemporary 25/70 single-sleeve-valve chassis.

So long a span of production is a notable feat for any Edwardian design, and really explains why the 30/98 remains to so many people the epitome of the Vintage sports car; for it is not, as are the contemporary Bentleys and Sunbeams, a modification for public use of a competition design, but the ultimate development of a fundamentally plain and sound touring car to give an outstanding performance with complete reliability. As such it remains remarkably tractable and flexible, and can be driven about in top gear like any Vintage tourer. The handbook counsels the driver to start from rest in bottom or second gear at 250 r.p.m. and endeavour to reach top with minimum variation in engine speed; and indeed, with its wide ratios, it is not a car on which much is gained by frequent gear-changing. Nor, since it is a fast touring car rather than a sports car, does the 30/98 advertise its performance by the shriek of pinions or the harsh crackle of exhaust. The sweet-running engine produces its power in becoming dignity, with merely a soothing rumble of exhaust noise, nor is this performance quite so inferior by modern standards as that of many Vintage cars. The E-type engines gave about 90 b.h.p. at 2800 r.p.m. and were light enough to pull a high (3:1) axle ratio, giving them a speed of about 85 m.p.h.; the OE engines ran up to 3500 r.p.m., at which they gave about 110 b.h.p., but the cars were heavier and a lower ratio gave a very slightly decreased maximum but better acceleration. *The Autocar* tested a fully-equipped "Velox" four-seater in 1923 at 82 m.p.h. and the makers were always prepared to guarantee a Brooklands speed of 100 m.p.h. after special preparation. If these speeds seem trivial to the modern motorist, let him consider the merits of having a car with a maximum 30 m.p.h. greater than most other cars on the road, and a cruising speed of 60 or 70 m.p.h. when most other traffic was proceeding at about 30 m.p.h.

The 30/98 was not, however, in all respects the king of the road. One of the penalties of developing any car, and particularly an Edwardian, to give a very superior performance is that in the process defects become more and more apparent. Vauxhall brakes had doubtless been adequate enough in 1913, but during the twenties they became less and less so, and remained a weak feature of the car under more competitive traffic conditions. Neither the hastily added front brakes of 1923, with their untidy exposed kidney-box compensation between the dumb-irons, nor the vast but somewhat crudely laid out hydraulics of the later cars were really good enough for the performance, though they seem to have satisfied the contemporary drivers. The chassis, too is alarmingly light and unbraced for so fast a car, and the engine accessories and their drives are manifestly afterthoughts rather than part of a carefully considered whole. The standard coachwork, too, pays for its lightness by a notable lack of comfort, especially in the back seats.

Nor was the 30/98 ever really outstanding in competition, although on Brooklands special versions were winning races long after production had ceased. Kent Karslake has put forward the theory that Hispano-Suizas were never entered at events such as Le Mans because no one had the least doubt of their capacity to maintain a very high speed for twenty-four hours. It would seem most unlikely that such considerations prevented Vauxhalls from appearing there, and it is in those particulars which they lack, such as heavy chassis, large brakes, and a generally unified design, that the successful Bentleys scored. Nevertheless, it must be put on record that in 1953 a 30/98, owned and driven by T. H. Plowman, covered 107 miles in one hour on the very rough track at Montlhéry, which is a performance of which any production car nearly thirty years old may well be proud. But it is on the open road that the combination of refinement and appetite is seen at its best and the 30/98 becomes in the words of its makers "a sporting car which has never known a superior".

4

Racing Cars

THE 1914–18 war came at a moment when new vistas of development were unfolding themselves before designers, among whom
the pioneer Ernest Henry was pre-eminent. This new movement
had started in 1912 and Henry completely dominated the racing
world for the following decade. Up to the war he had worked for
Peugeot and after it for Ballot. His cars were pretty consistently
the fastest present, but they were as consistently haunted by the
most wickedly bad luck, so that they very seldom won.

During the war Henry had worked with Bugatti on his successful straight-eight aero-engine, so that when Ernest Ballot entered
a car for the 1919 Indianapolis and asked Henry to design it,
Henry produced an engine very similar to the pre-war Peugeots,
but with eight cylinders in line. The straight-eight engine was to
dominate racing during almost the whole of the inter-war years,
so that the 1919 Indianapolis Ballot is very important historically
in having set the fashion. Actually Bugatti had made an even
smaller straight-eight racing car, of only $2\frac{3}{4}$-litres capacity, as
early as 1912. There had, of course, been earlier straight-eights,
but they were all of very large capacity and had no bearing on the
high-efficiency eight pioneered by Bugatti and Henry. Not long
after the Henry-Ballot came Duesenberg, who had also made
Bugatti aero-engines under licence, and in 1920 they produced a
straight-eight racer having a single overhead camshaft and three
valves per cylinder (one inlet and two exhaust). As it turned out
the Duesenberg was more successful than the Ballot, which it
beat in the 1921 Grand Prix at Le Mans, despite having only
a three-speed gearbox. It was also notable for having hydraulic
brakes (literally hydraulic, being operated by water contained
in the axles).

Duesenberg continued in racing, but with little further impact
on the European scene, as they concentrated almost entirely on
maximum speed and paid little or no attention to chassis design,

which played an ever-increasing part in successful Grand Prix racing.

The 1921 Coppa Florio race saw the first appearance in racing of a supercharged car. The American Chadwick had experimented with some success in supercharging as early as 1907, but Mercedes were the pioneers of its development after the war and the 1921 car was their first attempt. They entered for quite a lot of races up to 1924 but without notable success.

Racing in 1920–21 had been to a 3-litre formula, under which Henry's influence had been paramount, but under the 2-litre formula current from 1922 to 1925 it rapidly waned, although he was employed to design the unsuccessful 1922 Grand Prix Sunbeam. F.I.A.T. had produced a not very successful 3-litre car in 1921, but in 1922 they prepared an excellent 2-litre six-cylinder machine, and for a short time six cylinders remained the fashion, although the eight soon reasserted itself.

In 1923 Sunbeam discarded the outmoded Henry and brought Bertarione, the F.I.A.T. designer, over to replace him. They were rewarded for this by winning the 1923 Grand Prix, while F.I.A.T. evolved a new supercharged car, with a Roots compressor, which had its first win at Monza in 1923.

For 1924 Bertarione improved the Sunbeam (still basically a 1922 F.I.A.T.) and supercharged it, in which form it was undoubtedly the fastest car of the year. With a certain Grand Prix victory in their grasp, the night before the race Sunbeams allowed themselves to be persuaded by Bosch to fit new magnetos of faulty design, so that the race went to the new straight-eight P.2 Alfa Romeo. When formula racing came to an end in 1927, the P.2 was revived and modified to give substantially increased power. In this form it had considerable success.

The year 1923 saw Delage re-enter Grand Prix racing with a most advanced and tremendously complicated V-twelve machine, but it did not meet with success until 1925, the last year of the 2-litre formula, when, in supercharged form, it developed 190 b.h.p. at no less than 7000 r.p.m.

It was said that the Porsche-designed straight-eight 2-litre Mercedes could attain 8000 r.p.m., and this with cylinder dimensions of $61·7 \times 82$ mm. The classis design was very faulty and the car seems never to have raced without having a major accident; but the engine may well have inspired the 3·3-litre engine which powered the Mercedes 1934 Grand Prix car under the 750-kilogramme formula.

During four years the 2-litre formula therefore saw very great advances. The 1922 F.I.A.T. developed 92 b.h.p. and had a maximum speed of about 105 m.p.h. By 1925 the Delage had more than doubled this power output and could attain 140 m.p.h., a speed which was not greatly exceeded in Grand Prix racing for nearly a decade.

For 1926–7 the capacity limit was reduced to 1½ litres, but this was not really a new situation for designers, since there had been a series of important 1½-litre voiturette races since 1920.

The first of these, at Brescia, was completely swept by Bugatti, who took the first three places with a team of sixteen-valve cars which had been completed on the outbreak of war and kept in storage. In subsequent races, and throughout 1921–2–3, the 1½-litre field was dominated by Talbot-Darracq. As has just been said, Sunbeam employed Henry to design their 1922 Grand Prix car, but this was no more than a tardy (and, as it proved, belated) recognition of the fact that his designs had, without consultation, been supplying the Sunbeam racing stable since 1913! The 1921 Grand Prix Sunbeam was, in effect, a 1920 Ballot with a plain-bearing crankshaft and straight-forward lubrication, and as such it was an extremely fine car, although it never met with any outstanding success. However, when half the engine was used as a 1½-litre, and known as a Talbot-Darracq, it became invincible and remained so until the end of 1923. For 1924–5 Bertarione, by then working for Sunbeam, designed a worthy successor to the Talbot-Darracq, in the shape of a scaled-down version of his 2-litre Grand Prix Sunbeam. The result, surprisingly enough was known as a Darracq.

This, in turn, held sway until the Grand Prix formula dropped to 1½ litres for the years 1926–7. However, all former cars were pretty well put out of the running by a new ruling that mechanics might no longer be carried in races. This enabled designers to make a reduction in frontal area of some 15%, which almost exactly counterbalanced the reduced power of the smaller engines (which dropped 15% in power for a 25% drop in capacity). Maximum speeds therefore remained much the same, although acceleration suffered.

A somewhat inconclusive 1926 season gave Bugatti considerable success with a 1½-litre edition of his type 35 cars, but by 1927 Delage had perfected their Lory-designed straight-eight, which carried all before it during that year, which was to be the last of formula racing until 1934. This Delage must certainly be regarded as the climax of Vintage racing design, for when it was ten years old it made Richard Seaman's reputation and showed its absolute supremacy over the current E.R.A.s and all other voiturettes.

After 1927 Grand Prix racing, such as it was, became a *formule libre* affair, enlivened mainly by Bugatti, who during these years gained a measure of supremacy with his type 35 cars such as no other maker has ever enjoyed. Although developing very much less power than the 1927 Delage, Bugatti's larger engine (usually 2·3 litres) gave much better acceleration and this, coupled with great reliability and superior chassis design, enabled his cars to beat the Delages on most circuits. Undoubtedly the fastest Vintage racing car in England which survives in running order is a type 35B Bugatti.

The only new Grand Prix car to be introduced in 1928–9–30 was the straight-eight, 2½-litre Maserati, which was the most successful competitor for Grand Prix honours. For 1931 most manufacturers put out something new, so that although *formule libre* racing continued, 1930 really marked the end of an era.

The decline of Grand Prix racing focussed greater interest on sports car events, especially the great Twenty-Four Hour Race at Le Mans, where Bentley immeasurably enhanced the reputation of Great Britain by winning for four successive years from 1927 to 1930. The 4½-litre Bentley was really already obsolete when it was introduced in 1927, and got its victories more by brute force than mechanical finesse. But victory it did get, most convincingly, and its great stamina in standard form has enabled it to be developed to a point far beyond anything which its designer can have envisaged, so that over short distances it is still a force to be reckoned with in sports car events. In supercharged form developing 240 b.h.p. at 4200 r.p.m., it was able to show fight against genuine Grand Prix cars, and in the French Grand Prix of 1930 a blown 4½-litre Bentley, driven by Sir Henry Birkin finished second only to a type 35C Bugatti.

Mercedes produced their famous 38/250 car in 1929, and in its final development it probably put out 300 b.h.p. and was capable of 150 m.p.h. Its great size (7 litres) and rather poor brakes seriously handicapped its performance in racing.

In 1926–7 Amilcar and Salmson produced some superb machines for 1100-c.c. class racing. The Salmson was a straight-eight, 50 × 70·8 mm., with a Roots-type blower, which enabled it to develop 100 b.h.p. at only 5800 r.p.m. More successful was the Amilcar, which was a Cozette-blown twin-cam six-cylinder of 56 × 74 mm. These beautifully proportioned cars performed well in England and are still used successfully in current Vintage racing. Thirty-four of these twin-cam cars were made.

As with production cars, the great attraction and interest of Vintage racing cars lies in their infinite variety, ranging from the apparently lumbering Bentley bulldog to the infinitely lithe Bugatti greyhound, or from cars such as the V-twelve or straight-eight Delage (which must be the most complicated engines ever made prior to the V-16 B.R.M.) to such cars as the type 37 Bugatti, which many amateurs could well run and maintain.

In 1914 the world speed record stood at 131·7 m.p.h. and in 1929 it had been raised by Segrave in the Golden Arrow to 231·4 m.p.h. Sir Malcolm Campbell attacked it most persistently with a series of Sunbeam cars with aero-engines, but with two exceptions, the 1923 Delage and the 1926 Sunbeam, the successful cars were not of great technical interest. The Delage and Sunbeam are more fully described under their respective makes.

Most interesting of all was the Stutz "Black Hawk" designed by Frank Lockhart to attack the record. A straight-eight of only 3 litres capacity, it showed itself in tests to be capable of 200 m.p.h., but crashed on the record attempt, being completely wrecked, while Lockhart was killed. This tremendous speed was not again attained from a 3-litre for nearly fifteen years.

Racing at Brooklands attracted some superb and diverse Vintage cars, many of them developed from standard models such as the 30/98 Vauxhall; 3-, 4½-, and 6½-litre Bentleys;

innumerable Bugattis; the Leyland Thomas; the 8-litre sleeve-valve razor-blade Panhard; the Zeppelin Maybach-engined Chitty-Bang-Bang of Count Zborowski; or the 1913 21½-litre four-cylinder Benz. Brooklands demands a book to itself, and in W. Boddy *The Story of Brooklands* was fortunate in obtaining the author best qualified to write it. The development of the Grand Prix car is, of course, incomparably told in *The Grand Prix Car* 1906–1939 by L. Pomeroy, with illustrations by L. C. Cresswell.

In Vintage Grand Prix racing only five makes distinguished themselves consistently or made history. In chronological order they were Ballot, F.I.A.T., Sunbeam, Delage, and Bugatti, and these will now be described in greater detail.

BALLOT

Ernest Ballot's engineering firm made stationary engines during the 1914–18 war. Before the war it had made proprietary engines for such famous makes as Delage and others.

On Christmas Eve 1918 he entered a team of cars for the 1919 Indianapolis race, for which purpose the cars would have to be ready to leave France by the end of April.

He therefore reached the prudent conclusion that there was little time to be lost in starting to design them, and invited Ernest Henry to undertake this – apparently impossible – task. So successfully did Henry and the Ballot workshops apply themselves that the racing cars were running in 100 days from the time Henry set pencil to paper. In these days, when two years is considered barely adequate in which to design, build, and develop a new racing car, the Henry-Ballot feat seems almost incredible.

Nor was the result a mere re-vamp of a pre-war Peugeot, but a new conception which set the pace for practically all successful racing design in the inter-war years. Despite this, the 1919 Ballots were successful from the moment they ran and had a long and honourable racing history. One still survives in America.

Up to 1914 no successful racing car had more than four cylinders. The 1919 Indianapolis race was for cars with engines having a capacity of not more than 300 cubic inches (equal to

4917 cubic centimetres). Henry responded to this formula with an eight-cylinder in-line engine with cylinders measuring 74 × 140 mm. Following Henry's established practice, there were two overhead camshafts driven by a train of gears at the front of the engine. These operated four valves per cylinder via inverted cups placed over the ends of the valve stems. The sparking plug was between the camshafts, in the centre of the hemispherical head. There were two carburettors with very large chokes and barrel throttles.

Cylinder-head design was, in fact, Henry's strong point; the lower parts of his engines were not so felicitous. He employed a crankshaft with roller bearings for the mains, and very peculiar big-ends. The crankshaft journals themselves were small in size, and between them and the steel connecting-rod were floating bronze bushes, lined with white metal on their inner surface. Oil reached these, at times, via a rather haphazard system of dry-sump lubrication and centrifugal action of the crankshaft. The theory seems to have been that the bushes should revolve at half crankshaft speed, thus halving bearing speeds; but needless to say they never did so, and the high potential of a Henry top end could never be fully realised because of the frailty of the bottom half.

The 1919 engines were limited to 3500 r.p.m., but as the large-choke carburettors produced a very sluggish gas flow at low speeds, there was correspondingly little power below 2500 r.p.m., which seems to be a critical speed for all Henry's engines. The operative rev-range was therefore critically narrow, and although this was no special drawback on a course such as Indianapolis or Brooklands, it must have invested road racing with much the same problems as faced drivers of the B.R.M. more than thirty years later.

Again following usual Henry practice, the engine and separate gearbox were carried in a subframe, so that the chassis itself was virtually unbraced. Yet despite their apparent flexibility the 1919 5-litre and the 1920 3-litre cars handle quite beautifully. This is due to their excellently balanced weight distribution and the fact that the front and back springs were set at roughly equal centres, so that there was little apparent tendency either to over- or under-steer.

At Indianapolis the cars proved to be too high-geared (they pulled a 3 to 1 final ratio), so, having no spare ratio, smaller American wheels and tyres were fitted, and these gave constant trouble and cost Ballot the race, which, ironically, was won by one of Henry's 1914 Grand Prix Peugeots.

Later, at Brooklands, the Ballot proved to have a maximum not far short of 120 m.p.h. and on its twenty-first birthday, before it went to America, it attained 110 m.p.h. in road trim on a road in Oxfordshire, with power in hand.

Incidentally, the 1919 Indianapolis race produced one other very interesting multi-cylinder machine, in the shape of a V-twelve Packard. However, it was not very successful in the race. It was based upon a production model first introduced in 1915 and described in greater detail in the chapter on luxury cars.

The 1920 Indianapolis race was for 3-litre cars and so was the 1921 European Grand Prix, for which Henry designed another straight-eight Ballot, 65×112 mm., but mostly a scaled-down version of the 5-litre car. In 1920 it was fitted with front-wheel brakes which, at any rate in later years, were perilously erratic in operation.

The engine developed 82 b.h.p. at 2500 r.p.m. and 107 b.h.p. at its safe maximum of 3800 r.p.m. Once again the floating-bush big-end bearings were the Achilles heel of the engine and subsequent experience showed that any attempt to exceed this moderate speed for more than the shortest period was fraught with dire results.

The four-speed gearbox had ratios 3, 4·2, 5·4, and 7 to 1, and the latter, coupled with the usual Henry lack of low-speed torque and a very small cone clutch, made it virtually impossible to effect a rapid getaway.

Although the 3-litre cars were again the fastest of their size and date, they were persistently dogged by bad luck and won only one important race, the 1921 Brescia Grand Prix.

In 1922 Henry moved on to the Sunbeam firm, and Ballot retired from racing and concentrated on his very successful single-overhead-camshaft four-cylinder, 2-litre production model and his not so successful production straight-eights. But he had, with Henry's aid, written his name big in the annals of motor racing history.

BUGATTI

As the first of all Bugatti types, whether touring, sporting, or racing, must come the type 13, the first car made by Ettore Bugatti in his own name, from 1910, although the prototype was running in 1907.

It is impossible to say whether a Bugatti is ahead of its time or otherwise, because from whatever angle you view it, it is quite different from any other car, and ageless. You can only liken it to a Breguet watch. If Bugatti had lived a century earlier he would have made Breguet's incomparable watches; if Breguet had lived a hundred years later he would probably have made Bugatti cars. It was no accident that Bugatti collected Breguet watches. Bugatti certainly anticipated most modern trends, but in a way peculiarly his own. Everything in a type 59 Grand Prix car is inherent in the type 13. Thus, although the type 59 was an up-to-the-moment design in 1934, it had all really been said a quarter of a century earlier. The type 13 has already been described in the chapter on sports cars, and also how it ran second in the 1911 *formule libre* Grand Prix to a 10½-litre F.I.A.T.

In 1912 Bugatti foreshadowed the small-cylindered straight-eight engine which, in effect, dominated between-wars racing. This he did by joining two type 13 engines end to end. The resulting 2¾-litre car attained 86 m.p.h.

The type 30, although catalogued only as a touring car, was originally made as a racing car, for the Grand Prix de l'A.C.F. at Strasbourg. It will nevertheless be described in the touring section.

The engine of the Strasbourg cars was, however, an important innovation, being the first to have three valves per cylinder, two inlet and one exhaust. The two small inlet valves ensured a brisk gas-flow, greatly assisting the useful low-speed torque for which all Bugattis have been famous. Setting theory at naught, the single exhaust valve had a greater area than the combined area of the two inlet valves. This, coupled with the beautifully shaped exhaust manifold, testifies to the great importance which Bugatti attached to the scavenging of exhaust gases. Another unusual feature of the layout was that the sparkings plugs were on the inlet side. It is usual to place the plugs near the hottest part of the engine (i.e. the exhaust valves), but Bugatti evidently preferred to keep them cool.

The racing types proper of the Vintage years are the various denominations of types 35, 37, 39, and 47. The subdivisions of type 35 are as follows:

35 Grand Prix 2-litre unsupercharged, 1924
35A Modified Grand Prix 2-litre unsupercharged, 1926
35C Grand Prix 2-litre supercharged, 1927
35T Grand Prix 2·3-litre unsupercharged, 1927
35B Grand Prix 2·3-litre supercharged, 1927

Officially the 35A was designated Grand Prix "Imitation" and first appeared in 1924–5. Similarly the 35B was officially called the type "Targa Florio".

All, of course, were single-overhead-camshaft straight-eights, the 2-litre 60 × 88 mm., the 2·3-litre 60 × 100 mm. There was, in addition, a 1½-litre edition with cylinders 52 × 88 mm., first used in 1925 and then in 1926 for 1½-litre formula Grand Prix racing. In 1927, the last year of the 1½-litre formula, it was replaced by the type 39, with cylinder dimensions 60 × 66 mm., and the 39A, which was the same thing supercharged. This type 39 is really only a variant of 35 and need not be considered separately.

The type 35 engine was really a modified edition of the 1922 type 30, but having roller bearings throughout. Even so, the basic type 35 had only three main bearings. The later variants had a main bearing between each pair of cylinders, and this was achieved without any addition to the overall length. Other details of the engine may be found in the notes on the type 43 in the sports car section.

Bugatti was at one time much opposed to supercharging, saying that he could get as much power without it, but in 1926–7 he was won over to the system and his period of overwhelming supremacy in the racing field dates from this time. It continued into the 1928–30 era of *formule libre*, and beyond the Vintage limit into 1931, with the post-Vintage twin-cam type 51.

from fading, and the unsprung weight reduced to a minimum. Thereafter his fortunes in Grand Prix racing waned, although he had some successes in 1934, the first year of the new 750-kilogramme weight formula, with his 3·3-litre type 59.

But the type 35 has the remarkable record of having lived through three formulae – the 2-litre, 1½-litre, and *formule libre* – and of having become more successful with increasing age. It is also remarkable that although none of the variants came within 30 b.h.p. of the Delage which dominated the 1½-litre formula, the Bugatti consistently proved itself faster over any given road circuit.

This was partly due to the excellent low-speed torque of the larger Bugatti engine, which gave them their tremendous acceleration. Bugatti deliberately restricted maximum power to this end, and also to secure reliability. His cylinder head had very little room for the circulation of water, and Bugatti evidently took the view that if you had enough cast iron in the head, the heat would find its own way out. This naive faith was entirely justified in the event, but Bugatti was certainly wise not to attempt more than his modest 60 b.h.p. per litre.

But equally as much, Bugatti lap-speeds were due to his amazingly efficient chassis, which represented the ultimate in non-independent suspension. Bugatti clearly worked on the principle that as long as a chassis is extremely rigid forward of the steering box, what happens further back is relatively unimportant. This rigidity he secured by deeper chassis members than were then fashionable, firmly braced by the four-point rigidly-mounted engine.

Even the back part was a good deal more rigid than it looked and ended up with the famous reversed quarter-elliptic back springs. The merits of these have been hotly debated, but no very conclusive arguments have so far been produced either for or against them. Suffice it therefore to say that Bugatti used them on all models from 1912 onwards and secured better road-holding than anyone else using rigid axles. Even very few independently suspended layouts have shown themselves superior.

The cast aluminium wheels with integral brake drums also contributed to the success, the brakes being powerful and free

The extremely quick gearbox also enabled the most to be made of the power. There was a wide choice of back-axle ratios, but a typical overall set gave ratios of 3·85, 5·02, 7·12, and 9·35 to 1.

It was thus as a balanced design, combining many merits, that the types 35 and 39 achieved overwhelming successes over such a long period. It is, moreover, aesthetically satisfying in a way which perhaps no other car has ever been. It is no exaggeration to describe it as the most successful racing car of all time.

By contrast, the type 37 is uninspiring. It has a four-cylinder, plain-bearing, 69 × 100 mm., 1½-litre engine used for voiturette racing. It was introduced in 1925 and in 1927 acquired a super-charger, being then known as 37A. Its chief merit is that owing to its relative simplicity it is a particularly suitable mount for amateurs of moderate means.

Last of all in the series of Vintage racing Bugattis came the very rare type 47 of 1930, consisting of two type 39 engines placed side by side on a common crankcase, and having two super-chargers. The type 47 was also available as a 4-litre car having cylinder dimensions 60 × 88 mm. The type was made as a Grand Prix car (one driven by Louis Chiron broke the Bernina hill-climb record), but a specimen was prepared for Le Mans and

Front-wheel assembly on a 1924 Grand Prix Bugatti. The brake drums were built up integral with the cast aluminium wheel and rim. This type of wheel was used on all the successful type 35 Bugatti racing cars

still exists. Also listed as "Grand Sport", this was the most expensive car, except the type 41, ever made by Bugatti.

In 1931 Bugatti abandoned the single-camshaft engine for racing and turned to twin overhead camshafts operating two valves per cylinder. These later Grand Prix cars, in various capacities, have the basic type number 51.

DELAGE

Prior to the 1913 Grand Prix, Delage racing activities had been confined to voiturettes, including the winning of the 1911 Coupe de l'Auto event. Delage was notable for unconventional valve gear, and both in the 1911 Coupe de l'Auto and for the 1913 Grand Prix he used horizontally opposed valves, with the exhaust manifold emerging somewhat unexpectedly and inconveniently out of the top of the engine. For the 1914 Grand Prix he had two overhead camshafts with a mechanical linkage for closing the valves. These cars also had front-wheel brakes, but they failed to distinguish themselves.

Delage did not return to racing immediately after the war, but, for the 2-litre and 1½-litre years his efforts were heroic and crowned with abundant success.

In 1922 Delage employed a M. Plancton to design a Grand Prix car for the 2-litre formula and the resulting highly complex machine was built in the remarkably short space of four months. It was a V-twelve with a bore and stroke of $51 \cdot 3 \times 80$ mm., and ball or roller bearings were used in every possible situation. Each bank had two overhead camshafts and it must have been one of the most expensive engines in the whole history of motoring. It developed 120 b.h.p. at 6000 r.p.m., thus showing a marked improvement over the 92 b.h.p. of the contemporary F.I.A.T. Despite its bulky engine the car had slight and slender lines, and a very handsome pear-shaped radiator, reminiscent of a Bugatti. However, in unblown form the cars did not meet with success, and in 1925 they were considerably redesigned. The body was new, there was a more characteristically Delage radiator, and the engine was supercharged. In this form it achieved the remarkable (for the date) output of 195 b.h.p. at 7000 r.p.m. The maximum speed was about the same as the contemporary

93

2-litre F.I.A.T., namely 140 m.p.h.

In 1925 Delage had the satisfaction of winning three out of six *grandes épreuves* and was acclaimed the champion for the year.

For the 1½-litre formula, M. Plancton was succeeded by M. Lory, who proceeded to design one of the most – perhaps the most – outstanding racing cars of all time. This was a 57.5×75 mm. straight-eight following the general style and complication of the V-twelve; it had, in all, 62 ball or roller races. The cylinder block and head was an integral iron casting with side plates of steel for the water jacket. The crankshaft roller bearing were housed in split cages and lubrication was by jet, with a dry sump. The connecting-rods were exceptionally strong and beautifully designed. Two overhead camshafts driven by a train of gears at the front of the engine operated two large valves per cylinder, inclined at an angle of 100 degrees. The compression ratio was $6\frac{1}{2}$ to 1 and the supercharger pressure 7 lb. per square inch, yet with these moderate figures an output of 170 b.h.p. was obtainable at 8000 r.p.m.

To obtain full advantage of the potential output M. Lory reverted to a pre-war Delage practice in using five forward speeds with an overdrive fifth. Various back-axle ratios were available, but a typical overall set gave 4·4, 5·2, 6·6, 8·75, and 11·7 to 1. This arrangement enabled the maximum speed of which the car was capable, about 130 m.p.h., to be maintained at the safe engine speed of 6400 r.p.m. (a piston speed of only 3200 feet per minute).

To obtain full advantage from the new rule that a travelling mechanic need not be carried the engine was set at an angle across the chassis and was carried in a subframe, together with its unit gearbox. As the engine and gearbox were lengthy and the chassis of light construction, the latter was not notable for rigidity, and the lap speeds of the car suffered correspondingly. Like most racing machines of the mid-twenties, braking was via mechanical servo and Perrot shaft.

At first the engine had two superchargers, with the exhaust manifold on the offside, but as a result, so many pit stops were needed to cool the driver's feet that races were lost, and Bugatti was the most successful competitor for the 1926 honours. However, for 1927 the engine was modified so that the exhaust emerged from the nearside and a long, single supercharger was mounted in front. The front of the car, and especially the steering linkage, was also stiffened up as much as possible, and in this form the Delage proved practically invincible, winning four out of the five available Grand Prix races.

Ten years later, when Richard Seaman became dissatisfied with the servicing arrangements for his E.R.A., the brilliant mechanic Ramponi advised him to obtain one of the 1926 Delages, which he did, and was rewarded by a clear superiority over the E.R.A.s, despite their better chassis and braking. Ten years of development had failed to equal the amazing achievement of M. Lory. In Ramponi's hands the power output was increased to 195 b.h.p. with very little modification, and Laurence Pomeroy has calculated that with a 15 lb. boost the post-war Alfa Romeo type 158 could have been equalled.

Seaman ran his Delage through a whole season with no mechanical failure, including three successive full-length races with no overhaul of any kind. This is a performance probably without equal and in a ten-year-old car it is miraculous. Truly the 1926-7 Delage was the crowning achievement of the Vintage decade.

After 1927 Delage could well afford to retire from racing, but one other racing Delage must be mentioned. This was the V-twelve 10,688-c.c. car made in 1923 to attack the world land-speed record and also sprint hill-climbs. Despite this disparity of objectives, it achieved both with success, taking the speed record on a narrow road at Arpajon, driven by René Thomas, at 143·24 m.p.h. The car next came to Brooklands, where it probably had more successes than any other car and established the reputations of Oliver Bertram and John Cobb. Its best lap speed was 136·45 m.p.h.

After varying fortunes it was then acquired by Clutton, completely rebuilt, and raced in 1951–2 with some success in Vintage events on the Silverstone circuit, as well as being driven considerable distances on the road. Probably no car has ever had such a versatile and successful career, including the land-speed record, sprint records, track and road-circuit racing, and touring. After a fairly bad crash in 1952 as the result of catching fire, it is being rebuilt and will race again.

F.I.A.T.

Of the manufacturers who distinguished themselves in Vintage racing none had had a longer or more distinguished racing career than F.I.A.T. Among the barbarous crudities of the 1000-kilogramme formula, the 1905 F.I.A.T. stood out as a finely conceived and executed mechanical achievement, notable in particular for its inclined overhead valves. The 1911 Grand Prix winner had an overhead camshaft operating four valves per cylinder and this design appeared in various sizes up to the monstrous 300-h.p. record-breaker which in 1913 achieved an unofficial 143 m.p.h. at Ostend. This had the largest four-cylinder engine ever fitted into a motor-car, with a capacity of 28·4 litres. The cylinder dimensions were 190 × 250 mm. The 1914 Grand Prix F.I.A.T. had an overhead camshaft and four-wheel brakes, and was a most handsome machine.

For the 1921 3-litre Grand Prix they had a straight-eight designed by Bertarione, which is historically important, because Bertarione was the first man to break away from the Henry school. Thus his twin overhead camshafts operated two only valves per cylinder, while the cylinder block followed Mercedes precedent in having steel forgings welded together, with a steel water jacket. The cylinder dimensions were the almost universal 65 × 112 mm. Even more striking, however, was the bottom half of the engine, which was always the Achilles heel of Henry. Bertarione employed a one-piece crankshaft with roller bearings throughout, housed in split cages. These cars developed 120 b.h.p. at 4600 r.p.m. and were probably the fastest of all the 3-litre cars; but they met with no major success. It many have been for this reason that Bertarione seems to some extent to have been ousted as the top designer to F.I.A.T. and their 1922 2-litre Grand Prix car is credited to the joint efforts of Zerbi, Fornaca, and Cavelli. This may be one of the reasons why Bertarione allowed himself to be tempted by Coatalen into the Sunbeam camp for 1923. Nevertheless, the Zerbi-Fornaca-Cavelli trinity followed closely upon the design of Bertarione's 3-litre

14 The 1925 Type C.G.S. Amilcar Grand Sport – one of the most popular
of the small French Vintage sports cars

15 A 1929 Riley "9", with a four-seater fabric body

16   1925 Lancia "Lambda", 5th series short chassis

17   1927 Alfa Romeo 22/90

18　The first of the M.G. "Midgets" – a 1929 "M" type

19　One of the first M.G.s with obvious Morris "Oxford" parentage, 1923

20   The "twin-cam", 3-litre Sunbeam, 1926

21   The 3-litre Bentley, with Vanden Plas coachwork, 1924

22 Shelsley Walsh hill-climb, 1922: E-type 30/98 Vauxhall

23 The 1930 6½-litre "Speed Six" Bentley

24 1924 Alvis 12/50 with the famous "duck's-back" polished aluminium body

25 "International" Aston Martin two/three seater, 1927

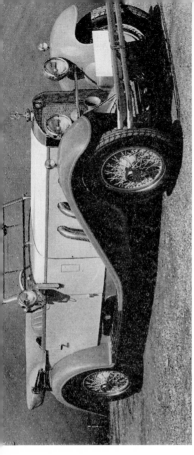

26 The 38/250 Mercedes-Benz, introduced in 1929

27 The 4½-litre "S"-type Invicta standard two/four seater, introduced in 1930

28   The most famous of all veteran racing cars: the 1902 Panhard "70";
Charles Jarrott at the wheel

29   The Métallurgique driven by Colonel J. T. C. Moore-Brabazon in the
1908 "Four Inch" Race in the Isle of Man

and were rewarded by winning six out of seven Grand Prix races in 1922–3.

For 1922 they used a 65 × 100 mm. six-cylinder engine. The two camshafts were driven by a train of gears at the back of the engine, and there was dry-sump lubrication. In the steel block, as before, the only novel feature was the wide-angle head (96°), which enabled the use of very large valves. These and the shorter stroke brought about a substantial increase over the 1921 machine in power per litre, and even though only one carburettor was used, 92 b.h.p. was obtained at 5200 r.p.m. This high crankshaft speed (and fairly high piston speed) could be attained with reliability because of Bertarione's sound notions on crank-shaft design and lubrication. The cars had an unladen weight of only 13 cwt. and a maximum speed of about 105 m.p.h.

For 1923 Zerbi, Fornaca, and Cavelli produced a 60 × 87·5 mm. straight-eight, with the important addition of a supercharger, by which means the power output was increased to 120 b.h.p. At first a vane-type instrument was used, but this proved unreliable and was quickly replaced by a Roots-type blower. In this form the car won the 1923 Italian Grand Prix and so made history by being the first supercharged car to win a Grand Prix. Mercedes had been using a supercharger since 1921, but with no important success. As in all superchargers at that time, air only, and not the mixture, was compressed.

These cars were timed at 137 m.p.h., yet despite a successful year in 1923, the honours for 1924 were about equally divided between Alfa Romeo and Sunbeam, and for 1925 F.I.A.T. retired from racing.

For voiturette 1½-litre racing F.I.A.T. also made a four-cylinder which was half of a 1921 3-litre straight-eight, and in 1923 a team appeared in the Brooklands 200-mile race with a supercharger, although both retired with mechanical afflictions. However, for the 1925–6 Grand Prix 1½-litre formula, F.I.A.T. evolved two extremely enterprising designs, neither of which, unfortunately, was ever fully developed.

One was a supercharged twelve-cylinder, with two vertical rows of six, having two crankshafts geared together. The cylinder dimensions were 50 × 63 mm. and the power output was 160 b.h.p. The only success of this model was at the Milan Grand Prix of 1927. The other design was a supercharged two-stroke, also with crankshafts, but the pistons were opposed, working in pairs in six cylinder barrels of 52 mm. bore. Each crankshaft had a throw of 58 mm., making a total effective stroke of 116 mm., although with a very low piston speed. The pistons of one crankshaft uncovered the inlet ports, and the other set controlled the exhaust ports. With a compression ratio of $6\frac{1}{2}$ to 1 and a boost of only 6 lb. per square inch, a power output of 174 b.h.p. at 6500 r.p.m. was attained. But this engine was never raced, and after 1927 F.I.A.T. retired altogether from racing.

THE SUNBEAM-TALBOT-DARRACQ COMBINE

Sunbeam started their racing career in 1912 by winning the Coupe de l'Auto race with a tuned-up edition of their production 12/16 tourer, but so little altered that it even ran with artillery wheels. Louis Coatalen, who was the power behind the firm, then conceived a devoted admiration for the work of M. Henry and proceeded to copy his Peugeot designs with scarcely the most thinly-veiled disguise. In this way he won the 1914 T.T. race and competed unsuccessfully in the Grand Prix.

By various subterfuges it was found possible during the war to build up a 5-litre six-cylinder car, which was entered for the 1919 Indianapolis race, but for some reason never satisfactorily explained the team was withdrawn. One of the cars still exists and the engines had considerable racing success in a later Grand Prix chassis.

For the 1921 3-litre Grand Prix Coatalen produced what was perhaps the best of all the many variants of the Henry theme. This was a 65 × 112 mm. straight-eight, like the Henry Ballot, with two overhead camshafts and four valves per cylinder, but it improved on the Ballot by having plain bearings and pressure lubrication throughout. Appearing variously with two and four carburettors, it was a non-starter in the Grand Prix, but won the 1922 T.T. (against, be it admitted, negligible opposition). However, despite its moderate success, this machine is one of quite exceptional charm and great reliability.

The $1\frac{1}{2}$-litre four-cylinder Talbot-Darracq, on the other hand, which had half the 3-litre engine, was invincible in voiturette racing during 1921–2–3.

For 1922, Ballot having retired from racing, Coatalen was able to obtain the services of his hero in person, but Henry had already said all he had to say, and other stars were brighter in the firmament. He accordingly only succeeded in designing a drably unsuccessful machine in which, for some unaccountable reason, he departed from his successful eight-cylinder formula and built a 68 × 136 mm. four-cylinder engine with, stranger still, a three-speed gearbox. In all other respects it closely followed his pioneer Peugeot work of a decade earlier.

Coatalen therefore next succeeded in luring Bertarione from F.I.A.T., and for 1923 he had a fairly close version of the 1922 F.I.A.T., but with the smaller bore/stroke ratio of 67 × 94 mm. By this means he put more than 10 b.h.p. on to the F.I.A.T. output, and using Henry's 1922 chassis (Henry had a very sure touch with chassis design, despite always carrying his engines in a subframe) the Sunbeam team finished the French Grand Prix in first, second, and fourth places. For 1924 Bertarione supercharged the car, being the first person to compress the mixture (as opposed to the air only), as is now the universal practice in supercharging. In this form it gave 138 b.h.p. at 5500 r.p.m. and was easily the fastest car of the year, although it only won one Grand Prix. The maximum speed was about 125 m.p.h. In later years the output was increased to about 170 b.h.p. Bertarione also made a 1½-litre four-cylinder, 67 × 105·5 mm. version of the 2-litre for voiturette racing, which gave 108 b.h.p. at 5500 r.p.m. with a 7-lb. boost.

For 1926 Bertarione made perhaps the finest of all his designs for the 1½-litre formula, the result being known, not any longer as a Sunbeam, but as a Talbot. The straight-eight engine was, on paper, about as good as the Delage, and the chassis was incomparably better, being remarkably stiff. But the machine was never adequately developed, and in the middle of 1927 the combine withdrew from racing. In the late thirties Powys-Lybbe tried to emulate Seaman by resurrecting a Talbot, but rearmament was already getting into its swing and the project could not be carried through.

Sunbeam produced various land-speed record machines throughout the Vintage decade, but only one was of technical interest. This was a V-twelve supercharged 4-litre, being, in effect, two 2-litre Grand Prix engines on a common crankshaft. In this form, driven by Segrave on the Southport sands, the record was taken in 1926 at 162·33 m.p.h. This is interesting not only as being by many times the smallest car to have held this coveted honour, but also because, at this time, it stood at a speed not 20 m.p.h. higher than the maximum of the fastest Grand Prix machines of the year previous. The engine was subsequently put into a more practicable, but excessively heavy, front-wheel-brake chassis.

Sunbeams contributed greatly to British prestige in the motoring world in the dozen years during which they competed with success in international racing.

5

Economy and Utility

IT is altogether too optimistic to suppose that English roads in the 1920s were wholly teeming with exotic and interesting cars. The motoring population was still extremely small; and the limited production of the sporting or luxurious models, which appeal to us so strongly in retrospect, rendered them exceedingly uncommon. Only about 500 Vauxhall 30/98s were ever made, for instance; and since a fair number of these were exported the chance of seeing them to any extent as new cars was remote. The total production of Aston Martins in ten years was fewer than a hundred cars; whereas by 1924 no less than 750 Morris cars were being made each week. The attraction, too, of such Vintage sports cars which has led to their preservation – probably far beyond their makers' hopes – has perhaps caused them to be regarded as typical, which they are not. Performance has always been costly, and they were, after all, the most advanced designs available at the time. The majority of cheaper production cars were by no means so interesting either in specification or behaviour. Any account of the period which did not recognise this would be incomplete, and we must now turn to the great mass of domestic and utility cars which formed the majority of the total production of our ten years. Many of these were of inferior design; many of them were dull and of negligible performance; hardly any were beautiful; but against this they were undoubtedly available in a tremendous variety.

The modern motorist requiring a family car of medium size has a limited choice, on the whole; and having made it, his car is likely to be very little different in characteristics from the others of the same price. In the Vintage period, however, there were literally dozens of small firms producing "11·9s" and "14/40s" for him to choose from, and design was not sufficiently standardised for them to be alike in behaviour or layout. The numerous ways in which designers attacked the new problems created by the vast new motoring public therefore renders these cars rather more interesting than might be expected. They were also frequently produced by firms with a long engineering history who were capable of excellent workmanship Their actual construction and finish are beyond reproach, except in the final two or three years of the twenties, and this, often aided by meagre power outputs, has given them an unexpectedly long life. While "character" is a dangerously vague term to apply to motor-cars, it perhaps best sums up their appeal, and has caused fair numbers of them to be rebuilt and put into use again today. This is quite as it should be; for the 3-litre Bentley is by no means so typical of the Vintage class as the Clyno, although it is more desirable and attractive in every respect.

Often the Vintage light car has controls which work with an agreeable precision and a range of fittings which is never found today on cheap cars; and such minor details compensate to a great extent for the lack of performance and uncomfortable ride. No two of them are alike to drive and many demand skill and patience which would unnerve the complacent motorist today; but to the eccentric who cares to use them now, this is all part of the fun. Nowadays the light-car designer, in this country anyway, is in a difficult position, for his public demands the contradictory qualities of orthodoxy, performance, and comfort; which all means weight. He is therefore forced to lower the overall gear ratios to the extent that his cars are disagreeably fussy to drive and record rather poor fuel consumptions. It is a matter for congratulation if a modern 850-c.c. car records a better mileage than 35 to the gallon when driven hard. In the twenties, however, the public was less exacting and standards of comfort and speed were lower, so that the early economy cars produced genuinely good consumptions. The very first Austin Sevens, for instance, weighed slightly less than 7 cwt. and as the engine gave only a modest 10½ b.h.p. they were capable of over 60 m.p.g. at the low speeds then considered correct for such cars. Against this, of course, few designers of cars of under one litre capacity dared to fit them with four-seater coachwork, and the standard light-car body was the two-seater with or without a dickey seat. The drawbacks of the latter were sometimes partly mitigated by the popular "chummy" body style, in which two persons of small size could be accommodated in an exiguous rear compartment. Saloons of this engine size were not general at all until the end of our period, though they started to be possible on 10-h.p. cars in about 1924, ensuring that their meagre performance was reduced even further.

Until about 1910 economy had invariably meant crudeness, the designer's avowed maxim having been "one cylinder or four". The typical cheap car of this time had a rough single- or twin-cylindered engine, no electrical equipment, and a lamentable performance, especially in hilly country; it was also noisy and tiresome to drive.

Two notable exceptions must, however, be named. The two-cylinder Renault of 1100 c.c., current throughout the Edwardian period, was a car of great charm and it achieved a widespread and well-merited popularity. The vertical engine was remarkably smooth and silent, immensely reliable, and (like all Renaults) extraordinarily durable. The car was comfortable, the steering excellent, and the controls to match. The maximum speed was about 35 m.p.h., and many of these cars have deservedly survived. The other exception is the Bébé Peugeot, introduced in 1911. This admirable car was designed by Ettore Bugatti, who was already a pioneer of the four-cylinder light car, with his type 13 Bugatti. Its 55 × 90 mm., 850-c.c., T-head engine was one of the smallest four-cylinders to be made commercially, and the little cars were by no means as impracticable as might be supposed some even carrying two-seater saloon coachwork. This model was not marketed after the war, but the Peugeot "Quadrilette" which succeeded it possessed an even smaller engine (680 c.c.) and had certain features which were certainly known to Herbert Austin when he designed the Austin Seven.

After the war the small multi-cylindered engine came into fashion for cheap cars and the progress in this field was much more marked than for larger sorts of car. The average 1924 touring car of 2 litres and more was very similar to the models of ten years before and in some cases, such as the Rover or Wolseley, virtually identical; whereas the Austin Seven, though costing about the same as the two-cylinder Renault of 1910–14, was in almost every way superior to it. After 1910 a few firms in this country produced well-made small cars of four cylinders on conventional lines, perhaps the most notable and popular of which were the 10-h.p. Singer of 1912 and the 10-h.p. Standard of 1913; but even these were heavy and pitifully slow. In a slightly more expensive category A. C., Calcott, and Lagonda were making creditable little cars, but in very small numbers. The fact had to be faced that the single-cylindered engine, after a distinguished career, was no longer acceptable to the public; the small four was still relatively costly.

The motor-cycle at that time was powerful and really quite fast, but suffered from wholly ineffective brakes, belt drive, and the lack of a satisfactory free-engine clutch; which usually meant one speed only. Its use was therefore restricted to those of robust constitution who were not liable to drop dead from heart-failure when inducing the high-geared engine to start after a traffic stop. By the outbreak of war, however, there were several quite efficient two-speed gears on the market and also a number of infinitely variable transmissions by expanding pulleys, of which the best was the sturdy and popular Rudge "Multi".

The gap between the motor-cycle and even the cheapest four-wheeler had to be bridged somehow, and as a result the cycle-car was born in about 1912 and acclaimed with enthusiasm by an enormous public of potential motorists. It consisted essentially of a moderately powerful two-cylinder engine of about 1100 c.c. in a crude frame with transmission by belt or chain; but on looking back it seems that the public would buy virtually anything so long as it was cheap enough, and the variety of improbable layouts is astonishing. Few cycle-cars were even moderately well made; and many of them combined grotesque mechanical features with phenomenal unreliability and frightening handling qualities. Wooden chassis-frame; suspension by coil springs or sometimes no suspension at all; final drive by flat belts, ropes, or friction discs; exiguous two-seater coachwork in hardboard, plywood, or even wickerwork – these caused the cycle-car to be rather less successful than its many optimistic sponsors had hoped. Some of the more extreme were tandem-seated, with the driver exercising his limited control from the back seat, where, at any rate, he had the comforting assurance that the passenger would reach the accident before he did.

A few makes of cycle-car became tolerably popular, and had a little more care been taken with their detail work and fewer quaint fancies been embodied in them, they could have found a greater degree of favour. "Wire and bobbin" steering was a popular feature of many cycle-cars, in which the expensive complication of jointed steering connections and steering boxes was conveniently obviated by a length of wire cable threaded round a number of bobbins. The obvious possibilities of crossing the wires was, of course, not lost upon practical jokers, and G.N.s themselves were by no means beyond dealing with difficult customers by this treatment.

Among the "wire and bobbin" brigade, none was more startling than the A. V. Monocar. This strange and splendidly dangerous device carried its driver only and came to a sharp point at the front. The usual air-cooled V-twin was immediately behind the driver – so immediately that it was not uncommon for him to receive electrical stimulation from the foremost sparking plug. The engine was started by pulling a chain, wound round an extension of the flywheel; back-fires thus had the dramatic effect of winding the operator back into the works. Its immensely narrow track made the A.V. extremely hazardous at speed, but at Brooklands one was persuaded to achieve 75 m.p.h.

Many peculiarities of the cycle-cars were attributable not so much to the mechanical optimism of their inventors as to the extremely homely equipment and almost complete lack of capital with which most of them had to work.

G.N., for example, would not for a moment have considered the wanton extravagance of having a separate set of taps and dies for left as well as right-hand threads for their screw-on hub caps, with the result that the loss of wheels was by no means uncommon, even with the "improved" type of hub. Yet the G.N. was really practicable, and A. C. Armstrong, the founder and first editor of the *Cycle-Car*, wrote: "Rather crude as was this vehicle, and I drove two models some 30,000 miles without

105

any serious breakdown, it was the most practical and simple type of cycle-car evolved."

The adaptability of the cycle-car to modification is well demonstrated by the story of a single-seater G.N. which was bought in 1913 by a customer, provided it could be made into a two-seater tandem in time for him to take it abroad with him two days later. Godfrey and Nash duly cut the car in half, let in a gusset, and delivered it on time.

Incidentally, in 1915 the chassis price of the touring G.N. was only 88 guineas.

For one brief moment the searchlight of royal patronage shone on the cycle-car, for at the 1920 Show, King Alfonso XIII of Spain (a notable motoring enthusiast who gave the "Alfonso" Hispano-Suiza its name) ordered a Carden cycle-car – one suspects that he coupled a sense of humour with his enthusiasm for motoring.

Not surprisingly, few cycle-cars survive today, so that it is not often possible to savour their discomforts at first hand. They were not taken up very seriously by large firms, although Humber produced one of the best of them in the little V-twin "Humberette"; and hardly any makers with the exception of G.N. were able to live them down. Although they had a brief revival after the war when anything could find a market, they were obviously a blind alley, and few were made after 1923. None the less, their designers did appreciate a favourable power-weight ratio for the first time in the low-price range, and the better cycle-cars had quite a snappy performance. One or two of the post-war cycle-cars, such as the Carden and Tamplin, met with considerable favour, though this was probably on account of low cost rather than absolute merit.

Such machines can hardly be taken seriously, and more worthy of attention from the point of view of the historian was the popularity before the 1914–18 war of the cheap American car in this country. After about 1910 the Model T Ford began to be seen in large numbers and was in fact built in Manchester from about that year; and in a slightly costlier class the Overland, Dodge, Studebaker and Chevrolet were imported in great quantities. Such cars attacked the problems of utility from a new angle and their vast potential market in the United States caused them to be turned out with far more of an eye to production costs than any English maker dared; they achieved reliability and economy by the use of large and astonishingly inefficient engines and no attempt was made to give them any sort of performance. Since they were simple, cheap, easy to drive and needed little maintenance, they were very successful in the more agricultural parts of this country, helped also by their continued importation during the war, when English makers were put on to munition work. After the war, though, they were penalised by the heavy tax on their large bores, and although the Ford maintained its unassailable position despite an R.A.C. rating of 23 h.p., they lost popularity.

American utility: a 1919 Dodge two-seater

It should never be forgotten that the Model T Ford was decidedly the cheapest car of any size on the British market; in 1926 when an Austin Seven Chummy cost £150, the Ford four-seater was only £120, and this first-class value for money caused it to have tremendous popularity over here. Even by 1923 no less than a quarter of a million had been made in this country alone. It was quite unlike any other car, with its short-stroke engine of 2.9 litres, two-speed epi-cyclic gearbox, and transverse suspension. The engine was of an unparallelled inefficiency, being limited by the small valves and porting to about 1600 'r.p.m., and this, with a high top-gear ratio of 3·6 to 1, caused the car to give an honest 30 m.p.g. in general use, and for the same reasons it was a hard car to wear out; front brakes were never standard-dised. Many of its mechanically peculiar features were, however,

107

common practice with American manufacturers at time of its birth in 1908, and it was only during the phenomenal production in span of nineteen years that they became so unusual. The Model T, like the "Silver Ghost" Rolls-Royce, is a timeless design.

With its high ground clearance and extreme ease of maintenance, it was the ideal farmer's car; and railway trains on remote branch lines were inevitably met by the immensely high and narrow saloon or landaulet versions.

The Model T was a car of tremendous character, and its vices and merits have become part of American folklore. The distinction which obtained in this country between the Ford driver and the motorist was very marked during our period; but its unmistakable silhouette was ever present in the background. The Model A, which succeeded it in 1928, was never quite the same.

The economy and simplicity of the Ford were found to a similar extent on the other popular American importations of the period. Despite the high tax on their large-bore engines there was always a strong following for the robust Chryslers and Buicks, whose chief appeal lay in their top-gear performance and general ease of handling, which was far superior to that of the majority of similar British cars. Thirty years later this remains much the same.

The first departure for the light car came in 1919. The development of aero-engines led to a great enthusiasm for air-cooling and the earliest post-war designs reflected this. While manufacturers could rely for a few years on their pre-war large designs suitably modified, the demand for a well-made light car caused many to bring out air-cooled twin-cylinders of about 1000 c.c. The Rover Company, who had not made a small car for some time, re-entered the market in 1919 with the famous Eight; Belsize built the ingenious 9-h.p. twin designed by Granville Bradshaw, who was also responsible for the more sporting A.B.C. G.N. were, of course, well established, and for a few years all these makes flourished exceedingly. Such cars, although crude and quite slow, were a decided advance on pre-war practice or on the cycle-car, and combined very low running costs with performance of an entirely novel kind; their relatively low gearing and light weight gave them brisk acceleration and their opposed or V-twin engines were fairly well balanced. The firms who made them also had sufficient resources to permit production in large numbers and for a short time it seemed that here indeed were the lines along which the economy car of the future would develop, particularly as excellent showings were put up in the Exeter and Land's End trials by teams of such cars. None the less they had their disadvantages: none were quiet, especially the Rover with its ball-bearing engine, and the public has always been wary of air-cooling. Many were the stories told among Rover Eight owners of the cylinder heads glowing a rich cherry-red after an ascent of Honister or Porlock, though this was almost certainly due to their incompetence rather than the shortcomings of the car.

For these reasons the novelty of such cars soon wore off. Manufacturers sought a new approach and it is fortunate for the historian with a tidy mind that several of them reached the same conclusion at the same time.

1922 decisively saw the birth of the modern light car. For in that year four makers, three of them of great distinction and fame, applied themselves to the problems of designing a fairly cheap light car, which would be a scaled-down large car with a water-cooled engine of quite high efficiency in a light chassis, but with a degree of refinement hitherto unknown. The Talbot and Humber 8/18s and the Gwynne Eight represented the conventional approach and are among the most charming small cars ever made; the fourth, the Austin Seven, was unconventional in most respects for the time, but succeeded nevertheless in becoming one of the most popular and best-loved cars ever produced in this country. For a few years after their introduction these were in a class of their own, and there were no real advances in the light-car category until the introduction of a further much less attractive batch in 1928. The Talbot, Humber, and Gwynne were certainly rather costly, but this was justified by the lively performance, coming from their low weight and efficient little pushrod overhead valve engines. The Talbot, originally designed by Louis Coatalen for Darracq, had a maximum speed of about

55 in top and 40 in second, with acceleration and brakes that do not disgrace it in traffic thirty years later. The Humber was undoubtedly the prettiest and best-made, and although rather slower than the others, scored by its extreme refinement and reliability, being a tiny replica of the larger touring Humbers of the time. It continued to be developed as the "9/20" and "9/28" until the end of the decade, although the later examples are heavy and uninteresting by comparison. The Gwynne was rather crudely constructed and unbeautiful in appearance but had an amazing performance for a 1922 950-c.c. car, with a maximum speed of nearly 60 m.p.h., and it performed with great élan in trials as a result.

But the Austin Seven was the outstanding car of them all. From the point of view of commercial success and technical excellence it must rank among the first half-dozen most brilliant designs ever. Having restored the failing fortunes of the Austin Motor Company, it continued to be produced in virtually the same form until 1938, when nearly 300,000 had been made. In a way it succeeded in spite of itself, for it had many faults; the brakes were inferior, the steering vague, the suspension uncomfortable. But against this the quality of all parts was superb, giving complete reliability under conditions of total neglect, the layout simple, providing the utmost ease of maintenance, and the light and unorthodox frame proved extremely robust. With such virtues available at such low cost, the cycle-car was totally redundant and motoring for the millions had indeed arrived.

These cars, however, although strictly designed for economy of running, were not all cheap; for example, the 8/18 Talbot cost as much as two complete Morris "Cowleys". We must turn to those cars of the period which were really meant for utility by reason of low first cost and economy of fuel. It is rather difficult to feel any burning enthusiasm for such cars as the Swift, Singer, or Clyno, whose virtues are really only those of reliability; but they were after all wholly typical of their period and also the first cars to be produced in any quantities in this country. The more obscure makes, such as the Deemster, Cluley, Rhode, or Horstman are not without a certain esoteric appeal; but by and large this class of car is not particularly interesting in itself. Many were

110

purely assembly productions, using the popular proprietary engines of the time by Anzani, Dorman, or Coventry Simplex with transmission by Wrigley or Moss; and for many of the less inspired concerns this was doubtless a very good idea, although the excellence of some of these engines tends to show up defects in the home-made gearboxes, and vice versa.

The most popular R.A.C. rating in the Vintage period was 11·9 h.p., which implied some 1½ litres capacity, producing, in most cases, about 30 b.h.p. This was regarded as about the smallest engine which would carry four passengers in any comfort at a respectable pace. The variety of such cars was remarkable, and there were no less than 45 different 12-h.p. cars on the British market in 1926, although, of course, not all of them were in the utility class. The best of them all, and the most successful and popular production of its time, was the Morris "Cowley", which was produced in larger numbers than any contemporary car, and was in some respects the British equivalent of the Model T Ford. Morris had made his name before the war, but he did not join to any extent in the post-war boom which saw so many hopeful attempts to enter the popular market, and it was not until about 1922 that, by a series of sensational price reductions, he captured this completely. From then on he went from strength to strength until production reached a thousand cars each week at one time. His cars offered first-rate value for money and the vast production enabled them to be particularly well equipped; in addition the basic design was excellent, with enough refinement and quality to ensure consistently high sales. Most light cars had some weak feature or another which their owners had to tolerate, but the Morris had none of importance. It had a robust side-valve engine and a three-speed gearbox in unit, and if it was never notable for performance or, indeed, extreme economy, it had the merits of being easy to drive, totally reliable, and particularly smooth and silent. Even today it remains a more attractive car to drive than others of its class, and is enjoying a revival of favour, helped by the fact that spare parts can be found under nearly every hedge and certainly at the back of every garage in the country. This is especially true in remote provincial regions, where the "Cowley" was for many years the typical farmer's car. The well-known and charming "bull-nosed" radiator was superseded in 1926 by the flat square type, but these later cars, perhaps because they mostly carry ugly saloon coach-work, lack the grace and appeal of the earlier versions and are altogether noisier and coarser.

The small Continental car, though handicapped by import duties, became popular on the British market in the 1920s by reason of its good brakes and generally rather high quality. The lively little Bébé Peugeot, the 7·5 h.p. "cloverleaf" Citroën, the "9/15" Renault, and the outstandingly good and durable F.I.A.T.s, types 501 and 509, were familiar over here.

From its introduction in 1919 the 10·4-h.p. Citroën swiftly became the most ubiquitous of all French cars, possessing as it did quite extraordinary powers of resistance to the worst iniquities of French drivers, and also fair economy. In this country it was best known in the rather quaint three-seater "cloverleaf" model of 7·5 h.p., a car whose total lack of performance was compensated for by its indestructibility.

The two F.I.A.T.s in particular were altogether excellent little cars. The 501, which appeared as early as 1919, had a long-stroke side-valve engine of quite unusual silence and refinement, and there was a balance and quality about the design that has caused it to be considered one of the most pleasing small family cars ever made, particularly in its steering and brakes. The 509,

Vintage all-weather equipment on a 1926 F.I.A.T. 12-h.p. tourer

which was a sensation of the Paris Salon in 1925, was another beautifully made light car with an overhead-camshaft 990-c.c, engine, quite lively, and with first-class brakes; though the low gear ratios on both these cars were perhaps better suited to Alpine motoring than British roads.

The Bugatti-designed Bébé Peugeot was not produced after the war, and was replaced by the Peugeot "Quadrilette", an almost absurdly small car which in its earliest form seated two people in tandem. The very narrow track caused this model to be very unstable, and a slight concession to safety and comfort was made in 1922 with the introduction of a staggered two-seater, although this still had to have the clutch pedal in the passenger's compartment. For all its tiny monobloc 680-c.c. engine, scarcely larger than the magneto beside it, it was by no means a toy but a quite serious and practical car which remained popular in France until 1930 in slightly larger and heavier form. Even today it has a performance closely comparable with the modern utility two-cylinder Citroën.

Such cars have not, unfortunately, survived in England to the same surprising extent as in France, where thousands of such Vintage cars are still in daily use, making a French country town on a market day a diverting spectacle to the Vintage enthusiast. This is presumably because that realistic nation has not suffered the malady of fashion which has caused countless British cars to be prematurely abandoned and destroyed before their time, but sees a car as something to be used until it is completely worn out.

Other cars in the utility class, but with rather more dignity than the Morris, were the popular Austin 12/4 and the Hillman and Standard Fourteens. It is really doubtful if they should appear in this chapter, or as touring cars. They were able to carry heavy and upright closed coachwork with complete reliability if very unspectacular performance. The Austin in particular was of thoroughly realistic and sound design and beautifully made for a cheap car. From its introduction in 1922 it sold in large numbers and would certainly have assured Austin's fame if the Seven had not been made, its basic design continuing until long after the Vintage period and being still current as a taxicab. The ponderous chassis and very wide gear ratios caused it to be exceptionally sluggish in performance, but the very low power output and enormous five-bearing crankshaft rendered it virtually indestructible. Before the introduction of this car the medium-sized utility market had been attempted by three post-war firms in particular, whose cars had come on to the scene with enormous publicity and promises of vast output. Despite this, however, the Cubitt, Angus-Sanderson, and Bean were not of sufficiently attractive specification to sell against the Austin 12, and soon disappeared from the market, though the Bean survived and achieved a certain popularity as a worthy family car until its production ceased in 1929.

The really cheap light car of conventional design did not become available until 1928, when five firms produced substantial, if charmless, little vehicles, selling at less than £200. The Singer "Junior", Morris "Minor", Triumph Seven, and Clyno and Standard Nine were not without certain merits, and their very low cost was remarkable considering their specification. All had saloon coachwork, while the overhead camshafts of the Singer and Morris would have been unthinkable on cars of this class a few years before. All had far better brakes than earlier light cars, the Triumph being one of the first British cars to use hydraulic operation; but their fairly brisk performance was only achieved by the use of miserably low gear ratios and fussy high-speed engines. Although Vintage by date they have few of the Vintage merits and belong more in character to the unhappy post-Vintage period, when motoring had become a purely utilitarian conception. None the less, the ability to buy a fully equipped four-seater 9-h.p. car for £130 was completely new, even if that car was only a Clyno Nine.

It would be tedious to discuss each and every popular car of the Vintage period. We have selected only those which were outstandingly successful, cheap, interesting, or merely amusing.

THE AUSTIN SEVEN

Unquestionably one of the immortal designs in motoring history

is the Austin Seven, for upon its introduction in 1922 it rendered
the cycle-car obsolete, set a high overall standard for the economy
car, and made motoring possible for the first time to thousands
of families. It is surely no exaggeration to say that it was as great
an advance in its own sphere as were the 1901 Mercedes and the
1907 Rolls-Royce in theirs. For sixteen years it maintained an
unassailable popularity, capturing the public imagination as few
cars have done before or since, by a notable combination of
durability and charm.

A 1926 Austin "Chummy" Seven

The design was of classic simplicity, being essentially a scaled-
down and lightened large car. The side-valve two-bearing engine
of 747 c.c., which produced 10½ b.h.p. at 2500 r.p.m., was set
in a light T-section frame which narrowed towards the front
to carry the transverse suspension; rear suspension was by
short but steeply cambered quarter-elliptics, and the suspension,
more than any other part of the car, seems to owe something
to the contemporary small Peugeot. Brakes were fitted to all
four wheels, an altogether unprecedented move on so small a
chassis. Although frail in appearance all parts were in fact
immensely strong, being made of the best materials; this is well
confirmed by the large number of Sevens of all ages which still
give faithful service. The coachwork was standardised from the
first on an aluminium "Chummy" four-seater which was to
remain the basic Vintage design, though a most charmingly
upright saloon was available from 1926. The prototype cars,

of 696 c.c. only, weighed less than 7 cwt. and with 10 b.h.p. to propel them, recorded exceptional fuel consumptions, rumours of 75 m.p.g. being current at one time. When production began in earnest in 1923 the weight had gone up to $8\frac{1}{2}$ cwt. and for the rest of its career the car gave about 45 m.p.g. The price was progressively lowered until in 1929 the tourer cost £125 complete, and a few years later it could be had for even less. The car's fame was world-wide, and it was built under licence in Germany as the B.M.W., in France as the Rosengart, and in the U.S.A. as the "Bantam".

Although the smallest car on the British market it was an essentially practical vehicle. Four adults could be carried if necessary and the performance was not entirely negligible, due to the fairly low gearing (top was 4·9 to 1). All models were capable of about 50 m.p.h., and would maintain 40–45 m.p.h. with great ease. Unlike other economy cars the Seven was of proverbial reliability. The tiny brakes were never particularly effective, and the steering inclined to be a little indefinite, but serious trouble was seldom known.

Almost its first public appearance was at Shelsley Walsh in August 1922, when amid great enthusiasm a somewhat leisured ascent was made in a minute and a half. But the engine design was happily capable of modification to produce considerable power, and very soon after its introduction special versions showed their paces in the 750-c.c. class, Gordon England taking the hour record in 1923 at 73 m.p.h. He later produced several cheap and pleasing little sporting models known as the "Cup" and "Brooklands" types which by reason of their light weight gave over 70 m.p.h. At the end of our period appeared the "Ulster" production model, which had a Centric-type Cozette supercharger delivering at up to eight pounds per square inch, a pressure-fed crankshaft in place of the jet-fed standard type, and various modifications to the valve gear and manifolds, giving 33 b.h.p.; these cars had a road speed of better than 80 m.p.h. and a safe engine speed of 5000 r.p.m. Also in the same year the standard model was modernised in appearance, and given coil ignition and a larger crankshaft (diameter $1\frac{5}{16}$ in. against the $1\frac{1}{8}$ in. of previous models).

The Austin Seven had its little ways. All owners, past and present, will recall with a certain affection the persistent tinkle of the starting-handle mounting; the relentless drip of oil from the steering column; the slower drip of oil from the dashboard indicator; and the notoriously vicious clutch, which rendered a smooth start virtually impossible by a pedal travel of about $\frac{1}{8}$ in. But these small details were as nothing against the very real merits of this outstanding light car.

CLYNO

The Clyno Engineering Company of Wolverhampton started life in a modest way with the manufacture of motor-cycles and it was not until 1922 that they entered the light-car market with a very cheap 10·8-h.p. four-cylinder light car of slightly more than usual crudeness. Unlike many other optimistic constructors whose cars were produced in a spasmodic and haphazard manner, the Clyno Company sensibly laid down an efficient production line from the first. They were thus able to keep up with the enormous demand for their cars, which enjoyed a quite astonishing and well-merited popularity for a few years. They were certainly one of the commonest sights on the roads in their heyday. No Clyno was of much technical interest; all models had side-valve four-cylinder engines by Coventry-Simplex with three-speed gearboxes, and no attempt was made to give them any but the most ordinary behaviour and speed. No special versions appeared in competition, though they made the obligatory attempts at the light-car trials of their time.

The Clyno was simply made, and quite pleasant to drive, for it had light steering and excellent brakes. But any car in direct competition with the Morris "Cowley" had to maintain a high standard in more respects than these, and the car soon failed, particularly as the Rootes Group (who were the selling organisation at that time) withdrew their support. Production ceased in 1929, but not before the firm had made a final attempt at a £100 car, a conception which had been worrying designers for some time (and which was finally achieved by Morris in 1932); but the Clyno Nine was not sufficiently good, even at £112 10s., to restore the *marque* to popularity.

FORD "T"

Henry Ford started making cars in 1891, and the world speed record-breaking "999" was made in 1902; but the Ford Motor Company, as it is known today, was not founded until 1903. Its early products covered quite a wide range, from economy "runabouts" to the 2500-dollar, 6-litre, six-cylinder Model K introduced in 1906.

The model which first gives a noticeable foretaste of the "T" is the 1906 Model N, while the "S" of the following year establishes the lines of the famous "T" brass radiator. Both of these had the stroke smaller than the bore ($3\frac{3}{4}$ in. × $3\frac{3}{8}$ in.). In the Ford catalogue of 1907 it is stated that; "The Model N was Mr. Ford's conception of a runabout that was 'all automobile' – in other words, all efficiency with none of the frills or fussings so dear to the hearts of some motorists."

The Model T was on sale towards the end of 1908 and the catalogue is unequivocal in its claims: "There are excellent features in other cars, but better features or as high-grade materials as are used in the Model T Ford cannot be found in any other car at any price. A better car is not and cannot be made."

With such a highly individual car, it was perhaps risky to compare its merits with others; but as to the high-grade materials there was no doubt, and this was one of the important reasons for Ford's success as a manufacturer.

Model T Ford coupé, 1924. (According to the catalogue: "Mechanically adjustable plate glass windows give ventilation as required")

118

The outstanding importance of the "T" is that it was the first car to be mass-produced in the fullest sense of the word. Others had gone considerable distances in this direction, and Ford himself claimed to have sold 25,000 cars before the "T", so that he had gained all the experience necessary for this great venture.

The engine had a longer stroke than the "N" and "S", its dimensions being $3\frac{3}{4}$ in. × 4 in., which give a capacity of 2884 c.c. It was designed for simplicity, strength, and flexibility. Very small valves limited the crankshaft speed to about 1800 r.p.m. and the power output to about the Treasury Rating of 22·4 h.p. Lubrication was by splash and maintenance was simplified by a detachable cylinder head, which was an unusual feature in 1908. A trembler coil facilitated starting and for normal running there was a magneto built into the flywheel. The limited power output ensured remarkable flexibility, and the lowest of the two speeds was intended only for starting and excessively steep gradients. Top-gear ratio was 3·64 to 1, which produced a top-gear range of 3 to 45 m.p.h., while the overall weight of $13\frac{3}{4}$ cwt. facilitated remarkably brisk acceleration. Petrol consumption was in the neighbourhood of 30 m.p.g. Bottom gear, which was 10 to 1, had an extreme maximum of 15 m.p.h. Reverse was even lower, and could thus be used as an emergency low. In moments of acute crisis it could even be useed as an emergency brake, since the gears were epicyclic, engaged by friction bands. The gearbox was in unit with the engine, another unusual feature at this early date. Although the gearbox gave extremely good service, it exerted so much "drag" when the oil was cold that it was almost impossible to turn the engine, and it became a matter of routine to jack up one back wheel as a preliminary to starting on a cold morning.

Control was effected as follows: the right-hand pedal controlled a transmission brake; the central pedal operated reverse; the left-hand pedal gave the two forward speeds and neutral – full depression produced low gear, neutral was half-way, and taking the foot off the pedal engaged top. The accelerator was hand-controlled only, by a long lever under the steering wheel, and a similar lever controlled the ignition advance and retard. The hand brake, when pulled on to the halfway position moved the left-hand pedal to its neutral position; further application operated the modest rear-wheel brakes.

Transverse springs were employed for both back and front axles.

Its simplicity, robustness, and very high ground clearance made the car ideal for the backwoodsman, and indeed it is extremely doubtful if the "T" has ever been improved upon for rough usage with minimum maintenance.

Over twenty styles of coachwork were available in the early years, but on colour Henry Ford was adamant – you could have any colour you liked as long as it was black.

In 1917 the Model T lost of its much attraction when its exterior appearance was drastically altered. The famous flat-sided brass radiator disappeared and the new style featured (in the words of the catalogue) "The stream-line hood, large radiator and enclosed fan, crown fenders, black finish and nickel trimmings" ("crown fenders" would be described in English as domed mudguards). Electric lighting and starting followed in 1919, and the model then continued with little alteration until 1927, when it was finally withdrawn. After a considerable pause it was replaced by the Model A, a very conventional machine with wire wheels, three-speed gearbox and four-wheel brakes, (the "T" had never made this concession to progress and continued to the last with two minute brake drums on the back wheels only). While it was in preparation, others had taken the lead, and the "A" never replaced the immortal "T" in the public fancy. Indeed, the "Tin Lizzy" or "Flivver" had become almost a national characteristic, and at the end of its eighteen years in production the total number sold was fifteen million.

GWYNNE

Gwynne's Engineering Company of Chiswick, who are still well known as makers of marine pumps, succeeded in producing during the Vintage period a remarkable and charming little car known as the Gwynne Eight. This appeared in 1923 and had a robust 950-c.c. overhead-valve engine of quite unusual liveliness in a conventional chassis, giving the car acceleration and a maximum speed (nearly 60 m.p.h.) really exceptional for its class. Although by no means comely in appearance or even very well finished, the performance of the car gave it a considerable popularity and it was very good value for money at its low price of £200 or so. It had the probably unique distinction of having been designed in Spain; but it was certainly a thoroughly realistic approach to the problems of light car design. The solid three-bearing engine was susceptible to considerable tuning and W. D. Chinery, who was associated with the firm at the time, drove a Gwynne in trials with considerable success, especially in the R.A.C. Light Car Trials of 1924, where he made brilliant climbs of the very tough Welsh hills and scored a class win, averaging over 45 m.p.g. for the 1000 miles. A very fetching aluminium two-seater sports model with a dashing pointed tail appeared in 1926 which was alleged to produce 25 b.h.p. at 3000 r.p.m. and each of these cars had a Brooklands lap certificate of 65 m.p.h. In a rather different category the makers produced a tiny fire-engine on the same chassis for attending small fires on country estates.

Perhaps fortunately, the Gwynne never grew up in the way of the contemporary small Humbers, and when production ceased in 1928 it was outclassed by the development of competitors with better brakes and fuller equipment.

THE HUMBER LIGHT CARS

All Humber cars during the Vintage period were of the highest quality, and any light car bearing the name could be expected to be of the most extreme refinement; the little 8/18 model was an immediate success from its inception late in 1922. It had a coil-ignition engine of 985 c.c. which gave 20 b.h.p. at 3000 r.p.m. and was notable for its use of overhead inlet and side exhaust valves, an arrangement which was to be consistently used by Humbers until about 1931. Although costly to produce it was certainly justified by the efficiency and smooth running of the engine. The little Humber weighed about 12 cwt., and the rather low gear ratios prevented a startling performance, while fuel consumption was about 35 m.p.g. On the other hand, the sound detail work and careful construction rendered it an exceedingly quiet and pleasing car to drive, and the equipment was unusually

121

comprehensive for such a car. The standard coachwork was a very pretty occasional four-seater "chummy" body. The limitations of this, however, caused the model to grow up in 1925 into the 9/20 which, with an engine only slightly larger, was burdened with a full four-seater body of remarkable length and ungainly appearance; but it retained all the Humber quality and was capable of an unexpectedly lively performance. Front brakes were added in 1927 and for a year or so the 9/20 was an unusually attractive economy car. But in 1929 saloon coachwork had become all the fashion and it grew further into the 9/28 a car which typifies the sad change which had come over light- car design by having the extremely low top-gear ratio of 5·5 to 1. Its performance is accordingly rather laboured, despite the greater power output of the engine. The excellent Humber light car of 1922 had in fact grown up into a very ordinary small saloon car with little but its quality to commend it, and production ceased in 1930.

JOWETT

The Jowett Brothers of Bradford built their first car in 1910 and it had a flat-twin water-cooled engine. After the war this same engine slightly enlarged was used when production started in earnest, and it was made in virtually the same form until 1953.

The car was not much known outside its native Yorkshire until 1921, when a team put up a notable performance in the Scottish Six Days Trial, and its reputation began to spread southwards. The basic Jowett design, which was to have such an unparalleled production run, was simple enough. The car was of unattractive appearance and slightly crude finish, but made up for this by the refinement of the well-balanced engine, which was also a model of reliability. Indeed, it was claimed in 1926 that every Jowett made was still in service. As might have been expected from its somewhat provincial background, the steering and brakes were not of the best, and there is little to appeal to the connoisseur in these cars, which were, after all, of a strictly utilitarian nature.

One brief venture into the sporting field took place in 1928, when J. J. Hall set out to capture the 1100-c.c. Twelve-Hour record at Brooklands. It is rather difficult to see why he chose a Jowett, but he did, and took the record in a special 8-cwt. two-seater at 55 m.p.h., a tribute to his patience as well as to the dependability of the car.

Despite the highly primitive production methods used by the firm, they established a faithful enough clientèle to enable them to remain in the market with the same twin-cylinder car throughout the 1930s, and it was not until 1937 that they made first four-cylinder, a forerunner of the brilliant post-war Javelin. As the excellent Bradford van, the horizontally opposed twin continued in production until 1952, thus establishing a record run of forty-two years.

LAGONDA

An American opera singer and engineer named Wilbur Gunn came to this country early in the century and in about 1904 started the firm of Lagonda Ltd. to produce motor-cycles and tri-cars; the name Lagonda was that of his home town. He prospered sufficiently to build powerful four- and six-cylinder cars for some years, and according to one contemporary report these were adroitly exported to Russia. In 1913 the company policy changed and Gunn, who seems to have been a far-sighted man, decided to set about the serious production of a small four-cylinder light car to sell at an extremely low price, and this was to be the basic Lagonda for the next thirteen years. For 1913 it was, and remained, a thoroughly unorthodox design, having a 1100-c.c. engine with overhead inlet valves operated by exposed pushrods and rockers, a three-speed gearbox in unit, and final drive by worm. This was set in a rather crude chassis of angle-iron to which the body panels were directly riveted; and with a weight of about 10 cwt. gave a most creditable performance for a car costing under £150.

After the war Gunn died; but the car continued to be made in 1500-c.c. form with few importants changes from the early layout. For a few years it became popular as a small car of quite high quality and extreme individuality, the detail work in particular being wholly unlike that of any other small car. This 11.9-h.p. Lagonda had no claim to sporting performance, for it was heavy and the gear ratios low, but its economy was remarkable, all but the saloon versions giving well over 40 m.p.g. It was also highly reliable, and in 1953 a 1924 four-seater was driven from London to Cape Town with no major disaster by a member of the Vintage Sports-Car Club, a really notable feat for a small car thirty years old.

Although special versions of the car were hopefully entered for the Brooklands 200 Mile Race from time to time, the cars were not seen much in competition, though one took the light-car hour record in 1921 at 80 m.p.h., being capable of 4000 r.p.m. with fair reliability. In the long-distance trials of the period, on the other hand, W. H. Oates was a consistent and successful competitor in his specially tuned version, and the low gearing and willing engine were very well suited to the poorly surfaced hills then favoured for such events.

By 1925, though, the standard car had become far too heavy and inferior in performance to other cars costing much less, such as the Morris "Cowley"; and as a result sales fell rapidly. Front brakes were added in 1926, but the general advance in light-car design had outmoded the little Edwardian chassis and the company wisely changed in that year to an entirely different type of car, the twin-cam 2-litre which we discuss elsewhere.

MORRIS "COWLEY" AND "OXFORD"

W. R. Morris, an Oxford garage owner, made his first production car in 1912. This, the Morris "Oxford" light car, was an orthodox 8·9-h.p. four-cylinder of 60 × 90 mm. with worm final drive. It bore the famous bull-nosed radiator and a practical, if hardly elegant, two-seater body; the engine was an extremely lively and fast-running monobloc T-head by White and Poppe, of Coventry. This engine contributed greatly to the success of the car, 50 m.p.h. and 50 m.p.g. being advertised as available according to the need of the driver. The car, being reliable and costing only £175 in 1913, sold well; and a production line was started in a disused school in the nearby village of Cowley in which a few hundred cars were assembled before the outbreak of war.

During the war the White and Poppe engine became unavail-

A late, front-wheel-braked example of the bull-nosed
Morris "Cowley", 1925

able, and in 1915 Morris began to import a "Continental" engine
from Detroit, largely modified to his own specification. After
the war this same engine was made under his supervision at the
Coventry works of the Hotchkiss Company; and although it is
one of the most widespread pieces of motoring folklore that it
is of French ancestry, there would seem in fact to be little
Hotchkiss about it. It was of 69 × 102 mm., giving a capacity of
1550 c.c., had a three-bearing crankshaft, and developed a
modest 25 b.h.p., giving the standard car a maximum speed of
50–55 m.p.h. and about 30 m.p.g. It continued as part of the
Morris range until 1934.

Production of the car was resumed in 1919 and by that time
the "Cowley" had been added to the "Oxford", being at first
only a cheaper version of the same chassis, costing about £60
less. Both cars sold well for a few years, while Morris set up a
really efficient production line, until he was able to announce a
series of drastic reductions in price for 1922. Since the cars were
in themselves excellent in quality and behaviour this provided an
enormous stimulus to sales and production soared in 1923,
until the bull-nosed Morris rapidly became the most popular
car on the roads; and it and its successors maintained this position throughout the Vintage period. In 1924 the "Oxford" was
given an engine of 1800 c.c., and this was to form the basis for
the first production M.G. a year or so later.

Most light cars at this time were equipped with coarse and

noisy gearboxes and fierce cone clutches. But the Morris three-speed box was fairly silent and the wet cork-lined clutch unusually smooth. Gear-changing by the rigid central lever was therefore a simple matter, and the general ease of handling which these cars possessed was far above the general standards in the utility. The best year was probably 1926, which combined the archaic yet pleasing lines of earlier models with four-wheel brakes of considerable efficiency. Also notable for so cheap a car was the quietness of the engine, started by a single-unit dynamotor on the gearbox; and the equipment throughout was complete and of the best quality. The car as a whole would stand the most fearful abuse without protest, and certainly deserved every bit of its success. Like the Model T Ford, it has become something of a legend, and is remembered with much the same mixture of respect and amusement by tens of thousands whose first motoring experience it provided.

THE ROVER EIGHT

In the early days of motoring one of the most popular of all small British cars was the single cylinder Rover, made from 1904 to 1910, which, by its extreme cheapness and reliability sold very well indeed. For some years the firm left the utility market in favour of a first-class medium-sized family tourer designed by Owen Clegg, who later joined the Sunbeam-Darracq combine; but immediately after the war the two-cylinder Rover Eight appeared. This had a horizontally-opposed side-valve engine of about a litre capacity, three speeds, and the customary Rover worm drive. Suspension was by quarter-elliptic springs and steering by rack and pinion. The chassis was crude in the extreme, even for so cheap a car, and the standard disc-wheeled two-seater coachwork was distinctly unbeautiful. For all this the car was low in cost and capable as a rule of nearly 50 m.p.g. due to its light weight, and sold well in spite of a somewhat dubious name for reliability – the early examples being prone to cast away their cylinder-heads at high r.p.m. The engine, though noisy, was very well balanced and lively enough to give the little car respectable acceleration and hill-climbing powers, though its maximum was only about 45 m.p.h.

The Rover Eight for a few years bridged the gap between the sidecar outfit and the orthodox light car, but obviously with the development of the latter it was handicapped by its rather crude nature. It was superseded in 1924 by a water-cooled four-cylinder Nine, a somewhat undistinguished little car which eventually grew into the popular "10/25", and continued in production until 1933.

SWIFT

Swift of Coventry was a pioneer British make, and one of the oldest cycle-manufacturing firms in the country, who established fame in the light-car world very early on, with a de Dion-engined voiturette. Their small cars remained popular throughout the Edwardian period and were quite outstandingly successful in the numerous reliability trials with single- or twin-cylinder cars; they even assayed racing and appeared in the 1905 Tourist Trophy race without ignominy. During the Vintage period their standard model was the Swift Ten, a small car which became exceedingly well liked and sold in large numbers, catering for the increasing middle-class market with great success. It was never a particularly cheap car, and the fittings and finish were generally of a quite high order. It was propelled by a very hard-wearing but feeble four-cylinder engine of 1100 c.c.; the mechanical parts were of alarming size and the car was throughout far too heavily made to give it a chance of any performance. It did have a certain solid appeal, however, and production ceased in 1931 only on account of internal difficulties in the factory and not through lack of demand. It has vindicated itself by a quite unexpected durability, and – particularly in the remote country areas of the British Isles – a good many Swifts may still be seen performing their agricultural duties.

THE TALBOT EIGHT

The 8/18 Talbot, which appeared early in 1922, was designed by Louis Coatalen and proved, as might have been expected, to have an exceptional performance for a light car at that time. It was also a distinct departure for the Clement Talbot factory, which had previously built only fast and rather heavy touring cars. Despite its somewhat high price, it had an instant appeal on account of its speed, efficiency, and elegant appearance; and was hailed in the contemporary press as the pioneer of a new sort of economical motoring. It had an overhead-valve engine of just under one litre capacity, coil ignition, a three-speed gearbox, and final drive to the solid rear axle by torque tube. Suspension was by quarter-elliptic springs all round, this being the first Talbot to have them at the rear, where they remained as long as genuine Talbots were built. The engine was capable of unusually high speeds for such a car, by reason of its careful balance and light moving parts. It was able to give the 8/18 in standard two-seater form the satisfactory maxima of 40 m.p.h. in second and about 55 m.p.h. in top, which made it substantially faster than the majority of its competitors. Nor was the engine rough in any way, but, like all Coatalen's productions, of extreme smoothness and flexibility. The finish throughout was excellent, and the coupé body light, comfortable, and of pleasing appearance.

The demand for more roomy coachwork led, in 1923, to the introduction of the 10/23, which had a stronger rear axle with bigger brakes and a slightly enlarged engine capable of carrying a very long four-seater or Weymann fabric saloon body. The 10/23 was the first Talbot to receive the attention of Georges Roesch.

These small Talbots were among the most pleasing small cars of the entire decade and demonstrated the merits of a miniature orthodox design for almost the first time; but in 1926 production of both ceased, superseded by the remarkable new 14/45.

TAMPLIN

The Tamplin cycle-car was one which acquired some fame after the war and is described here as being fairly typical of the genus cycle-car.

In essence, it was a motor-cycle with four wheels. A 1000-c.c. V-twin J.A.P. side-valve air-cooled engine drove a Sturmey-Archer three-speed motor-cycle gearbox, whence the power was conveyed to the back axle by a belt. True to its motor-cycle character, the engine was set going by a kick-starter, operated from the driving-seat.

A more modern note was struck by the body-cum-chassis, which consisted of an ash frame with waterproof fibre-board panels, reinforced where necessary by steel plates. A pair of planks, running the full length of the car on each side, did duty for mudguards. The front suspension was independent, with coil springs and vertical sliding guides, like a Morgan; rear springs were quarter-elliptic.

By contrast, the braking arrangements were entirely in the motor-cycling tradition, for the foot brake exerted its slender influence on the gearbox belt pulley and the hand brake pressed a block into the rear belt-rim. Such modest attempts at retardation were, however, matched by an equally moderate performonce and an all-up weight of about 6 cwt.

The road wheels, as usual, carried motor-cycle tyres of only $2\frac{3}{4}$-in. section, and the track was extremely narrow, being 2 ft. 10 in. in front and 2 ft. 7 in. behind. As a result, passenger space was remarkably limited. The driver sat slightly off-centre to the right and the passenger was placed centrally behind him, with his feet in a small space to the left of the driver. A passenger was at all times a very desirable adjunct, since there was no reverse gear, the passenger doing duty in its absence. When there was no passenger, reversing presented obvious problems.

It is really remarkable that anything so primitive could be sold as late as 1921, for the standard of engineering was deplorable, and will stand no comparison even with the homely construction of a contemporary G.N. Its short-lived success can only be explained by the great cost and shortage of real motor-cars for the three or four years immediately following World War I.

TROJAN

The two-stroke engine has always been more attractive in theory than in practice for motor-cars, and until recently very few have caught the public fancy. In the Vintage period there was one such design which sold extremely well and deserves mention as one of the oldest and most eccentric of British cars.

The Trojan was the work of a clever inventor named Leslie Hounsfield, who shortly before the war conceived the idea of a car to carry four people at minimum cost, to be of the utmost mechanical simplicity, and to be absolutely foolproof in operation. Two Edwardian Trojans were in fact built, and after the war Leyland Motors took up the idea with some enthusiasm and began serious production in 1922. The specification was entirely peculiar: a pressed-steel tray formed the chassis and had attached to it below the front seat a horizontal four-cylinder two-stroke engine in unit with a two-speed epicyclic gearbox, which drove the solid back axle through a single roller chain of extraordinary length. The disc wheels carried solid tyres of very small section whose unyielding quality was, however, mitigated by the suspension, which used four enormously long and narrow cantilever springs. Starting was by an internal handle and equipment was reduced to a minimum throughout the car, the standard coachwork being a four-seater of uncouth appearance.

Backed by the great resources of Leyland, the Trojan could be sold at a low enough price to attract buyers despite its highly curious nature and it was also sufficiently well-made to be very reliable. This was just as well, for quite a number of garages bore notices stating "No Trojans". For several years the price was below that of an Austin Seven, to which it offered far superior roominess and comfort. It found considerable favour among the clergy, and is probably the only make to have advertised in the *Church Times*. Nor was its sole merit that of cheapness, for although the 1500-c.c. engine produced only 11 b.h.p at the peak speed of 1200 r.p.m., the low-speed torque was of course formidable, and the little car would climb virtually any gradient and could be driven over the roughest country without damage. On the other hand, it was possibly the slowest production car of the entire decade; even the gloomiest of orthodox light cars could probably attain a rousing 45 m.p.h. on occasion, but the Trojan's inexorable maximum was 38 m.p.h. and no more. So that despite a modest fuel consumption the initial enthusiasm for the car waned.

The original solid tyres eventually gave way to the conventional pneumatic system – not, it was said, from any dictates of comfort, but because cars which fell in with a tramline were unable to disengage themselves except by following the line to its terminus. Pneumatics had, in any case, been an optional extra since 1922.

Its end was hastened by the attempt of the makers to modernise it (against Hounsfield's advice) by placing the engine vertically in the boot of a very large and weighty saloon while retaining the chain drive and other curiosities, and after 1929 the Trojan Utility Car was no more; though a light delivery van on the same chassis was subsequently made in large numbers.

6

Touring Cars

THE tourer was the most typical car of the Vintage era, so it may seem paradoxical that probably fewer survive than any other true Vintage type. The reason, however, is not far to seek. The various other categories have all continued through the intervening years to exercise some specialist appeal or other. That of the sports and racing car is the most obvious and needs no further explanation than the two thousand-odd members of the Vintage Sports-Car Club. The luxury car, too, is evident enough. The aesthetic and nostalgic appeal of a machine made by skilled craftsmen regardless of expense, whether it be a motor-car or a watch, is irresistible to anyone with a love of mechanical perfection. Also, many Vintage luxury cars survive as hire vehicles, while a few even continue in their original ownership and use, magnificent survivals. The Vintage utility car has always appealed to the "marginal motorist" because of its honest, frill-free approach to economy motoring. It is even beginning to exercise an appeal to collectors. The cycle-car is certainly now a great rarity, but that is mainly because it never really had an appeal: you only owned a cycle-car if you could afford nothing better (this does not, of course, apply to the faster G.N.s, which had real performance). In any case, they were so abominably designed and made that in the course of nature nothing could prevent their early and unmourned disintegration. A surviving cycle-car has therefore become an object of the utmost curiosity and interest.

But the touring car was the bread and butter of Vintage motoring. Accordingly, it had no enthusiast-appeal and during the nineteen-thirties it sank gradually down the social scale while the more unusual types continued to find an appreciative market.

Right up to the war innumerable Vintage touring cars were to be seen in country districts performing more or less agricultural duties, in varying stages of disrepair and neglect. The war brought shortages of spares, such spares as there were going for scrap metal; and obsolete tyre sizes were difficult to obtain. Even so, some of them staggered heroically through the war and went on working through the acute shortage of new cars in the immediately post-war years. But in the past three or four years they have suddenly disappeared. Too expensive for the marginal motorist, too slow for the sporting driver, too draughty for anyone else, the English Vintage touring car in good condition – or in any condition at all – may soon disappear almost completely into the limbo. Yet even in the last year or two there has been evidence of a revival of interest in the tourer, and in the membership of the Vintage Sports-Car Club are appearing some superbly restored examples of Humber and the less sporting sorts of 12/50 Alvis. Sunbeams are in a class by themselves and have always enjoyed an enthusiastic following.

12/50 Alvis with sports-touring body, 1924; "balloon tyres and front-wheel brakes" were an "optional extra"

Nowadays it is taken as a matter of course that a family car is a saloon, and only the sporting driver wishes to expose himself to the elements; at most, the family man drives about in a permanently shut convertible, comforting his *amour propre* with the thought that he could open it if he wanted to. The cheap family saloon is, however, a growth of the late Vintage period. In the early twenties, building enclosed coachwork was quite an expensive undertaking, and even then it usually developed numerous rattles fairly early in its career. Moreover, the horse and cart was still a common enough from of transport and it was accepted as a natural and obvious thing that if you went out on a cold day you dressed accordingly, and if it rained you got more or less wet.

The Vintage tourer was, moreover, a long-established type. The Vintage luxury car was an entirely different thing to its Edwardian predecessor, as also was the sports car. But many early Vintage tourers were only slightly modified editions of an Edwardian design, and it is often quite hard to distinguish between 1913 and 1920. Indeed, as soon as the Edwardian tourer developed full-height sides and doors to the front seats, in about 1911, it became one of the most charming vehicles imaginable. The occupants sat in superbly upholstered, leather-covered seats, high enough to see the view over the hedgerows, carried along at a cruising speed of 35 or 40 m.p.h. (but usually, by choice, much less) by an immensely smooth, silent, flexible, and inefficient engine of between 2 and 4 litres capacity.

After the war things went on in much the same way, at any rate for a considerable time. Sunbeam, for example, continued with substantially pre-war models until the end of 1924, while gradually building up a post-war programme. One of these survivals, the 24/60, one of the most handsome and altogether delightful cars Sunbeams ever made, comes near the top limit of 5 litres arbitrarily set for the purposes of this book as the dividing line between luxury cars and other categories. The first new post-war Sunbeam model, by contrast, was the 2-litre "14", and this was by far the most popular size for the Vintage tourer, both here and abroad.

Typical of the larger variety of tourer, in the medium price range, were the Crossley, direct descendant of the valiant "W.D." model which gained a tremendous reputation for its war service, and the ugly but honest Austin "Twenty". How great was the margin of safety of this lethargic vehicle was shown when the manufacturers ran a "Twenty" at Brooklands with a single-seat body and recorded a lap-speed of 94½ m.p.h.

Continental cars generally had a higher performance than the English. The normal speed of English traffic in the early twenties was amazingly low, but in France and Italy cars were habitually and mercilessly driven at or near their maximum. Certainly

French roads encouraged fast driving, and there was relatively little traffic on them. A 2-litre car could therefore afford to pull a high enough gear to enable 60 m.p.h. cruising to be maintained, at some expense of top gear performance. Flexibility was more important for English roads and driving habits. Correspondingly, the French and Italian motorist demanded really powerful four-wheel brakes from 1919 onwards, while the English remained content with rear-wheel retardation until about the end of 1924. It is remarkable how these acknowledged national characteristics have changed since the second war. Traffic in France has palpably slowed down and the standard of driving has deteriorated, while in England speeds have risen and the level of driving skill has improved out of recognition with a new generation of war-trained, mechanically-minded motorists.

Humbers made a tourer of quite exceptional charm and refinement, and Sunbeams must be regarded as providing the peak of Vintage touring. Although all the Vintage range of Sunbeam tourers had overhead-valve engines their power output was almost inexplicably low and few aspired to give as much as 20 b.h.p. per litre. For example the "16" newly introduced in 1927, which was a 2-litre six-cylinder, with the not inconsiderable compression ratio of 5·7 to 1, could only manage to provide 44 b.h.p. at 4000 r.p.m. – which is at least 12 below what might reasonably be expected by the lowest standards of efficiency. But this self-denying ordinance by the Sunbeam designers did certainly achieve a standard of flexibility, refinement, and durability which later became a lost art, but which modern technique has lately rediscovered in conjunction with an increase in power of 50% or more.

A unique position was enjoyed by the little Rolls-Royce, introduced with a six-cylinder, overhead-halve, 3·1-litre power plant in 1922. This was really a luxury car in miniature, and it was provided not so much for those who wanted a cheaper as a smaller Rolls-Royce. Despite our definition, it has therefore seemed logical and convenient to describe the "Twenty", together with the "Phantom", in the luxury chapter. More often than not, the "Twenty" was regarded as a town carriage and carried bulky closed coachwork, but many of these beautiful chassis were fitted with two and four-seater open bodies and became the very acme of the Vintage touring car. The first model developed only about 50 b.h.p.. and although this was slightly increased in capacity and power as time went on, no Vintage "Twenty" had a maximum appreciably over 60 m.p.h.; the comfortable cruising speed was 50 m.p.h.

As long as saloon coachwork was heavy and often very prone to rattle, people cheerfully accepted the inevitable penalties of open coachwork, but the death-knell of the tourer was struck all unwittingly by the Standard Company, who in the early twenties introduced their "all-weather" equipment. This consisted of detachable metal-framed celluloid side panels which afforded something approaching the protection of a saloon. At once people began to look askance at the meagre protection of a cape-cart hood. The introduction of the Weymann saloon was another contributory factor. This construction consisted of a wooden frame, insulated from the chassis, and covered with fabric or leather. It was thus both light and rattle-free. Yet another reason was the gradual increase of driving speeds, which made the back seats of an open four-seater by no means an enviable position.

The French also espoused the Weymann saloon with enthusiasm, and many of their touring-type chassis are so fitted. Elegant open coachwork is also found, often with boat-decking for the top surfaces. If English Vintage sports cars enjoy a general pre-eminence, the French must be allowed to excel with their fast tourers of 2 to 3 litres capacity. Such makes as Delage, Schneider, Chenard Walcker, Voisin, Panhard et Levassor, Bugatti, and Mors come readily to mind. Although the DIS Delage described itself as a 14/40 it must surely have developed 50 b.h.p. at least, with its maximum of 70–75 m.p.h. and cruising speed of 60 m.p.h.; the same must equally be true of the splendid 2LTS Ballot. All these were really big, impressive-looking cars, and if their engines fell short of the English in sheer refinement, they reached a very acceptable standard, and they have deservedly survived in considerably greater numbers; the owner of a DIS Delage in still a person much to be envied. The sleeve-valve cars such as the Voisin, Panhard, and Mors were,

30   The winner of the first Grand Prix: Szisz and the 1906 13-litre Renault

31   The winner of the 1914 Grand Prix: Lautenschlager and the 4½-litre
      Mercedes

32 British success – a 2-litre Sunbeam, winner of the 1923 French Grand Prix

33 The 1924 "P. 2" 2-litre, straight-eight, supercharged Grand Prix Alfa Romeo

34 The 1919 5-litre Indianapolis Ballot – parent of all straight-eight racing cars; Louis Wagner at the wheel

35 Vintage versatility – the 1923 World Speed Record 10½-litre, V-twelve Delage, taking part in circuit racing nearly thirty years later; Cecil Clutton at the wheel

36 The culmination of the Vintage racing car: the 1927 straight-eight, supercharged Grand Prix Delage. Triumphant in its own day, it was equally invincible in 1½-litre racing in the hands of Richard Seaman ten years later

37 The type 35B Bugatti, introduced in 1927; the outstanding Grand Prix car of the late twenties; seen a quarter of a century later at a Vintage Sports-Car Club Silverstone meeting

38 Family Saloon – a 1924 Austin "heavy twelve-four"

39 A typical Vintage light car: the 11.9-h.p. Lagonda

40 Refined economy – the 1923 Humber 8/18. In the background are an American-made Rolls-Royce and a "blue-label" 3-litre Bentley saloon

41 1927 Jowett long chassis 2-seater tourer. The Jowett horizontally-opposed twin had the longest run of any production car: 1910-1953

42   1924 2LT Ballot

43   1926 DIS Delage

44   The 1924 six-cylinder Sunbeam 24/70

45   A type 44 Bugatti (straight-eight, 3-litre, touring chassis), introduced in 1927, with coachwork by Gangloff

of course, the very peak of refinement, though generally at corresponding loss of performance. The 4-litre sleeve-valve Peugeot was, however, a really brisk performer, somewhat on a level with a 3-litre Bentley, while the 3-litre type 44 Bugatti, specifically – and quite properly – catalogued as a tourer, could out-perform most avowed sports cars of comparable capacity.

Much the same was true of the Italians, who produced several straightforward machines of about 2-litres capacity, such as the O.M., Ansaldo, and, of course, the incomparable Lancia. The Lancia "Lambda", although certainly envisaged as a touring car, has by its outstanding performance and handling qualities earned universal acceptance as a sports car and is so treated in this book.

Germany produced no desirable touring car, although the supercharged 16-h.p. Mercedes, by the drabness of its performance, certainly deserves no other category. This expensive machine, the first supercharged European production car, had a maximum of 60 m.p.h. unblown, which might be raised to $66\frac{1}{2}$ m.p.h. (according to a 1923 road-test) by use of its much-vaunted and unbearably noisy compressor. In 1927 they struck rock-bottom fairly and squarely with a six-cylinder 2-litre touring model which was geared at 6 to 1 in top gear and had a maximum of 55 m.p.h. It is most remarkable that a firm which produced such consistently successful racing cars from the earliest times made so very few desirable production models. Even the legendary Edwardian "60" and "90" are much over-rated and, like the big supercharged cars of the late twenties, owed their reputation more to their bark than their bite. It must certainly be conceded that Mercedes have convincingly altered this state of affairs in their products since World War II.

America produced one or two superlative touring, near-luxury cars, notably the V-twelve and straight-eight Packards. The Packard Eight of the late twenties is a connoisseur's car, combining a beautifully balanced rigidly mounted side-valve engine with a three-speed gearbox which, for once, is really matched to the power-curve. Performance is well ahead of contemporary touring standards and, most surprisingly, the steering is distinctly on the firm side, extremely accurate, and not excessively low-geared. Right up to the middle thirties the Packard

Typical American tourer: the 1919 Studebaker "Big Six"

Super Eight was one of the finest cars that money could buy, and its basic engine design is still in use. Also of a high order were the Lincoln and Cadillac. No less than 80,000 Cadillacs had been made by 1922. Some of these cars are described in greater detail in the chapter on luxury cars, where perhaps they more properly belong.

But enough has been said to show that the Vintage touring cars are at once varied, commendable, and interesting, and they undoubtedly give a great deal of pleasure to the people who still use them and have the placid temperament necessary for their enjoyment.

A.C.

A.C. stands for Auto-Carrier. The company was formed in 1904 to make a light three-wheel commercial delivery van. These had a great success and continued to be made up to the outbreak of war in 1914. The first four-wheeler was built in 1913, but production was not started until 1918. The engine was the famous 1½-litre side-valve Anzani. The car was an immediate success because of its high finish, brisk performance, and good lines.

From the first the design incorporated the three-speed gearbox and transmission brake in the back axle, and so light was this assembly that there was no serious increase of unsprung weight. It was also logical enough to keep the transmission brake where it did not have to operate through the propeller-shaft and universal joints. Unfortunately, it was not a good brake. Westall, one of the works competition drivers, was exceedingly scathing about this brake, proclaiming that it was only fit for making toast, although his attempts to demonstrate his statements never quite succeeded in producing any toast. Brownsort, a confederate of Westall, had a similarly dry sense of humour, and both of them sharpened their wit incessantly upon the impetuous and at times mechanically wayward designer John Weller whom, having conceived an idea, however impracticable, neither demonstration nor argument could shake.

It was on the occasion of some record attempt that the car was about to be restarted after a routine check, including changing the oil. People were beginning to push the car. "I shouldn't, if I were you," said Brownsort. Pressed for his reasons, he held up the big-end nut of a connecting-rod which he had seen in the discarded sump-oil.

The four-cylinder model continued until 1927–8, when it was dropped, for in the meantime Weller had introduced and firmly established the model upon which the fame of the firm still rests. This was his light 2-litre six-cylinder. The prototype was made in 1919 and in 1954 basically the same design is still in production. For length of production the thirty-five years of the A.C. "Six" is exceeded only by the upwards of forty years of the Jowett horizontally opposed twin.

The "Six" was astoundingly light, the complete engine with starter and dynamo weighing only 350 pounds. Apart from the iron cylinder head, the whole engine was made of light alloys

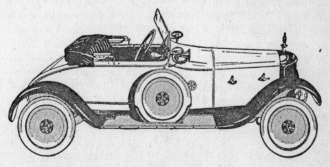

1920 Anzani-engined A.C.; perhaps the best of the early
Vintage light cars

139

with wet steel liners. Apart from the 1919 prototype, the overhead camshaft was driven by an extremely long chain, made possible by the Weller spring plate tensioner. The first engines developed only 40 b.h.p., but this has now been more than doubled, showing the remarkable soudness and advanced design of the original. In 1923 the "Six" began to take class records and (among other things) covered 50 miles at Brooklands at 91 m.p.h., while in 1925 Mr. T. Gillett at last beat S. F. Edge's twenty-four hour record of 1907, by driving (single-handed like Edge) for twenty-four hours at an average of 82·58 m.p.h.

Edge himself had joined the company in 1921, and he was the Governing Director from 1922 to 1929. Immediately, as in the Napier days, the correspondence columns of *The Autocar* were bombarded with letters from Edge proclaiming the unique advantages of all the features to be found in the A.C.; especially the use of only three speeds and the gearbox on the back axle. Under Edge's guidance the "Six" was steadily improved, and was endowed with some extremely handsome coachwork, especially the drophead coupé.

Edge was always thinking up new publicity stunts and these were enthusiastically executed by the Hon. and Mrs. Victor Bruce. Their greatest success was that of winning the Monte Carlo Rally in 1926, it being the first time this had been achieved by a British car.

But despite these triumphs, the company failed to weather the financial blizzard of the late Vintage period, and it went into voluntary liquidation in 1929. As is well known, it was later re-formed and continues to market the "Six". In 1954 the famous engine has been put into a very light four-wheel-independently-suspended chassis to make one of the most advanced and formidable modern 2-litre sports cars. But in the Vintage era the A.C. "Six" occupied a unique position as a small touring car of great refinement and flexibility, coupled with a lively performance and comfortable, comely coachwork.

BALLOT

The Ballot firm made its name in racing, and its achievements in that connection will be found in the chapter on racing cars. No production car was made until 1921, and then it was closely related to one of the racing cars – a 2-litre, 70 × 130 mm., four-cylinder with two overhead camshafts. The maximum speed was over 90 m.p.h. and about fifty in all of these cars were made. Unfortunately none is known to survive.

In 1922 Ballot retired from racing and in 1923 the firm market-ed a very remarkable car, known as the 2LT (2-litre Tourisme). With cylinder dimensions the same as the twin-cam car, the maximum was only 65 m.p.h. There were powerful suction servo-operated four-wheel brakes. In 1925 the 2LT was supple-mented by the 2LTS with slightly inclined valves. These cars had a really outstanding performance, and they usually carried an immense, four-square, very roomy and comfortable Weymann saloon body. Even thus encumbered they would cruise indefin-itely at about 64 m.p.h., with a maximum just over 70 m.p.h. Acceleration certainly was not outstanding; nor was this helped by a very slow gearbox. Cornering was excellent and free from roll. Everything about the car was impressively massive, especial-ly the engine, which was also most commendably smooth and flexible up to its 4000 r.p.m. maximum. The top-gear ratio, as was almost universal with this type of Continental, gave 20 m.p.h. at 1000 r.p.m.

In 1927 started a series of somewhat less successful cars. First came the 2LT6, with chain-driven overhead camshaft, of which very few were made. Also in 1927 came the 3-litre straight-eight RH2, with cylinders 63 × 105 mm. In 1928 the bore was increased to 66 mm., and finally, in 1930, to 68 mm., giving a capacity just over 3 litres, and then known as the RH3. This car had a maxi-mum of 75–80 m.p.h. but had a bad reputation for bearing failure.

In 1931 the company was taken over by Hispano-Suiza.

Both in their racing and production models Ballot adhered to very high and advanced ideals. The 2LTS was a particularly fine achievement having regard to the large size of the car and the small size of the engine. It is a pity that so few examples have survived.

BUGATTI

Once again the story starts with the 1910 type 13, which was

141

equally in its element as a sports, touring, or racing car. Enough has been said of this model in the sports and racing chapters, to which the reader is referred for details of it. Its longer-chassis derivatives, the types 22 and 23, often carried definite touring and even saloon coachwork.

The touring models, so-called, of the Vintage decade were the types 30, 38, 38A, 40, 40A, 44, and 49. All have a single overhead camshaft and three valves per cylinder.

The types 30, 38, and 38A may all be considered together and they are perhaps the least successful or likeable of all Bugatti types. The type 30 was introduced in 1922, being a touring edition of the 1922 Grand Prix car. Rough, noisy, and not very fast, its main interest lay in its being the first small straight-eight to be put into production. The "38", introduced in 1926, was a long-chassis edition of the "30", and had the characteristic tubular front axle, as against the H-section axles of earlier types. The type 38 was also the first Bugatti to be fitted with a central gear-change. A supercharged edition of the "38" became available as the "38A" in 1927.

The type 40, introduced in 1926, was really a touring edition of the racing type 37, with its $1\frac{1}{2}$-litre, 69×100 mm., four-cylinder, plain-bearing engine. The type 40 has been described as Bugatti's Morris "Cowley" and it certainly achieved widespread popularity as the cheapest and most simple model of the whole Bugatti range. It had a maximum of about 75 m.p.h. and very similar overall performance to the contemporary Anzani-engined Frazer-Nash. The standard body with pointed tail is very much on the lines of the type 43. The shiny black seats were said to be stuffed with hay. They felt like it.

Closely allied to the type 40 is the type 44, which is a straight-eight 3-litre employing two type 40 blocks, fed by a single Schebler carburettor. This was perhaps the best of all touring Bugattis, even including the much renowned type 57. Although not quiet in the Rolls-Royce sense, the engine was perfectly smooth and refined despite its rigid mounting. Silence alone is no criterion of refinement, and many modern sound-proofed, rubber-mounted engines which pass for refined would compare poorly with a type 44 if similarly mounted. Although not marketed until 1927, it is known that the prototype existed in 1919, when it was shown at the Paris Salon, and it probably continued as a listed model until 1934; it is a curious fact that Bugatti models were seldom quite superseded, and it seems quite possible that if anyone had walked into the works in 1939 and ordered a type 13, his order both could and would have been executed. This was possible because Bugatti designs were conceived as a series of machining processes, and little or no jigging up was involved. On the other hand, innumerable components were interchangeable between all types. This not only accounts for many seeming eccentricities of Bugatti design, but for the large number of models Bugatti could bring out without going bankrupt. The early types 40 and 44 had jet lubrication to the big-ends, but later examples had a pressure-fed crankshaft and these cars had tremendous stamina and reliability. Maximum engine speed was 4500 r.p.m., giving 90 m.p.h., and the cars would run indefinitely at 4000 r.p.m. Many long-suffering type 44s were fitted with quite upstanding saloon bodies and these, together with the somewhat long, narrow chassis, could give rise to an uncontrollable degree of roll oversteer. In recent times private owners have tuned and raced the type 44, and witht wo or even four carburettors it has proved itself a formidable competition car, capable of 100 m.p.h.

Analogous to the "40" and "44" were the "40A" and "49", introduced in 1931 and 1930 respectively. The "49" was popular in France but not very many came to England. It was a 3·3-litre, 72 × 100 mm. straight-eight, and the "40A" was one block of a 49. No English example is known.

The type 49 was even smoother than the "44" and had a remarkably quiet and quick gearbox. It also had sixteen sparking plugs, all in a row, fed from a single distributor and two coils, which contributed greatly to its flexibility, and these cars could easily be started from rest in top gear. Conversely, there was a marked tendency for cracks to develop between the plugholes, although no harm seemed to result. The type 49 had the very handsome cast aluminium wheels also found on the types 41, 46, and 50. Later examples had dry-plate instead of the usual Bugatti wet multi-plate clutches. This was achieved by having alternate plates lined with Ferodo, and made the cars much easier to maintain. The type 49 was, in fact, widely known as "the Doctor's Bugatti". Limited to 4000 r.p.m., it was said to produce only 92 b.h.p., as against 99 b.h.p. from the type 44.

CROSSLEY

Before the war one of the most fashionable and attractive of all fast light sporting cars had been the 15·9-h.p. "Shelsley" Crossley. This had a very straightforward side-valve four-cylinder engine of $2\frac{1}{2}$ litres, in unit with a four-speed gearbox, and was deservedly ranked high by the sporting motorist of the time. Maximum speed was about 60 m.p.h., and with its shapely pointed radiator, elegant touring coachwork, and wire wheels it was undoubtedly one of the prettiest cars on the road. One of them ran in the 1914 Tourist Trophy race in almost standard form save for the addition of an oil-cooler between the dumb-irons; it was driven by Cecil Bianchi, who was unfortunately forced to retire on the second day with clutch failure.

In 1908 Crossleys had introduced what was to become their best-known car, the $4\frac{1}{2}$-litre 20/25 model, which had a side-valve engine producing about 50 b.h.p. This was adopted quite early on by the War Office on account of its extreme robustness and reliability and was made in very large numbers during the war as a staff car, R.F.C. tender, ambulance, and mobile workshop; about forty-five a week left the Manchester works throughout the war. Although considered a bit slow by the more dashing R.F.C. drivers, in comparison with the D-type Vauxhall, its durability and smoothness added tremendously to Crossley prestige and it went back into production almost unaltered as the 25/30 in 1919. It is impossible to drive a Vintage Crossley today without being bombarded at every stop with affectionate reminiscences of these cars on active service. The 25/30 survived with modern additions until 1926, a good run for a 1908 model. Crossley were always reluctant to abandon a useful design and the same engine was used in some of their commercial vehicles until the mid-thirties.

The "Shelsley" model was discontinued during the war, which was a pity, for its performance and character could easily have

144

enabled it to hold its own during the early Vintage period. Its place was taken in 1920 by the 19·6-h.p., a large and excellent touring car combining Edwardian and modern features in a particularly pleasing manner. It had a side-valve 3·8-litre engine of unusually longstroke (90 × 150 mm.), probably producing about 55 b.h.p. A separate four-speed gearbox with excessively low intermediate ratios was fitted, though top was 3·5 to 1. The three-bearing crankshaft was carefully balanced with vast counterweights. The heavy flywheel and long stroke consequently produced particularly flexible and effortless running with good acceleration in the 30–50 m.p.h. range and a maximum of about 60 m.p.h. The Smith five-jet carburettor gave a very useful economy, over 20 m.p.g. being obtainable from the 30-cwt. tourers.

Although allegedly designed for the owner-driver requiring a lighter car than the 25/30, the 19·6 is massively built throughout, with a deep and well-braced chassis, very long springs, and surprisingly light and accurate steering. Crossleys had pioneered front brakes in this country in 1910 but they did not reappear until 1924. Although rather disappointing in performance due to its low power, the 19·6 could be satisfactorily tuned; Leon Cushman raced a special four-seater at Brooklands which lapped at well over 100 m.p.h., with a maximum of nearly 112 m.p.h. In 1922 the makers realised its potentialities more fully by producing a special version known as the 20/70. This, given 75 b.h.p., differed from standard in having slipper pistons and a high-lift camshaft, while the gearbox had revised intermediate ratios. Later Perrot-type front brakes were fitted, and with its Rudge wheels and flared mudguards the 20/70 Crossley was quite one of the most elegant sporting outfit of its day. Maximum speed was a guaranteed 75 m.p.h. fully equipped on Brooklands. The four-seater was considerably cheaper than the chassis of the 3-litre Bentley. Although this highly desirable car was catalogued for four years it is most unfortunate that none is thought to survive.

Current with all this heavy metal was the Crossley Fourteen, a 2·3-litre tourer somewhat lacking in character. This model was quite popular as a family car. Crossley also entered the very cheapest market by sponsoring the Willys-Overland, a deplorably crude American vehicle which was made in large numbers at the W.D. factory in Stockport. Due to the association of that great pioneer Charles Jarrott with the firm as well as with the British Bugatti agency, Crossleys undertook in 1923 to make the "Brescia" under licence, but this venture met with no success and few, if any, were actually made in Manchester. Certainly subsequent productions bear no traces of Bugatti's refining influence.

Crossley had always stood out against six-cylinder engines, claiming that four of their cylinders were quite as good as six of anyone else's. Fashion, however, led them to capitulate in 1926, when the early range of big fours was dropped in favour of a series of overhead-valve sixes. The best known of these are the 1928 15·7-h.p. 2-litre and the 20·9-h.p. 3-litre. The former, a quite potent engine, was used in the semi-sporting "Silver" Crossley tourers and a rather handsome "Shelsley" fabric saloon. It was also built for Lagondas for a few years and installed into a somewhat dull and heavy post-Vintage Lagonda known as the 16/80. The 21/60 "Golden" Crossley was a beautifully made car of extreme smoothness, marred by great weight and low gearing; none the less it survived to the end of private-car manufacturing by the firm in 1937. Crossleys maintained their traditions of small production and high quality until the end of the Vintage period; but in 1932 they attempted a new market with a series of most depressing cheap family cars having negligible performance and rough Coventry Climax engines. Like that of so many other makes, the Crossley story really ends in 1930.

DELAGE

It is not invariably the case that manufacturers successful in racing are so felicitous in their production models, but Louis Delage was almost consistently good at both. Before the war he had, in particular, produced a most charming and refined 11-h.p. model, with a remarkably modern-looking four-cylinder monobloc engine (made by Ballot).

After the war Delage was among the first to offer front-wheel brakes, as was to be expected after his use of them in the 1914 Grand Prix. In 1919 a 24-h.p. side-valve tourer was so fitted, and when this model developed overhead valves in 1921 it was guaranteed to attain 80 m.p.h. Excellent performance throughout the speed range was also ensured by the remarkable output of 88 b.h.p. at 2830 r.p.m.

Delage was also among those who offered a luxurious 40/50, of advanced design with front brakes, but his success during the Vintage decade rested mainly on the series of magnificent 2¼-litre touring models. All had four cylinders, 75 × 130 mm., pushrod-operated overhead valves, and a permitted crankshaft speed of 3200 r.p.m.

The forerunner of these was the "new" 11-h.p. of 1921, which was a 75 × 130 mm. side-valve, and the overhead-valve models did not appear until 1924.

First came the DI, followed by the DIS in 1925, and both of these were current until 1927. The DISS was made in 1926 only. It is commonly supposed that the performance goes up as the number of Ss, but in point of fact there is little or nothing to choose between them, although the DIS and DISS did have a more efficient camshaft and larger valves than the DI. When the DISS was dropped at the end of 1926 an improved DIS was continued with a new closer-ratio gearbox, which was a great improvement.

Like so many of the Continental 2-litre tourers, the Delage gives a remarkable performance for its modest power output and considerable size and weight. Thus, although it took nearly 20 seconds to reach 50 m.p.h., the maximum was about 75 m.p.h., and a gearing of 24 m.p.h. at 1000 r.p.m. gave a comfortable cruising speed in the neighbourhood of 60 m.p.h. This was coupled with comfortable springing, excellent cornering, light and sensitive steering, and a very high standard of smoothness and silence from both engine and gearbox. The brakes were adequate but not outstanding, and the clutch was the weakest part of this outstanding example of the Vintage touring car.

H.E.

The H.E. was made in Reading, and started life immediately

after the first war as a modest sort of 11·9-h.p. touring car propelled by a four-cylinder side-valve engine. This was of 69 × 120 mm., and gave a highly conservative 26 b.h.p. at 2650 r.p.m., despite the use of Ricardo pistons. It underwent various modifications during the next few years, growing from a 13/20 into a 14/30 of just over 2 litres. The basic design must have had its merits, for in October 1921 several class records were taken at Brooklands by its designer Sully, including a flying start half-mile at 87·63 m.p.h.

Outwardly the H.E. was very much the family touring car of the period, with four slightly low gear ratios and a most massive final drive by overhead worm; but the firm announced a sports model on the same chassis late in 1922. This, the 14/40, was a singularly handsome two-seater with boat-decking and an upswept pointed tail. Certainly it was one of the most rakish turnouts of its day. For a light 2-litre car the performance was creditable, if not really outstanding, with a maximum of about 65 m.p.h. on its 4·5 to 1 top gear, and quite lively acceleration from the well-tuned side-valve engine. The complete car weighed only 22 cwt., and like the 30/98 Vauxhall and Aston Martin, used the Hele-Shaw multi-plate clutch. Front brakes were added late in 1923, and the car survived until 1926. If it deserves to be remembered more as a fast tourer than a sports car, it was certainly the most distinctive of all the Vintage 14/40s.

It was succeeded in 1926 by the 15·7-h.p. six-cylinder of only slightly larger capacity (2290 c.c.); this was a very smooth side-valve unit which could readily attain 4500 r.p.m. This indeed it needed to do quite often, for the gear ratios were rather discouraging. Maximum speed was, however, about 70 m.p.h. Although not distinguished for their lively acceleration, the H.E. Sixes were decidedly robust and well-braked touring cars which could be wound up to a cruising speed of nearly 60 m.p.h. A few years later the firm toyed with a supercharged 1½-litre six which recorded the by no means remarkable maximum speed of 66 m.p.h. and gave 18 m.p.g., showing the disadvantages of a 5·5 to 1 top gear. The 16/50 was given a 6 to 1 compression ratio to become the 16/60, and remained the staple H.E. until the company sank in the economic depression of 1930.

148

The Humber Company during the Vintage period never produced anything resembling a high-performance car, or catalogued even a nominally sporting model. Such homely concerns as Wolseley, Rover, and Hillman listed special sports versions from time to time, and were seen in much modified form at Brooklands; but Humbers concentrated for ten years solely on medium-sized family cars of great distinction. A brief, costly, and unexplained venture into the world of competition took place in 1914 when a team of three Humbers was entered for the Tourist Trophy Race; they were designed by F. T. Burgess, who later joined W. O. Bentley in the design of the 3-litre. They had twin overhead camshaft engines of long stroke, and although none finished the race they were exceedingly rapid and attractive cars, with a higher maximum speed than any Humber which has left the works subsequently. One has happily survived, and is beautifully maintained by a member of the Vintage Sports-Car Club.

Humbers from 1920 to 1930 represent the very best touring practice of the period, although perhaps a little conservative in design. Characteristically, they were among the leaders of the school which maintained that front-wheel brakes were dangerous, and retained the obsolete transmission brake until 1928. All their cars were of the highest quality, beautifully made, and singularly sweet running and durable; none were bad cars, and none had any pretensions to performance. We have already traced the rise and fall of their economy car, the 8/18, and must now

Early Vintage fixed-head coupé: a 1920 10-h.p. Humber

consider the larger versions, though none was larger than 3 litres.

After the war the Edwardian side-valve cars of 10 and 14 h.p. were continued for four years. In 1923, with the advent of the little 8/18, the sole real advance in Humber design took place. This was the adoption of overhead inlet and side exhaust valves, an arrangement to which the firm was to remain faithful until the early 1930s, and which was not used so consistently by anyone else. Although rather costly and complicated this system gives very nicely shaped combustion chambers and allows excellent water circulation round the exhaust valves. Although Humbers neglected its potentialities for high output it probably accounts more than anything for their hard wearing and silent qualities. The power output of these engines is always extremely scanty; the 2·8-litre four-cylinder 15/40 of 1923, for instance, gave only 40 b.h.p. at 2000 r.p.m. On the other hand, their complete equipment and careful workmanship renders them extremely attractive and pleasing touring cars. It has been calculated by a leading Humber fancier that no less than 30,583 cars left the Coventry works during the Vintage years, of which less than one half of one per cent. are known to have survived, but these few survivors are now beginning to be sought by connoisseurs.

The 1919 10·5 h.p. developed into the 12/25 and the 15·9 h.p. into the 15/40; and the first really new touring design did not appear until 1927. This bore the very popular "14/40" rating and is certainly a thoroughly willing and pleasant car, with a maximum of about 60 m.p.h. Simultaneously with it appeared the 3-litre 20/55 six, a very smooth and handsome car which was ultimately to develop into the "Snipe". The Vintage range was completed in 1929 by the addition of the light six 16/50 model. All these sold well in a particularly specialised market, that of the wealthy middle class who were above an Austin and yet not quite in the Sunbeam category; and Humbers catered extremely well for their demands. In 1930 financial difficulties caused the firm to become part of the great Rootes organisation, who entered a much wider market using the same name.

STRAKER-SQUIRE

The firm of Straker and Squire was alone throughout the Edwardian period in concentrating on one chassis of medium size from 1907 onwards. Certainly this side-valve short-stroke 3-litre 15/20 model was an exceedingly refined and pleasing car which was capable of considerable development, for a special version took a large number of class records at Brooklands in 1914, includin ga flying start half-mile at 98·74 m.p.h. The firm also built two very advanced 3·3-litre racers for the 1914 T.T. having single gear-driven overhead camshafts and delivering 83 b.h.p. at 3200 r.p.m., designed by A. H. R. Fedden. But there was not enough time to prepare them, and the competing cars had the side-valve engines. One retired with a broken piston and the other ran with complete consistency, and took a highly creditable fourth place, driven by R. S. Witchell. This was an excellent showing in a race where it was rather unusual to finish at all.

The firm's interest in competition was reflected in their post-war chassis, which was announced early in 1919 and was certainly one of the most remarkable specifications of its time. It was designed by A. H. R. Fedden, and had a six-cylinder engine 80 × 130 mm. (3920 c.c.), with separate cylinders and an overhead camshaft driven from the front by shaft and bevel gears. The rocker gear was enclosed in a single neat aluminium casing but the valve springs were exposed. This extremely unusual unit owed a great deal to aero-engine practice, while the valve mechanism was very similar to that of the T.T. cars; it must have been very difficult and expensive to produce. Although by no means neat or silent it was highly efficient for its day, being alleged to produce 90 b.h.p., with 70 b.h.p. at 2500 r.p.m.; maximum engine speed was 3750 r.p.m. A very carefully balanced seven-bearing crankshaft was used and drove through a plate clutch to a separate four-speed gearbox with quite well-chosen ratios. The chassis was conventional enough save for rather long cantilever rear springs.

Unfortunately this extremely interesting car hung fire from the production point of view and none seem to have reached the market until 1922. A few prototypes were made and one was raced with considerable vigour by the famous Kensington Moir (who was Sidney Straker's nephew), before he joined Aston Martin. This car held the test hill record at Brooklands, and also lapped at 103 m.p.h.; it scored many successes in speed trials and hill-climbs. This car has survived, and is now undergoing restoration.

For about three years from 1922 these cars, known as the 24/80, were made in small numbers, but the firm did not have the financial backing to make them a success. Straker himself was killed in a hunting accident about this time. This was very unfortunate, for the Straker-Squire Six was potentially one of the most interesting cars of the early Vintage period, and certainly deserved greater fame than it achieved.

SUNBEAM

The Sunbeam Motor-Manufacturing Company was founded in 1899 by John Marston, who had already amassed a large fortune by making Sunbeam pedal cycles.

A six-cylinder chassis was brought out in 1904, only a very short time after the pioneer six-cylinder Napier. Of the later pre-war touring models, none is more famous than the 3-litre side-valve 12/16 which, in tuned form, won the 1912 Coupe de l'Auto race against a full field of Continental opposition. Encouraged by this success, Coatalen embarked on a bold racing policy which is related in the chapter devoted to racing cars.

After the war the firm continued its pre-war models while building up a post-war programme. The first of the latter, the "14", was produced in 1921, and the last of the old programme the 24/70, went on until the end of 1924. But in 1919 there were two models, both with cylinder dimensions of 80 × 150 mm. and side-valve, fixed, L-head blocks. The four-cylinder 3-litre, known as the "16", was in fact no more than the old pre-war 12/16. The six-cylinder 4½-litre was known as the "24". Both these models continued until the end of 1921, when they were endowed with pushrod-operated overhead valves and detachable cylinder heads, and reappeared in 1922 as the 16/40 and 24/60. The latter must be accounted as one of the prettiest and also one of the best Vintage touring cars. Long, slim, and sleek, the 24/60 was immensely refined, and fast for its day, although acceleration was not outstanding. Geared at 29 m.p.h. per 1000 r.p.m., it could maintain an effortless high cruising speed. In 1924 the

Sunbeam refinement: a 1927 16-h.p. saloon

16/40 was dropped but the 24/60 continued for another year, fitted with front brakes and known as the 24/70.

In 1922 the 16/40 and 24/60 were also available in more rapid form with the "O.V." engines, which had an overhead camshaft driven by a shaft and bevel gears, operating four inclined valves per cylinder. These were, in fact, closely related to the 1914 and 1921 Henry-type racing cars. Very few of these desirable cars seem to have been made and none is known to have survived.

This completes the list of more or less pre-war designs continued after the war. In 1921 they were joined by the first completely new design, called the "14". This was a four-cylinder, 72 × 120 mm., 2-litre with pushrod-operated overhead valves. The cylinder block was aluminium, with shrunk-in-liners. Ignition was by coil, with automatic advance and retard. There was a wide-ratio three-speed gearbox and the back axle was attached to full cantilever springs. Final gearing gave about 20 m.p.h. at 1000 r.p.m. In 1923 the block became solid iron, and ignition was by magneto, with hand control.

Also in 1923 front brakes were offered as an optional extra, Sunbeam being among the first English firms to adopt this system in the face of pronounced sales-resistance and opposition from certain quarters of the technical press. For 1924 they became standard on all models.

Also in 1924 came a complete range of new models, known

as the 12/30, 16/50, and 20/60. The "14" continued as the 14/40 and, as previously stated, the old 24/70 continued for the rest of this year.

The 12/30 was a 1600 c.c. four-cylinder and very few were made. The 14/40 was a 75 × 120 mm., 2120 c.c., four-cylinder, which was also available in sports form, giving 50 b.h.p. at 3000 r.p.m. The 16/50 was a six-cylinder, 70 × 110 mm., 2½-litre with a seven-bearing crankshaft and the 20/60 was a 75 × 120 mm., 3181 c.c., six.

For 1925 this rather bewildering range was reduced to two effective models, the 14/40 and 20/60. The twin-cam sporting 3-litre was shown at Olympia this year but was not on sale until 1926. This famous car is described in the sports car chapter. This year and the next represent about the peak of the Sunbeam achievement, as indeed they do of the Vintage tradition generally. Thereafter weight went up and axle ratios went down, and a steady decline set in. In the case of Sunbeam this process was accelerated by the removal of the racing department to the French Talbot-Darracq factory, and with it went most of Coatalen's guidance and aspiration and initiative (Sunbeams had combined with the Talbot-Darracq concern in 1920, whereafter the identification of models, especially racing cars, within the S.T.D. combine becomes a matter of the utmost complexity).

1926 saw a new pushrod eight-cylinder of 5½ litres capacity known as the "30".

In 1927 the 14/40 was replaced by a new 2-litre, 6·7 × 95 mm., six-cylinder, known as the "16". This engine produced the remarkably low output of 44 b.h.p. at 4000 r.p.m., despite the quite high compression ratio of 5·7 to 1. One would have thought it quite difficult for such an engine, at this date, to have produced less than 56 b.h.p. The 20/60 gave way to an equally inefficient "20", of 2·9 litres capacity, having six cylinders measuring 75 × 110 mm. A six-cylinder, 80 × 120 mm., 3·6-litre "25" gave 72 b.h.p. at 2900 r.p.m. and the eight-cylinder "30" continued from the previous year.

These models, in fact, represent the first signs of the downward trend which led to the failure of the company in 1935, and the name now continues as part of one of the large combines, with no separate identity.

The Sunbeams of the Vintage period and early thirties occupy a unique position. They combined smoothness with reasonably high performance and good handling. Mechanically they showed considerable Continental influence, especially in the clean external design of the engines. In appearance they combined dignity and dash with remarkable success. To drive them is a delight, in a peculiar way, not unlike the small contemporary Rolls-Royce. They fully deserve the enthusiasm and loving care which they still receive from their numerous and enthusiastic owners. You practically never see a shabby Vintage Sunbeam.

VAUXHALL

As we have seen, the Vauxhall 30/98 was made in quite small numbers during the Vintage years. While it was the most distinguished car produced by Vauxhall Motors they did not depend on it, as Bentley depended on the 3-litre, but marketed in addition a number of smaller and more domestic motors. These were of excellent quality, and certainly deserve a mention in any account of the period.

One of the best known staff cars during the war was the D-type Vauxhall, which had been introduced as a touring car in 1912 and whose engine had been used in modified form in the "Prince Henry" models. This engine was a four-cylinder side-valve unit of 95 × 140 mm., giving a capacity of 3969 c.c., and producing some 50 b.h.p. at 2000 r.p.m. After the war it went into production as the 25-h.p. model, and touring versions were capable of just under 60 m.p.h. In July 1922 it underwent the same changes as the 30/98, overhead valves being added to turn it into the OD-type, or 23/60; but the engine gave only 10 b.h.p. more and maximum speed was not substantially enhanced. The 23/60, although outwardly very similar indeed to the 30/98, was designed as an entirely different sort of car, which would easily carry saloon or limousine coachwork. Consequently the chassis was extremely robust and heavy and the performance, even in touring form, only slightly above the average for the period. On the other hand, the engine was fitted with a peculiar device

155

known as the Lanchester Harmonic Balancer, a series of geared weights living below the centre main bearing and driven from the crankshaft; and this, coupled with its small valves and heavy flywheel, produced a most notable sweetness of running. The gearbox was identical to that of the 30/98, but the final drive ratio considerably lower. As a quiet and smooth formal car of its period the 23/60 is very hard to beat, but it naturally suffers by comparison with the 30/98. Looking back it seems that it would have been more intelligent to de-tune the engine of the latter rather than build another differing from it in so many small details. The notorious "kidney-box" front brakes were added late in 1923 and the 23/60 stayed in production until 1926.

The first post-war Vauxhall design, and the first small Vauxhall car to be made for some time, appeared late in 1921. This was the LM-type 14/40 Light Car, a model which was to be the mainstay of the factory for the next few years and which was to be made by 1925 at the high rate (for Vauxhalls) of thirty cars a week, giving employment to about 2000 workers there. It had a four-cylinder side-valve engine of 75 × 130 mm. (2297 c.c.)

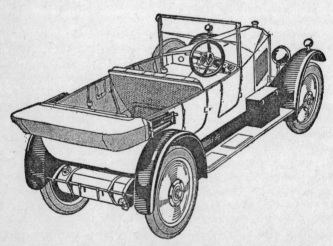

1924 Vauxhall 14/40 "Princeton" tourer. The engine was designed by H. Ricardo and the model produced concurrently with the "30/98"

in a light chassis with cantilever rear springs. The aluminium cylinder head embodied Ricardo patents. A unit gearbox was fitted, giving three somewhat low ratios, and the Hele-Shaw multi-plate clutch of the larger cars was replaced by a single disc. In its original disc-wheeled form the small Vauxhall was not a very lively car, with a maximum speed of only about 50 m.p.h. During the next few years it developed into a very pretty touring motor, with wire wheels, four-wheel brakes, and a much improved gearbox. Later examples would attain about 65 m.p.h., and the combination of light controls, a well-balanced small engine capable of 3000 r.p.m., and a four-seater car weighing only just over a ton produced one of the most pleasant of the many Vintage "14/40s". In appearance too it was handsome enough, resembling a baby 30/98; it remained current until 1927.

In September 1926 the last and strangest of the true line of Vintage Vauxhalls was announced, and this, the S-type, was made for about a year in very small numbers. Vauxhall Motors always tended to miss the boat by building obsolete racing cars, and in the S-type they extended this activity into the domestic field. It had a six-cylinder single-sleeve-valve engine designed under Burt-McCullum and Ricardo patents, and was the first six to leave the factory since the war. This beautifully neat unit was set in a heavy chassis, but had a four-speed gearbox of high and fairly close ratios and hydraulic brakes working on the front wheels and transmission, many of the chassis features being identical with the last year's production of 30/98s. It was an extremely costly machine, the chassis price being about on a par with the Rolls-Royce "Twenty". The engine was unusually lively for a sleeve-valve; but the car did not perform particularly well due to its great weight. None the less, a limousine weighing 45 cwt. was tested at 65 m.p.h. in 1926. It is particularly unfortunate that there are thought to be no surviving examples of this very curious Vauxhall.

The Vauxhall story is rounded off in a rather dismal fashion. General Motors assumed control of the concern in 1925 and although production continued normally for a few years the old line was discontinued in 1927 and an entirely new one-model policy adopted. This was the R-type 20/60, a 2·7-litre car of moderate price, roomy, well-braked, undergeared, and very much the family car. Although a sound enough car in its way it was an unworthy successor to the immortal 30/98.

Voisin

Gabriel Voisin, a pioneer aeronaut and the earliest manufacturer of aeroplanes in France, began car production immediately after the first war. His sole model for some years was a four-cylinder Knight-engined car of nearly 4 litres (95 × 140 mm.), known as the 22/30. Voisin cars were always of the greatest individuality, elegant, and beautifully made; and their sleeve-valve engines certainly gave a higher degree of performance and efficiency than anyone else could manage. These wonderfully neat units operated on fairly high compressions and used very lightweight sleeves; and such is their silence and refinement that it is not difficult to understand the French enthusiasm for the "valveless" engine during the early Vintage period. For a big four-cylinder of long stroke the 22/30 is almost unbelievably well-balanced, and there is none of the feeling, so marked in the contemporary Daimlers, that the engine is working to its limit all the time.

Even in 1921 these cars were capable of 70 m.p.h., and in that year one made a 50 m.p.h. average between Paris and Nice. By 1925 the very handsome boat-decked tourers, despite a weight of nearly two tons, would touch the 80 mark with remarkable silence. The Dewandre vacuum servo brakes, working in very large drums, were among the most effective fitted to any Vintage car. The gearbox, although of quite high and close ratios, was marred by coarse noises in the intermediates, a not uncommon fault on expensive French motor-cars. Another understandable failing was a rather high oil consumption, but by and large these cars are among the most attractive of their period.

Towards the middle twenties Voisin produced smaller four- and six-cylinder cars, still with Knight engines. The best known of these, the 16/50, had a capacity of 2·3 litres and was alleged to give 66 b.h.p. at 3200 r.p.m., maximum r.p.m. was no less than 4000, a pretty alarming thought for double sleeve valves. These cars were quite lively performers, although rather low-geared, with a maximum well into the 70s. Voisin coachwork was always striking in appearance, particularly on the square-rigged late Vintage saloons with cane panelling and piano-type door hinges. The aerial background of the firm had led from the earliest time to a keen interest in streamlining, and a team of extremely bizarre-looking cars had been entered for the 1923 Fuel Consumption Grand Prix.

In 1929 Voisin announced a 4-litre twelve-cylinder which was supposed to give over 100 b.h.p. and embodied a tremendously complex safety device to prevent damage should any of the sleeves become detached and fall into the Vee. He even produced a straight twelve in which the rear part of the engine had to live in the front part of the driving compartment. Throughout the thirties the firm remained faithful to the Knight engine, being beaten for sheer conservatism in this only by Panhard. To the last they remained high-performance cars of great distinction.

7

Luxury Cars

IT would hardly be expected that the greatest technical interest among all the different types of Vintage car is to be found in the luxury class; but such is undoubtedly the case. For in these giant cars no expense was spared to give the customer, who was in general paying £1500–£2000 for his chassis, the benefits of all the advanced design and craftsmanship that the makers knew. Consequently they embody the very highest standard in execution and finish, and have a great connoisseur appeal. It is very unfortunate that so many were hampered by grossly heavy bodywork, and Rolls-Royce thought it necessary to recommend that the total weight of a "Silver Ghost" should not exceed $2\frac{3}{4}$ tons. The most desirable and elegant versions are unquestionably those with comparatively light touring and two-seater coachwork but they are all too rare.

Before 1915 large cars had been slow, silent, and luxurious; or noisy, tough, and fast. In the luxury class the "Silver Ghost" Rolls-Royce, with its normal maximum of about 65 m.p.h., was regarded as outstandingly lively. The really fast cars were mostly based on racing designs and were quite unsuited to luxurious coachwork, although limousine bodies were occasionally found on the larger Napier chassis.

Nevertheless, closed coachwork played an important part in the development of the Edwardian car. The coachbuilder demanded a long wheelbase to give adequate space for a practicable body with side-entry and, equally important, he forced the manufacturer to make his chassis more rigid so that it should not subject the coachwork to excessive twisting strains.

Closed coachwork was always of tremendous height to accommodate the fancy headgear then fashionably affected. Fast cornering on such a car would never have been contemplated, although in fact many of them roll much less than is now thought necessary on some cars only half as high. Nevertheless, although the springing of a Rolls-Royce was quite firm it was also truly and luxuriously comfortable. The ability of extremely soft springing to absorb all road-shocks completely is by no means synonymous with real comfort, quite apart from its propensity for making people vomit.

Before the war, too, there was little limit to the size of engine which could be found in a luxury car, and vast motors of 10 litres and more were not uncommon in the highest price-range, often having R.A.C. ratings of 60 or 70 h.p. The tradition of increasing power by a simple increase in engine capacity died hard in this class, despite the move towards greater efficiency found in racing cars. Side valves, often in a T-head, were virtually universal, and, coupled with enormous flywheels, they give the larger Edwardians a silence and flexibility in their limited range which is unsurpassed and outstandingly agreeable. Very few designers trusted overhead valves for public use on account of their noise and supposed liability to breakage, even though overhead inlet valves had been used in early days by Napier and Rolls-Royce. The overhead camshaft, admittedly used by Maudslay from the first, was never found on luxurious cars, though it appeared on some of the very fine sporting tourers built for the "Prince Henry" Trials of 1910–13, such as the superb 27/80 Austro-Daimler.

After the war the Edwardian monster car disappeared, though Renault continued to produce in their famous "45" a side-valve six-cylinder of 9¼ litres which owed virtually nothing to any advance in design since about 1908. Overhead camshafts were all the fashion and technical advances had caused them to be entirely reliable and acceptably silent, especially with the complicated drive by worm gears or coupling rods as devised by Lanchester or Bentley. The market for sheer size and weight had disappeared and few big Vintage cars exceeded 7½ litres capacity. Even so their numbers thinned throughout the period and of the half-dozen or so British luxury cars which were current in 1920, only the Rolls-Royce survived into the next decade.

The war changed the outlook of the wealthy car owner. For one thing, many more wealthy people took a pleasure in driving, previously regarded as a menial function for the hired man.

Henceforward the luxury car had to be fast as well as luxurious. The "Silver Ghost" hung on until 1925, but it was no longer abreast of the times. Aircraft practice had imbued designers with the idea of making engines which were at once silent, smooth, and powerful and light. To make this new potential high performance practicably useful, overall height had to be reduced, and entirely new standards of braking were necessary to stop two tons of motor-car travelling at 70 m.p.h. or more.

All this was first found in the 37-h.p. Hispano-Suiza, which created such an overwhelming sensation when it was shown to the world in 1919. The light-alloy overhead-camshaft engine developed 135 b.h.p., and although this does not sound much from $6\frac{1}{2}$ litres, it was nevertheless a great advance on anything pre-war that could lay claim to comparable refinement. This was housed in a really deep, stiff chassis, and incorporated brakes of almost modern efficiency, actuated by a mechanical servo motor. Previously luxury cars had always been chauffeur-driven, and considerations of lightness and convenience of control had not unduly swayed the designer. The Hispano, by contrast, was wonderfully easy to control, either as to steering or pedal pressure and the gearchange was one of the easiest of the pre-synchro-mesh era. Indeed, so flexible and powerful at low speeds was the engine that the gearbox could practically by ignored in the course of all normal English motoring. At the other end of the scale was a maximum of 75 to 85 m.p.h. according to coachwork. The handling qualities were in no way behind the performance, yet true comfort had not been sacrificed in the process. In this the large car was at a great advantage compared with the lighter, definitely sporting machines. The great weight of the luxury cars made for a high ratio of sprung to unsprung weight, of which that great authority Mr. Reid Railton has written: "The greater the ratio between the sprung and unsprung weight the better, and the greater this ratio the more flexible the springs that will give the optimum conditions of safety." Conversely, with the light sports or racing car the ratio was low, and to compensate for this manufacturers had to resort to uncomfortably stiff springing and damping. It was not until the mid-thirties that the

German B.M.W. showed how light, fast cars could be made at once comfortable and safe. But this presented no special problem to the designer of a Vintage luxury car, and the combination of comfort and controllability in Hispano-Suiza set a standard which no one ever seriously improved upon, although the general standard was remarkably good.

In the light of modern knowledge it often seems remarkable that the Vintage designer would go to extravagant lengths to produce a highly efficient engine, and then deliberately strangle it by extremely scanty porting. It hardly seems necessary to have the complicated and inherently noisy overhead camshaft to produce a meagre 20 b.h.p. per litre, which could have been got as effectively from an ordinary side-valve unit. It does, however, seem that designers had become deeply interested in an efficient combustion chamber and there is no doubt that thereby they obtained very good thermal efficiency and correspondingly good fuel consumption. Also, it must be remembered that the state of the roads was not conducive to high speeds, and it was the 25 to 50 m.p.h. range in top gear that really counted. For this purpose restricted valves and manifolding, and a slight or nil valve-overlap, provided the kind of flat-topped power-curve which the customer wanted. A high ultimate power output, at the expense of low-speed torque and top-grade flexibility, would have had little appeal or practical use. In modern times the B.R.M. has shown that such considerations have considerable force even in the racing field, since it is little good to have a huge power output which is only available at such high engine speeds that it requires an infinitely variable torque-converter to make the power conveniently available.

Throughout the Vintage decade designers continued to produce luxury cars of the utmost variety and interest, whether in the form of sleeve-valve Voisins, the fabulous Bugatti "Royale", the straight-forward Rolls-Royce "Phantom" I, or the superb straight-eight Packard. Even at the extreme end of the era came two cars perhaps the finest of all – the 8-litre Bentley and the 9½-litre V-twelve Hispano-Suiza. Both, for the first time, brought 100 m.p.h. within the reach of superbly luxurious saloon coachwork, coupled with the utmost mechanical silence and smoothness, sports car standards of control and cornering, and more than normal sports car standards of acceleration.

Bodies were normally coachbuilt, but in the mid-twenties the Weymann body enjoyed a considerable and well-deserved vogue. This consisted of a fairly light wooden framework, insulated from the chassis, and covered with leather or fabric. Such bodies were, accordingly, both light and free from rattles, but the outer covering would not take a high polish, and needed renewing from time to time. Its construction and flexible character also limited the number of curves that could be introduced, although this was no disadvantage to the French coachbuilder, whose clients were demanding razor-edged square saloons of truly "Regency" elegance. Nevertheless, the Weymann saloon went out of fashion towards the end of the twenties.

A remarkably chic finish which sometimes covered the lustreless surface of a Weymann body was imitation cane basket-work, in imitation of the real thing on earlier horse-drawn carriages. It is especially found on another speciality of the Vintage era, the "coupé de ville", in which the owner lived in a little house at the back of the car and the hired man sat out in the rain. This was considered particularly smart; a superb example is the one illustrated on Ettore Bugatti's own "Royale".

Yet another type of coachwork found in luxurious form which has now quite disappeared is the touring body. Nowadays only coachwork of definitely sporting type is open, but these were full-scale, high-sided affairs, with a complicated screen for the back passengers which was adjustable in as many directions as a dentist's chair. Some of these bodies were heavy and lumbering in appearance but others, especially those finished on top with polished mahogany boat-decking and having flared mudguards, are the height of elegance and absolutely redolent of the Côte d'Azur.

Less successful was the full cabriolet or "all-weather" body, with a vast leather hood, and glass windows which wound into the panelling. At the expense of considerable time, blasphemy, and labour a series of cunning folds and hinges permitted the closed car to be converted into a sort of tourer, albeit with an untidy protrusion of material above the back seats. A few seasons' use generally caused rattles and draughts of such magnitude that the whole affair then combined the worst features of both closed and open types.

In diversity and technical ingenuity France undoubtedly led the field during the Vintage decade, although the English Rolls-Royce easily maintained its place as the outright luxury car *par excellence*. Of advanced design we could claim the 40/50 Napier and Lanchester 40. But of whatever nationality, in no age or type of motor-car are individuality and technical interest so general as in the luxury cars of the Vintage years.

THE 6½- AND 8-LITRE BENTLEYS

The larger Bentleys are so closely linked with the out-and-out sporting models that it was necessary to mention them in the chapter on sports cars. But equally they were envisaged only as fast luxury cars, and must certainly have a section to themselves in this chapter. For a certain amount of technical information the reader is referred to the sports car chapter.

The first 6½-litre chassis appeared at Olympia in 1925 and caused a considerable sensation. No attempt was made at performance, and the six large cylinders were fed from a single carburettor. Thus great flexibility and power at low speeds were obtained, yet even with a large saloon body the maximum speed was usually in the neighbourhood of 75 to 80 m.p.h. All this was done in great silence, and on merit alone the car should have been a powerful rival to the newly introduced "Phantom" I Rolls-Royce. But the two makes so firmly held their reputations for quite different sorts of car that this rivalry never materialised. The Bentley therefore sold mainly to people who were interested in high-speed luxury motoring. In 1929 they were rewarded with an even more remarkable machine in the "Speed Six". This is readily distinguished from the "Standard Six" by the radiator, which in the case of the standard model tapers from top to bottom, while the radiator of the speed model has parallel sides.

The "Speed Six" had two carburettors and was in all other ways a moderately tuned version of the earlier model. It thus gained considerably in performance, having a maximum of well over 90 m.p.h. with very little sacrifice in silence or flexibility.

Mostly fitted with compact Weymann saloon bodies, the "Speed Six" was, indeed, a most formidable motor-car and tremendously handsome as well. It was perhaps the best car to come from the Bentley factory.

In 1930 came the even more fabulous 8-litre, although only a few reached the market until 1931. This gave genuine 100-m.p.h. motoring with luxurious saloon coachwork, and silence and flexibility which surpassed even the 6½-litre models. The 8-litre must be accounted one of the great achievements in the history of automobile design.

But people still would not really believe that a Bentley could be a luxury car, and only a hundred 8-litre chassis were sold in 1930 and 1931. The whole history of the Bentley company had been one continuous struggle against insufficient capital, and when the great slump of 1931 set in, the great reputation and secure financial position of the Rolls-Royce firm carried it through and the Bentley sank. The name was bought up by Rolls-Royce, whose reincarnation of it has faithfully maintained the great reputation of the "Winged B".

BUGATTI

Under our arbitrary definition that cars of over 5 litres capacity are classed together in the luxury category, the Bugatti types 41 and 46 fall to be considered under this heading, and rightly so.

The type 41, known as the "Royale", was introduced in 1927 and only seven were made, which at a chassis price (in England) of £5250 is understandable. No 1 was wrecked in an accident which landed Bugatti in hospital, but the other six survive. The engine follows the usual Bugatti layout, having eight cylinders in line, with a single overhead camshaft, three valves per cylinder, a single carburettor, and dual ignition. The cylinder dimensions are 125×130 mm., giving a capacity of 12,760 c.c. The overall length of one of these engines is 4ft. 7 in. Like the type 50, the cylinder block and crankcase are in one piece, so that the crankshaft has to be removed in order to grind in a valve. The valves were, Bugatti said, of special material and needed no attention. Permitted engine revolutions were 2000 per minute, at which 300 b.h.p. was said to be produced. The gearbox was mounted on the back axle and had three speeds, of which the middle one was direct. The maxima were about 55, 95, and (theoretically) 125 m.p.h.

The track was 5 ft. 3 in. and the wheelbase 14 ft. 2 in., which is about the same as a London omnibus, yet so perfectly proportioned are these regal cars that their great size is by no means obtrusively apparent unless they are standing beside a car of normal stature. They are also remarkably light for their size, and a complete car weighs only about 45 cwt.

Bugatti originally intended to make twenty-five "Royales", but having failed to dispose of more than seven he then adroitly sold "Royale" engines to the French railways, where the Bugatti railcars became famous and put up some very high speeds.

The type 46, introduced in 1929, is an almost exact scale model of the "Royale". Popularly known as the "5-litre", the actual capacity is 5350 c.c., produced by cylinders measuring 81×130 mm. As a result the type 46 tends to get mixed up with the type 50, which is almost exactly a 5-litre but is popularly known as the "four-nine."

Considering the long stroke, the type 46 ratios gear are rather low, being 3·91, 5·45, and 9·8 to 1. However, the car was essentially regarded as a luxurious touring car with a maximum not much in excess of 80 m.p.h. It is, in fact, an excellent and most reliable car, with the sole shortcoming that it is most difficult to keep the long propeller-shaft in reasonable balance, and as the gearbox is mounted on the back axle, so that the shaft always rotates at engine speed, this can produce a most disagreeable vibration. In 1931 the "46" was made available with a supercharger blowing at about 6 lb. per square inch. It was thus known as the "46S" and is probably the smoothest of all Bugattis as well as one of the most silent. It is indeed a most impressive car, and so highly did Bugatti think of the type 46 that it was the only model he kept in regular production after the introduction of the type 57 in 1934, and one could be bought right up to the outbreak of war in 1939.

DAIMLER

An essential feature of the Vintage luxury car was its versatility.

The Rolls-Royce, and the Hispano-Suiza in particular, were equally at home carrying full enclosed limousine coachwork or the most dashing of sporting two-seaters. Daimlers, on the other hand, were alone in concentrating purely on dignified formal motors with closed coachwork; and so, while they achieved a very high standard in these, their cars have not a wide connoisseur appeal. Touring or coupé coachwork was occasionally fitted to their chassis, but it somehow looked out of place. The combination of great weight, low gears, and the silent but feeble Knight double-sleeve-valve engines produced a rather uninspiring series of cars by the exacting standard of the Vintage enthusiast.

Unlike Rolls-Royce or Lanchester, Daimler production was not rationalised round two models only. A tremendously wide and complex range was marketed, from a 12-h.p. 1½-litre six-cylinder to an 8½-litre of 52 h.p., and there is accordingly no classic Daimler type for the period. In 1927 the purchaser had the choice of no less than 23 models. On the other hand, the qualities of silence and reliability were developed to a very high degree and it is not really fair to criticise these cars for what they were not meant to be. Perhaps more than any other big Vintage cars they were intended for the chauffeur, a being whose comfort and convenience were notoriously and persistently neglected from the earliest days of motoring. Their Knight engines, even with the light steel sleeves fitted in 1924 to replace the cast-iron type, produced singularly little power; but they did so in a pleasantly unobtrusive manner. The Daimler gearbox was always notable for its quietness, with a distinctively melodious note in the intermediate speeds, and the Lanchester type of "hourglass" worm final drive was absolutely silent. Top gear was invariably low enough to give great flexibility, but correspondingly limited the maximum speed. Daimler coachwork, insulated from the chassis by great rubber mountings, was exceedingly comfortable in the limited range required. It was also peculiarly archaic in appearance, and Daimlers of 1924 are often virtually indistinguishable from those of ten or even fifteen years earlier. The same conservatism is apparent in Daimler fittings, from the Victorian push-on handbrake lever to the complex ring of controls above the five-spoked steering wheel. Nevertheless, Daimler designers were not averse to unorthodoxy and the celebrated "Double-Six" appeared late in 1926. This had a V-twelve 7½-litre Knight engine, but was still heavy and sluggish, with an awful thirst, but it gained some popularity and during the next four years it could be had in five different sizes from 3½ litres upwards.

Laurence Pomeroy, senior, had been in the U.S.A. since his retirement from Vauxhalls, but he returned to this country in 1929 to become Managing Director of the Daimler company, and set about the reorganisation of their design policy. His first move, in 1930, was the introduction of the famous fluid flywheel in conjunction with a preselector gearbox, giving extreme smoothness and ease of control. Gradually, too, the Knight engine was replaced by conventional overhead-valve units it became completely obsolete in 1935. Daimlers had in fact become up-to-date, and their current range now includes some cars of quite high performance.

DUESENBERG MODEL J

Fred S. Duesenberg was an idealist of the highest order and his rare products are quite unlike the run of American automobiles. In his Model J he sought to provide the ultimate in very fast and luxurious travel regardless of expense.

The "J" first appeared in 1928. As befitted a luxury car, the chassis was of ample dimensions, having a wheelbase of 11 ft. 10½ in. It had deep side members, and was copiously provided with tubular crossmembers. The engine was a 7-litre, 95 × 121 mm., straight-eight. The cylinders were in an integral casting with the crankcase, and the detachable head had two overhead camshafts, operating four valves per cylinder. The whole block and head was stove-enamelled green and the engine was rubber-mounted. It was said to develop 265 b.h.p. at 4200 r.p.m., and while such an output is feasible at this crankshaft speed, an output of 38 b.h.p. per litre, at this date, is to be regarded with some suspicion. Not content, however, Duesenberg next proceeded to the Model SJ, which was supercharged. In accordance with usual American practice, the centrifugal compressor was employed. These revolve at immensely high speed (usually at least five times engine speed) and produce very little pressure at low revs. Their purpose, in fact, is to become operative only at the point when the efficiency of atmospheric induction begins to fall off. With a maximum boost of 5 lb. per square inch, the "SJ" was said to produce 320 b.h.p. In this form the car had a top-gear range of 3 to 130 m.p.h. and would exceed 100 m.p.h. in the silent second of its three-speed gearbox. The acceleration time from rest to 100 m.p.h. was of the order of 20 seconds, and all these figures accord with what should be expected from such a power output and a car of this size.

The brakes, of course, were hydraulic, as Duesenberg had been a pioneer of this system. His winning car in the 1921 Grand Prix had hydraulic brakes in the fullest sense of the word, as they were operated by water – an arrangement which must have strained the confidence of the drivers to the utmost.

With such an unrivalled performance, the Duesenberg J and SJ should have got for itself a reputation second to none, but its handling characteristics were said to be disappointing, and whether for this or other reasons, it failed to catch on, and very few indeed reached this country. The appearance, certainly, was somewhat ungainly, with its usual drop-head body, and somehow it does not give the impression that it would handle very well. It is quite extraordinary how seldom instinctive impressions of this kind prove to be unfounded. It seems to be an almost infallible rule with motor-cars that what looks right is right, and conversely.

HISPANO-SUIZA

It would be unthinkable for anything with so high-sounding a name to be a failure, and the Hispano-Suiza was certainly no failure. Perhaps some of the legendary fame of the car was due to its name (and its superbly proportioned lines, especially the radiator), but the Hispano-Suiza also made history in its own right. The model shown in 1919 was unquestionably the first fully developed Vintage car.

To novelists it was irresistible. Here is a typical passage from *The Green Hat* by Michael Arlen, published in 1922: "Open as a yacht, it wore a great shining bonnet; and flying over the crest of this great bonnet, as though in proud flight over the heads of scores of phantom horses, was that silver stork by which the gentle may be pleased to know that they have just escaped death beneath the wheels of a Hispano-Suiza car, as supplied to His Most Catholic Majesty."

Before the war Hispano-Suiza had made various luxury chassis, but their fame mainly rested upon the long-stroke, four-cylinder, T-head car which won the first Coupe de l'Auto race in 1910. This was known as the "Alfonso" after the then King of Spain.

Hispano types are always confusing because there were two quite separate factories, one in France and one in Spain. The first foretaste of post-war policy came from the Spaniards, who before the war marketed an overhead-camshaft, four-cylinder, 85 × 130 mm. car, known as the "Barcelona", which continued in production until 1924.

During the war a very successful V-eight aero-engine was manufactured and a V-twelve was contemplated.

Immediately after the war, in 1919, Hispano-Suiza startled the motoring world with a car so far ahead of its time it may be said to have set the pace for the whole of the Vintage years. This was the famous 6½-litre 37·2-h.p. model. Its overhead-camshaft 100 × 140 mm. engine was, in fact, half of the projected V-twelve aero-engine. The light-alloy block had screwed-in steel liners. Maximum power was deliberately sacrificed to immense power in the middle speed range. The valve timing, in particular, was most unusual, since the exhaust valve closed and the inlet valve opened no less than 8 degrees after top dead centre and there was no overlap whatever. The engine gave no less than 100 b.h.p. at 1600 r.p.m., 115 b.h.p. at 2000 r.p.m., and peaked at 3000 r.p.m. with 135 b.h.p. The maximum permitted crankshaft speed was 3500 r.p.m. The compression ratio was the very low one of 4½ to 1. Ignition was by twin coils, firing two plugs per cylinder, with centrifugal-governor advance and retard, with a manual over-ride.

The gearbox had the rather depressing ratios of 3·3, 6·3, and 10·7 to 1. Most of these gearboxes have become very noisy with the passing of the years, but one or two little-used examples show that they were reasonably silent when new. In any case, they were not meant to be used. All normal running was done in top gear, and it was something quite unusual which demanded a lower gear. As may be imagined, the torque at low speed is entirely remarkable; but when seeking maximum acceleration, the wide ratios are an undeniable handicap, and there is a gap between about 35 and 40 m.p.h. when no gear really seems to fit.

But contemporary road-testers detected no such shortcoming and they described it as "one of the most lively cars ever produced – if not the fastest, nothing can touch it for rapidity of acceleration to 50 m.p.h." and "a car more than capable of holding its own with the world's best".

Attached to the gearbox was a mechanical servo mechanism, for operating the four-wheel brakes. It was the first of its kind and the braking power of a 1919 Hispano-Suiza in good adjustment concedes no points to most modern cars.

Like most cars of its period, the springing was fairly firm, yet truly comfortable. The road-holding and cornering were about as good as such a large car can be, and the steering was perfection; wonderfully sensitive and reasonably light despite its high gearing, taking only $2\frac{1}{2}$ turns of the steering wheel from lock to lock.

Maximum speed was usually from 75 to 80 m.p.h.

The appearance of the car was as strikingly modern as was the design, and it can truly be said that there has never been a car of more regal appearance.

In 1922–3 followed the "Monza" model, with a short chassis and the bores increased to 102 mm. This fairly rare type had a maximum of about 90 m.p.h., and it was followed in 1924 by the 100-m.p.h. "Boulogne", of 8 litres capacity, 110 × 140 mm. This engine had the compression ratio increased to about 6 to 1. One of these cars participated in a famous challenge at Indianapolis with a Stutz car. £5000 was wagered on a 24-hour race and the Hispano won easily, averaging 70 m.p.h.

Also in 1924 the old four-cylinder "Barcelona", made by the Spanish factory, gave way to a new "Barcelona", which was in effect a miniature of the French 37·2. The six-cylinder engine had dimensions of 85 × 110 mm., giving a capacity of $3\frac{3}{4}$ litres. These cars suffer from the inordinately low axle ratio of 5 to 1, enforcing a quite modest cruising speed.

Lastly, starting just within the Vintage years, came the fabulous V-twelve. The $9\frac{1}{2}$-litre engine had equal bore and stroke of 100 mm., and in the interests of silence the overhead camshaft gave way to pushrod operation for the valves. With a 6 to 1 compression ratio 220 b.h.p. was evolved at 3000 r.p.m. and with overall ratios of 2·72, 4·1, and 5·44 to 1, luxury coachwork could be moved about at 100 m.p.h., or accelerated from rest to 60 m.p.h. in 12 seconds – a figure of which any modern sports car may be proud.

The Hispano-Suiza is probably the only car that, in its day, was mentioned in the same breath as Rolls-Royce. It was magnificently made, perfectly proportioned, years ahead of its time, and a joy to drive. The Hispano-Suiza was one of the world's very great cars.

HOTCHKISS

The Hotchkiss type A.R. is now so rare that it would not merit a section to itself were it not for the 1922 chassis which may be seen in the Conservatoire des Arts et Métiers, Paris. This excellent museum is roughly the equivalent of our Science Museum and, having been founded during the French Revolution, contains some remarkably important exhibits. The vehicle and aeronautical sections are housed in a large disused church adjoining the museum and comprise such varied exhibits as the 1770 Cugnot steam-wagon, various Serpollet steamers, an 1893 Peugeot, and many later cars and aeroplanes.

From the Vintage point of view, undoubtedly, the most important exhibit is the 1922 Hotchkiss type A.R. chassis, which is illustrated here, and displays the chassis of a Vintage luxury car at its superlative best.

The 12-feet-wheelbase chassis has the respectable maximum depth of 8 inches, as well as a tremendous cross-member. An open propeller-shaft runs aft from the gearbox to this cross-member, after which, contrary to expectation (being a Hotchkiss), a torque tube carries the drive to the back axle. The back springs

173

are 6-feet-long cantilevers with a special girder arrangement under the front half to stop it working. The front axle has Hartford shock-absorbers and tremendous ribbed brake drums with Perrot-shaft operation via a servo motor. The hand brake works on the transmission and the unit-construction gearbox has ball-change.

The six-cylinder, 100×140 mm., $6\frac{1}{2}$-litre engine is arranged to give 130 b.h.p. at 3000 r.p.m. (slightly less than the equivalent Hispano-Suiza). The overhead camshaft is driven by an offset shaft at the front of the engine and is in the form of a miniature crankshaft which directly operates a series of hinged flaps which, in turn, bear on and depress the valve-stems. The supposed advantage of this cumbersome and complicated arrangement is not apparent, but it is quite typical of the strong individuality displayed in most of the early Vintage luxury class. And to emphasise the new interest in high-speed luxury, the model is described as "Voiture de Course ou de Grande Luxe".

Isotta Fraschini

With a name hardly less romantic than "Hispano-Suiza" and a specification to match, the vintage Isotta Fraschini should have been a serious rival to the Hispano; but in fact this was not the

1930 Isotta Fraschini

case. The two cars have quite a lot in common, even in appearance, but on almost every point an Isotta is palpably the inferior of the two.

The Isotta Fraschini firm was founded in 1899, and in 1910 they were pioneers of four-wheel braking. However, unlike other pioneers at that date, they did not subsequently abandon the idea, but from 1910 onwards all Isotta Fraschinis have had a brake at each corner.

The straight-eight was introduced in 1919 and remained in production for over fifteen years. The 85×130 mm. engine had a capacity of 6 litres and the overhead valves were pushrod operated. Originally the power output was the modest figure of 80 b.h.p. at 2200 r.p.m., but in 1925 the bore was enlarged by 10 millimetres, giving a capacity of 7372 c.c., and the power went up to 120 b.h.p. at 2400 r.p.m. A more sporting edition, the "Tipo Spinto", had two carburettors and other modifications and gave 140 b.h.p. at 2600 r.p.m.

The three-speed gearbox contained ratios as inept as those of the Hispano-Suiza, the overall reductions being $3\frac{1}{4}$, $6\frac{1}{4}$, and 11 to 1. Flexible as the engine is, the lack of more and closer-spaced indirect ratios is greatly felt in present-day English road conditions, but in its day the Isotta was doubtless regarded, in effect, as a one-gear car, and so it certainly can be used.

Two lengths of chassis were available, giving a wheelbase of 11 ft. $2\frac{1}{2}$ in. or 12 ft. 1 in. Like the Hispano, the brakes were worked by a mechanical servo, and they were equally effective.

In fact, if the Isotta Fraschini did not suffer its inescapable fate of always being compared with an Hispano-Suiza, it would be regarded as a very good car, and so indeed it is. But things being as they are, it must always take the second place.

LANCHESTER

Most British manufacturers in the very early days were content to copy Continental practice and there were all too few original thinkers. One name, however, stands out, that of F. W. Lanchester, a brilliant mathematician and engineer. In 1895, when he was working as a designer of gas engines in Birmingham, he built an experimental motor-car, which was almost certainly the first four-wheeled petrol vehicle to be made in this country. This little car owed nothing to the work of others, and after a few years' experimental work, was put into production in 1900; it was to be the basic Lanchester design for the next five years. The production version had a perfectly balanced, opposed twin-cylinder engine with forced lubrication, an epicyclic gearbox, full cantilever suspension, and silent worm drive. The engine was centrally mounted and air cooled. This model soon became one of the best known and most popular of all British cars on account of its extreme reliability and relatively effortless performance. Certainly in an age of ill-balanced vertical twin engines, noisy and difficult gearboxes, haphazard lubrication, and chain drive they showed up their contemporaries in a very poor light. Several of these most comfortable and elegant veterans, immortalised by Kipling in a splendid short story called "Steam Tactics", survive today.

Throughout the Edwardian period Lanchesters, though never seeking publicity by competition work, produced luxurious cars of the greatest individuality. Many highly unorthodox and advanced features were stubbornly used, such as four and six-cylinder "square" engines with horizontal valves closed by leaf springs; disc brakes; tiller steering; and the unusual engine position between the front seats which was current until 1914. They also used a wick carburettor, which had no jets but vaporised the warmed fuel by drawing it through a series of fabric folds. This bulky arrangement was alleged to provide an even mixture under all atmospheric conditions, and was of course immune from the none too clean motor spirit of the period. Lanchester controls, too, were quite unorthodox, a factor which must have caused considerable sales-resistance. Like Bugattis, Lanchesters never became wholly obsolete, and throughout the Vintage period their catalogues emphasised the availability of all spare parts back to 1900. They remain an outstanding example of cars built successfully from first principles, caring nothing for orthodoxy, and bearing in every detail the marks of truly original thinking.

In 1914 George Lanchester, another of the talented band of brothers, designed a more conventional chassis with a forward-mounted six-cylinder side-valve engine of 5½ litres, giving over 80 b.h.p. About a dozen of these most handsome cars, which could be had in sporting torpedo form, were produced during the early part of the war, but the firm soon turned to the production of aero-engines, and of an armoured car on the same chassis.

In the Vintage period the firm produced three models of great technical merit, though much of their individuality had gone. Many of their unique features were abandoned, or so they announced, owing to imperfect understanding on the part of the public. They were quick off the mark with their post-war model, the "Forty" which came out in 1919 and continued in production throughout the next decade. This, if rather heavy, was an extremely imposing car and of advanced specification; throughout its career it cost £50 less than the Rolls-Royce. It had a six-cylinder engine of 6178 c.c. (101 × 127 mm.), in two blocks of three, with an overhead camshaft driven by little Lanchester worm gears top and bottom; it was identical in dimensions and similar in layout to the 40/50 Napier. It gave 90 b.h.p. at 2000 r.p.m. on the standard compression ratio of 4·8 to 1 and would run at 2500 r.p.m. A three-speed epicyclic gearbox was retained, having very high ratios for such a chassis and giving a cruising speed of 60 m.p.h. at well under 2000 r.p.m., despite an all-up weight of two tons. It was alleged that engagement of reverse at 40 m.p.h. simply slowed the car, which would then rush backwards without protest; a feat of somewhat limited application. Final drive was by worm, and cantilever rear suspension was used, the chassis being very similar to the 1914 cars. The shapely radiator had a little glass window in the header tank through which the water level could be observed. Maximum speed in touring form was nearly 80 m.p.h. and even the heaviest saloons of the middle twenties were capable of 75 m.p.h. Front-wheel brakes were added in 1925 and given hydraulic operation in 1926. A Lanchester "Forty" chassis had the attention of Parry Thomas, who made it into an inelegant but effective coffin-shaped single-seater which took nearly two dozen class records at Brooklands in 1924, including one thousand miles at over 95 m.p.h. About 400 of these magnificent cars were made in all, but hardly any of them survive today.

In 1923 the company produced a "Twenty", to combat the small Rolls-Royce; and again the chassis price was a tactful £50 less. This car had a very similar layout to the "Forty", but for the first time the epicyclic gearbox was replaced by a conventional four-speed type having rather low and wide ratios. Large four-wheel brakes were standard from the first and despite its greater weight the car was superior in power and performance to the Rolls "Twenty" (not that that was very difficult in itself). Maximum speed was about 70 m.p.h., with quite lively acceleration. This small Lanchester survived until 1931 and about 700 were made.

The "Thirty", last of the true line of Lanchesters, appeared late in 1928. It had a 5-litre straight-eight engine of identical bore and stroke to the "Twenty", giving 82 b.h.p. at 2800 r.p.m. This beautifully silent and flexible unit gave the car a maximum of rather less than 80 m.p.h., with comfortable cruising up to 70. This was a highly inauspicious time for the production of such a car and only about 120 were made before the firm got into financial difficulties in 1930. The assets were bought by the B.S.A. group against, it is alleged, strong competition from the Rover Company. Thereupon Lanchesters lost their individual character completely and became merely cheap and uninteresting versions of the contemporary small Daimler cars.

THE LEYLAND EIGHT

The most famous figure at Brooklands during the middle twenties was Parry Thomas and his Leyland Eight.

Thomas began his association with the Leyland company in about 1910 and during the war he undertook control of their aero-engine production. In 1916 the company began to think of producing what was intended to be the finest luxury car in the world as soon as the war ended, and they invited Thomas to build it for them. Design work was started in 1916–17 and the finished result, in which Reid Railton also had a hand, was shown at Olympia in 1920.

The engine had eight cylinders in line, cast in one piece with the top half of the crankcase. The dimensions were 89 × 146 mm., giving a capacity of 7266 c.c. An overhead camshaft was driven by connecting rods and a three-throw eccentric gear such as was later used on the six-cylinder Bentley. It operated two valves per cylinder opposed at an angle of 90 degrees. The valve springs were of cantilever leaf type, which was said to eliminate valve bounce. Power output varied according to the number of carburettors employed, but with two it was 145 b.h.p. at 3000 r.p.m.

Transmission was via a normal four-speed gearbox and open propeller-shaft to a most unusual back axle located by a torque tube. The axle had two spiral bevel gears, and the two driving shafts could be inclined to each other at an angle to counteract the highly cambered road surfaces then common, particularly on the Continent.(Thomas later took advantage of this arrangement at Brooklands, where, the banking being concave, he turned the axle upside down.)

In a car intended to be the last word in luxury and technical prowess it is remarkable that braking was on the back wheels only, the pedal brake being vacuum-servo-assisted. This was typical of British practice of the time, for the great Continental luxury cars, headed by Hispano-Suiza, had been marketed with four-wheel brakes in 1919.

The steering ratio was remarkably low-geared, requiring three turns of the wheel from lock to lock. The chassis was offered in three lengths of wheelbase, 10 ft. 6 in., 11 ft. 9 in., or 12 ft. 6 in., and incorporated automatic lubrication. The system of suspension was unique. The front was fairly normal, consisting of semi-elliptic springs shackled at the back end, and located by radius rods hinged to the front dumbirons. The back suspension consisted of quarter-elliptic leaf springs mounted on torsion bars inside the frame. There were anti-roll bars at back and front. The chassis price in 1920 was £2500, but in the following year this figure was reduced to £1875.

Thomas was most anxious to show the paces of the car at Brooklands, but the Leyland company was equally reluctant, and eventually agreed to its appearing in 1922 only on condition that it ran in full touring trim, with a view to demonstrating its ability to attain 90 m.p.h. Thomas ignored this to the extent of running it stripped, and throughout this season he consistently apped at 113–115 m.p.h., a most remarkable effort for an otherwise standard luxury car.

After this initial success he set about tuning the engine and fitting a streamlined racing body. So effective were these operations that the big car gave a fuel consumption of 15 m.p.g. at a steady 110 m.p.h., on a gearing of 46 m.p.h. at 1000 r.p.m. Thomas also eliminated the torsion bars, although he preserved the anti-roll bars. He persistently raised the Brooklands lap record and finally, in 1925, put it up to 129·36, only 15 m.p.h. below the ultimate established by John Cobb and the Napier-Railton ten years later. In 1927 Thomas was killed at Pendine attacking the World Speed Record in the ex-Zborowski, Liberty-engined Higham Special. It was not until after his death that the Leyland's lap record was beaten.

About eighteen of these impressively massive-looking cars were made between 1920 and 1925. It is doubtful if more than one now survives.

LINCOLN

When the Lincoln company got into low water and was bought by Ford, most people imagined that the plant would be turned over to making something consistent with the established Ford range. But there is no doubt that Henry Ford had a very strong feeling for cars of high quality, and even the famous Model T was in fact a car of quality (at any rate prior to 1917), although it was produced in such a way as to sell very cheaply. So far as materials were concerned, Ford would use nothing but the best. Nor was he without experience in making expensive cars, for in 1906 he had considerable success with his fine Model K, 40-h.p. six-cylinder. To quote from the 1908 catalogue, "Ford does not, ordinarily, build to meet a limited demand. But there are exceptions to every rule – even Ford rules. The demand for a high-class, high-powered, high-speed, highly specialised gentleman's roadster, is necessarily limited to those persons who want the last degree of automobile up-to-dateness, and who have the wherewithal to gratify their desires. Such persons are invariably enthusiasts and men who like to feel under their own hands a car that will respond to the slighest touch – almost the hought – of the driver, and which will on occasion attain any speed of which the road is capable. Conservatism has no place in the consideration of such a machine. The ability to do and to look the part are qualities demanded by persons who can afford to gratify their tastes for this twentieth-century luxury."

To anyone familar with these words it should have come as no surprise that Henry Ford carried on the Lincoln tradition for cars of the highest quality. And incidentally, it is doubtful if anyone has ever stated more precisely the qualities of a perfect car than in this 1908 Ford catalogue.

The new Ford-Lincoln came out in 1928. The motor was unusual in having eight cylinders arranged in a 60-degree V, whereas most V-eights are 90-degree, and the smaller angle is reserved for the V-twelve, the difference being due to considerations of balance. The cylinder dimensions were $3\frac{1}{2}$ in. $\times$ 5 in., giving a capacity of just over 6 litres, and they had an L-head. Ford had a marked liking for the L-head, having adopted it at a very early date, when the T-head was still the fashionable arrangement. With pressure lubrication throughout, and five main bearings, the Lincoln was well able to maintain the tradition that no Ford ever suffered from lubrication failure. The power output was 100 b.h.p., and the 11 ft. 4 in. wheelbase chassis usually carried luxurious and heavy saloon coachwork, so that silence and flexibility were clearly rated above performance.

Everything in the Lincoln was made to the highest standard and their lines were always in dignified good taste, so that even today a well-preserved example is impressive. The Lincoln bears admirable testimony to the fact that Henry Ford was a connoisseur of fine motor-cars.

MERCEDES

Mercedes were pioneers of the supercharger and marketed a supercharged car as early as 1922. This was a $1\frac{1}{2}$-litre tourer, and the system of supercharging was that employed by Mercedes with dogged perseverance up to 1939.

For normal running the engine was unsupercharged. If, having reached the full-throttle position, the driver persevered with further pressure on the accelerator pedal, he engaged the supercharger by means of a clutch. The supercharger was of Roots type and (necessarily, because of its being only for occasional use) supplied compressed air to the carburettor; it did not compress the actual mixture. It made a tremendous screaming noise and, if it made little difference to the very moderate performance, at least encouraged the occupants to imagine they were going a lot faster.

The famous Mercedes Vintage models were the 33/180, 36/220, and 38/250.

The 33/180 /orginally 33/140) was introduced in 1926 and had a 6¼-litre, six-cylinder, overhead-camshaft engine of 94 × 150 mm. It was said to be capable of 100 m.p.h., but under road test conditions could manage nothing better than 86·5 m.p.h. In 1927 the bore was increased by four millimeters to become the 36/220, and finally in 1929 came the 100-mm. bore 7-litre 38/250 SS, which was advertised as having a top-gear range of 8–114 m.p.h. Later came the SSK (Super-Sports Kurz, or "Short") with a 9 ft. 8 in. wheelbase, and finally, for racing, the much-drilled SSKL (Leicht), which with the very rare "elephant blower" gave a 12-lb. boost and nearly 300 b.h.p. In 1931 one of these cars, with a streamlined body, was timed at 156 m.p.h. One of the greatest racing successes of the SSK was the 1929 T.T., which was run in pouring rain and was won by Caracciola; it was one of his greatest personal triumphs.

It is difficult to account for the hero-worship accorded to these cars, unless it be due to their appearance, with all it Teutonic emphasis on sheer brute power, and the adolescent

1929 Mercedes-Benz SSK

appeal of the supercharger scream. Perhaps, too, distance lent enchantment, since very few could afford to assuage their insatiable thirst.

On the other hand, despite the grotesque unsuitability of the 38/250 for English roads, it had certain merits on its native soil, where its battleship construction was well calculated to stand up to sustained high speeds on mid-Continental pavé, and the high-geared, low-efficiency engine would effortlessly sustain a high cruising speed once it had been attained by means of the blower. But on crowded and tortuous English roads it needs a true nazi to keep using the strident supercharger, while without it the performance is negligible. Moreover, Mercedes were very guarded about its use, which they did not recommend unless with a 50/50 benzole mixture – and then not for more than 20 seconds continuously, and never in bottom gear. Neglect of these precautions caused frequent cylinder-head gasket failures, while it was also all too easy to provoke clutch-slip, this component being hardly equal to its commitments.

Whatever the 38/250 may have achieved in its day, with factory tuning, it certainly fails lamentably to reproduce in modern competition, when there is not one now in use which cannot be routed convincingly by a well-tuned $4\frac{1}{2}$-litre Bentley. Moreover, unless meticulously maintained, the brakes are even less adequately matched to the performance than are those on a 30/98 Vauxhall.

Even in its day the acceleration was far from dazzling, for a contemporary road test states that the 38/250 required no less than 18 seconds to attain a modest 60 m.p.h., although it would then advance to 90 m.p.h. in a further 27 seconds. But even a figure of 45 seconds for 0–90 m.p.h. compares very feebly with such an ostensibly comparable car as Forrest Lycett's unsupercharged 8-litre Bentley, which will reach 100 m.p.h. in less than 20 seconds.

On the credit side, it must be admitted that the road-holding and cornering are outstandingly good for so large and heavy a car, and if properly looked after the steering is commendably light, sensitive, and accurate.

In 1926, the ancient firms of Mercedes and Benz were amalgamated, and their products have subsequently been known as Mercedes-Benz.

NAPIER

The old-established London engineering works of D. Napier and Son produced a prototype car in 1899 which was really a Panhard chassis with a home-made engine. Encouraged by that great pioneer S. F. Edge, production of original two- and four-cylinder cars began in 1900, and Napier cars were soon seen in competition both here and abroad. All credit must go to them for their particularly early appearances in the now legendary Continental road races. Their best performance came in 1902 when Edge and Napier won the coveted Gordon Bennett trophy over the Paris-Vienna course, by a combination of great good fortune and tenacity. At home their prestige was enormous and for a few years Napier was undoubtedly the premier English marque.

A prototype six-cylinder car appeared in 1904 and the firm was undoubtedly the first to develop and market this type successfully. Edge lost no opportunities to push the merits of these cars and it is due to his flair for publicity as well as to the soundness of Montagu Napier's design that they achieved such fame. His feat on the opening of Brooklands in 1907 with 24 hours at an average of more than 65 m.p.h. has already been mentioned. In addition he threw out constant challenges to other makers to equal the performance of his cars, but these were rather carefully worded and seldom taken up. In 1908, however, a terrific battle took place on Brooklands between Felice Nazarro on the 90-h.p. F.I.A.T. and Ernest Newton on the immense six-cylinder Napier called "Samson". This was won by the F.I.A.T., which put in a lap at an alleged 120 m.p.h., after retirement of the Napier with a derangement of the crankshaft.

Unlike Rolls-Royce, Napier did not confine themselves to one type of chassis, but produced an extreme variety of types throughout the Edwardian period, from a two-cylinder taxicab chassis to a series of six-cylinder monsters of 90 and even 110 h.p. It was not until 1913 that they concentrated production on a particularly refined and pleasing 35-h.p. 5-litre, with a maximum speed of about 60 m.p.h. The war caused this to be shelved in

46   Early Vintage luxury tourer: a 1919 Napier 40/50

47   The 57-h.p. Daimler, with State Limousine coachwork by Hooper, built for H. M. King George V in 1924

48   Rudolph Valentino at the wheel of a sleeve-valve Voisin

49 The 1922 Hotchkiss "AR" chassis

50 1919 40 h.p., o.h.c., six-cylinder Lanchester saloon, with coachwork by Lanchester

51 Type 41 Bugatti, "La Royale", introduced in 1927: Ettore Bugatti's own coupé-de-ville

52 The Leyland straight-eight, designed by J. G. Parry Thomas, 1920

53 "The famous 45": a 9-litre Renault of 1925 competing at Silverstone in 1954, with Mr. R. Gibson Jarvie at the wheel

54, 55   The incomparable Hispano-Suiza: a 1928 "Boulogne" with Gurney
Nutting coachwork, and its 8-litre engine

56   American luxury tourer – a 1928 V-eight Lincoln "sport phaeton"

57   The late Forrest Lycett's 8-litre Bentley at Lewes Speed Trials, 1938

58   1930 "Phantom II" Rolls-Royce

favour of four-cylinder staff cars and the first successful aero-engine made by the firm, the famous twelve-cylinder "Lion", which gave 450 b.h.p. at 2000 r.p.m. from 24 litres, and remained in production until the recent war.

The post-war Napier 40/50, which was to be the firm's last venture into the private car market, appeared in September 1919 and was an exceedingly advanced and attractive car, designed by A. W. Rowledge, who later joined Rolls-Royce as aero-engine designer. The engine was a six-cylinder of $6\frac{1}{4}$ litres with an overhead camshaft operating inclined valves. The cylinder block and crankcase were of aluminium with wet steel liners pressed in. A similar method had been used in the 1903 Gordon Bennett racers. Pistons were of light alloy. On the standard 4·8 to 1 compression ratio this engine gave 82 b.h.p. at 2000 r.p.m., a very conservative output even by the standards of the time, but which presumably justified itself by the extreme refinement and quietness, the valve gear in particular being completely silent. This engine was light, and very clean and neat in appearance, far more compact than the very similar Lanchester "Forty". It was also unusual in having a low compression ratio on the rear cylinder, a curious expedient hastily adopted to cure a very severe low-speed vibration which occurred on the early engines. This feature was retained on all subsequent cars and worked very well. The four-speed gearbox, with a top ratio of 3·3 or 3·75 to 1 according to coachwork, and fairly close intermediate speeds, was centrally controlled, a very unusual feature on such a car. Rear suspension was by cantilever springs, whose tendency to roll was combated by a patent stabilising device at the forward end of the torque tube. Brakes were on the rear wheels and transmission, though a few of the last series were fitted with a heavy front-braked axle. Although the first chassis were alleged to weigh only 25 cwt. the complete car was always rather heavy, and even the tremendously elegant Cunard-bodied tourers scaled about two tons. As a result the performance was never outstanding and the cars do not seem to have been as fast or lively as the Lanchester "Forty"; maximum speed was between 70 and 75 m.p.h.

Nor were Napiers backed as before the war by the showmanship of Edge, who had accepted a stupendous bribe to leave them in 1912 on condition that he also left the motor industry for seven years. He was now campaigning for the A.C. company with equal vigour. The 40/50 never indulged in the spectacular contests of its forebears and production at the Acton Vale works slowed down until, in 1925, Napier cars ceased to be made. The firm turned to the production of aero-engines, a field in which they gained great distinction.

An interesting postscript to the Napier story came in 1931 when the assets of the bankrupt Bentley company were for sale. It is now known that Napiers were actively interested in their purchase and proposed to make a car called the Napier-Bentley; the form which this might have taken is a fascinating subject for speculation.

PACKARD

American Vintage cars conjure up a picture not particularly attractive to the connoisseur, but it is a mistake to think that there were no worthwhile examples. Certainly they were rare, and what the American enthusiast thinks of as a "classic" is usually post-Vintage, since America recovered from the 1930 depression more quickly than Europe. It was the "Three P's" that dominated the Vintage years – Packard, Peerless, and Pierce-Arrow. All of these spared nothing to attain mechanical perfection as they saw it, but Packard sales easily topped the list, and may be taken as typical of the American luxury car at its best. Right at the end of the decade came the Duesenberg "J", but that was a special case, apart the from normal run of American design, and it is described separately.

Although Packard spared nothing to produce a quality car, it is perhaps due to differing national temperament that their cars seem strangely unattractive to European connoisseurs. This is mainly due to the instrument panel, which cannot be faulted from the functional standpoint, but incorporates features aesthetically depressing to the European eye, such as pressed metal panel with tiresome decorative scrolls, and the ubiquitous ribbon-type speedometer. Nevertheless, this difference of aesthetic standards should not bias the judgment towards a really splendid car.

186

European early Vintage cars were either post-war and very modern in outlook, or really old Edwardian survivals. This was not so in America, owing to her late entry into the war, and the twelve-cylinder Packard which was current until 1921 had been introduced in 1915. It was known as the "Twin-Six" and was the answer to the new Cadillac V-eight.

The 60-degree engine was a perfectly conventional side-valve unit in which flexibility was the main objective, rather than a high maximum, and an acceleration figure of 12 seconds from 3 to 30 m.p.h. in top gear was proudly mentioned. As this means 10 seconds or less for the more usually quoted 10 to 30 m.p.h., it is a useful time, even by modern standards; while extremely few cars can run steadily at 3 m.p.h. in top. With cylinder dimensions of 3 in. × 5 in. the unit was also commendably compact, and one carburettor inside the V fed all the cylinders. The capacity of the "Twin-Six" was 414 cubic inches, or rather more than 6 litres. By 1921 over 35,000 had been sold, and in this year it was supplanted by the side-valve straight-eight, which has been the staple Packard product until 1955. The "Eight" had cylinders scaling $3\frac{3}{8}$ in. × 5 in., giving a capacity of 385 cubic inches (5·77 litres). Four-wheel brakes followed in 1923 (an early date for England or America). Pulling as low a top gear as 4·33 to 1, flexibility was again rated higher than maximum speed, which was generally below 70 m.p.h., although acceleration was prejudiced by the immense all-up weight of the average car, which exceeded two tons. Steering and springing were firm and taut, making these cars a real pleasure to drive, and their

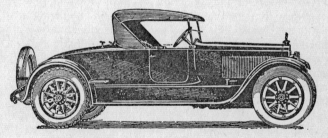

American quality car: a 1921 Packard "Twin-Six"

cornering ability was good for a luxury car; the rigidly-mounted engines were wonderfully smooth and apparently free from any period, which is unusual in a straight-eight.

The Packard Eight completely dominated the Vintage market, and its peak year was 1928, when no less than 50,000 cars were sold. In the lean years which followed, Packard alone weathered the storm, maintaining its high-quality models by a line of cheaper articles, such as the "120". The "120" subsidised the "Super-Eight", and the prestige of the "Super-Eight" sold the "120". In the middle thirties Packards went back to their old love, by introducing a "Twelve" (so called, as distinct from the earlier "Twin-Six"), but this time it was supplemental to the "Eight". These topped 7 litres and with a power output of at least 175 b.h.p. they had a maximum of over 90 m.p.h. with all the flexibility of the "Twin-Six". With lines of dignified and classic simplicity these great cars compare strangely with the voluptuous and chrome-bedecked curves with which Packard is once more attempting to capture the American luxury market.

RENAULT "FORTY-FIVE"

The pioneer firm of Renault had actively supported the great town-to-town races of the heroic age of motoring and appeared in the French Grand Prix until 1908; but their production models throughout the Edwardian and early Vintage period were chiefly remarkable for their comfort and longevity. They were alleged to improve with age, and certainly those which have survived to the present day seem completely indestructible. Probably, too, no firm produced a greater variety of different cars, from the popular but lethargic little "9/15" economy car to the famous "Forty-Five". This was undoubtedly the largest car to be made in any quantity during the Vintage period and quite a number came to this country. The design was an extraordinary mixture of archaic and modern practice, and many of its features would have occasioned no comment at all in 1909. Renault alone stood out against the move towards higher-efficiency engines and pinned his faith to sheer size.

The engine was a vast monobloc six-cylinder of 110 × 160 mm., with side valves and a fixed cylinder head; its capacity was no less than 9123 c.c. It was beautifully finished in black stove enamel, had a single carburettor and ignition by magneto only, which was unusual in a luxury chassis. The gearbox was centrally mounted in the chassis and rear suspension was by very widely splayed cantilevers. A wheelbase of 12 ft. 6 in. and a total weight of about 2½ tons did not prevent the "45" from having a quite respectable performance, with a maximum of about 90 m.p.h. on its 3·5 to 1 top gear. The engine was reputed to give 140 b.h.p. at 3000 r.p.m., but the maximum permitted r.p.m. on production cars was 2750. Powerful four-wheel brakes operated by mechanical servo were fitted from its introduction in 1923; the detachable wheels were of wood, a truly conservative touch. Renault were the most consistent advocates of thermo-syphon cooling and the radiator was behind the engine as on their smaller cars; the rear cylinders thus disappeared into a vast cavern of ungilled tubes. The flywheel had a vaned rim which was alleged to draw air through this radiator, but even so the driving compartment of a "45" could become disagreeably warm. The long sloping bonnet gave the car an imposing, almost aggressive look.

It was not a particularly costly monster, as monsters went in those days, the chassis price at one time being only slightly more than that of a Rolls "Twenty". To anyone who could tolerate a fuel consumption of some 8 m.p.g. this was pretty good value, for the long-stroke engine was extremely silent and flexible, with a terrific reserve of power. The only real drawback was the difficulty of starting the car. The standard dynamotor on the nose of the crankshaft was inadequate for the task, despite a tremendous reduction gear; and it seems something of an admission of failure that the makers mounted a decompressor and starting button on the near-side dumb-iron, just by the cranking handle.

A sporting version was introduced early in 1925 with a plate clutch, three-speed gearbox of higher ratios (10·3, 5 and 3 to 1), and oil-cooler between the dumb-irons. Some of these were fitted by the makers with the then fashionable mahogany-decked touring coachwork, producing a tremendously handsome and well-proportioned vehicle. A series of ventures into record-breaking took place in May and June 1925 at Montlhéry.

Garfield and Plessier drove a wire-wheeled Grand Sport four-seater to considerable effect, breaking more than a dozen records for endurance and speed in their class. The 500-mile record, previously held by Parry Thomas, in the Lanchester "Forty", was taken at 103·9 m.p.h., and the 12-hours at 97·5 m.p.h. This high speed might have been maintained for a much longer period had not some of the flywheel vanes snapped off, causing overheating and frequent stops for water. None the less the coveted 24-hours fell at 87 m.p.h. After this excellent performance the "45" was carefully compared by officials of the A.C.F. with a standard chassis taken at random from 28 which were awaiting delivery. It was found to comply with specification in all important points save for a higher axle ratio and larger carburettor jets. All working parts were to be perfect.

In the next year at Montlhéry a single-seater saloon driven by Garfield improved on these performances considerably; it now had a 2 to 1 top-gear ratio. This car covered 500 miles at 109·9 m.p.h. and took the 24-hours at no less than 108·3, covering its last lap at a little over 119 m.p.h. While for so large and high-geared an engine these records cannot have been a very arduous task, they were a most creditable performance for a heavy luxury chassis. The fuel consumption was apparently not recorded.

Despite this, the market for cars of over 9 litres was declining rapidly in the late Vintage period, and in 1929 the "45" was superseded by a side-valve straight-eight of only 7 litres. The last of the Edwardians had ceased production.

ROLLS-ROYCE

In 1904 F. H. Royce, a Manchester electrical engineer, produced a few experimental two-cylinder cars of modest size but high quality; and late that year these attracted the attention of the Hon. C. S. Rolls, a wealthy and discerning amateur. As a result the world-famous Rolls-Royce partnership was formed and within a very short time the name came to represent, as it has done ever since, the absolute height of excellence in automobile design. Various models left the Cook Street works in those early days, including two, three, four, six, and even eight-cylindered types; and the firm was only a year old when a four-cylinder car gained second place in the 1905 Tourist Trophy race in the Isle of Man, followed by an outright win in the same contest the next year. All these models had overhead inlet and side exhaust valves. Despite the considerable success of the production models and especially of the very silent and lively 30-h.p. six-cylinder, an extremely bold move was proposed in 1907 by Claude Johnson, the organising genius of the firm. Henceforth production was to be standardised round one model only, the 7-litre six-cylinder "40/50", which had appeared at Olympia the previous year. This model, soon to become known as the "Silver Ghost", was to remain in production for no less than nineteen years. For so young a firm to rely solely on so large and costly a chassis (£950 in 1907) was an unprecedented piece of daring, but it was completely justified by the tremendous success of the car. The "Silver Ghost" must be reckoned as one of the first two or three classic designs in the history of motoring, and it was only in the last few years of its amazing span that it was seriously outclassed in some respects by its competitors.

The first "Ghost" had a six-cylinder side-valve engine of 114 × 114 mm. (7036 c.c.), producing its rated horsepower, 48, at 1200 r.p.m. on the standard 3·2 to 1 compression ratio; a fabric-lined cone clutch working in oil, a four-speed gearbox with overdrive top, and an immensely robust chassis with semi-elliptic suspension. Ignition was by magneto and a coil and distributor of Royce's own design; he also designed the single-jet carburettor. The engine was in two blocks of three cylinders, and at a date when even the costliest of cars relied upon the inconvenient drip-feed lubrication, with a row of sight feeds and adjusters on the dash, Royce used a drilled and fully pressure-fed crankshaft. The engine was moreover absolutely silent and smooth throughout its range.

Royce was a perfectionist whose determination to produce the best car in the world was never affected by fashion or the temptation to make innovations for their own sake; and although his designs appear somewhat conservative on paper, this is compensated by their legendary durability and the exquisite workmanship upon which he, as a master craftsman himself, insisted. Nor did production costs mean much to him, as may be established by a glance at a Rolls-Royce torque tube and rear-axle unit sewn together (in his own phrase) by innumerable rings of tiny bolts. The "Silver Ghost" engine is by no means neat, and a French motoring journal once maliciously captioned a photograph of it "under the brushwood". Another famous designer called it "the triumph of workmanship over design".

Maximum speed of the early "Ghost" was about 55 m.p.h., and the flexibility and power made it absolutely in a class of its own by contemporary standards; by judicious manipulations of the controls it could be made to travel at a walking pace on its top gear of 2·7 to 1, or if necessary accelerate in no mean fashion with the smoothness of a steam engine. Various details were modified through the Edwardian period. The overdrive top gear was abandoned in 1909 as too noisy and in the same year the stroke was lengthened to 121 mm., giving the capacity of 7410 c.c. which was to be standard for the rest of the car's life. Rear suspension was modified to three quarter-elliptic and then in 1912 changed to cantilever. The longer-stroke engine, having higher compression, probably gave about 65 b.h.p. at 1750 r.p.m., giving the late Edwardian "Ghost" a maximum in touring form of around 65 m.p.h. according to the axle fitted, which varied from 2·9 to 3·4 to 1. A stripped and streamlined chassis covered a flying start half-mile at Brooklands in 1911 at 101·8 m.p.h. Shortly before the war a few cars were fitted with four-speed gearboxes. aluminium instead of cast-iron pistons, and a modified camshaft. These scored a great success in the arduous Alpine trials of 1913 against the opposition of much larger cars. In 1914 the sole entry, driven by the brilliant amateur James Radley, made the only non-stop run out of 75 starters. These so-called "Alpine Eagle" models formed the basis of the post-war "Silver Ghost" when production began again in 1919. At the outbreak of war the Derby factory employed 1300 workers, by 1919 the vast productions of aero-engines and armoured cars had raised this to 8600; there can be no doubt that the engineering skill and absolute integrity of this firm contributed greatly to the Allied victory in both world wars.

The "Silver Ghost" of the Vintage years differed only slightly from pre-war. The transmission brake was replaced by a dual system working in enormous rear drums, probably the most effective two-wheel brake layout yet devised. The electrical system now included a dynamo and starter of Royce design, the latter driving silently through a chain and clutch on to the gearbox mainshaft. The maximum engine speed was still a modest 2200 r.p.m., which produced about 75 b.h.p. on the standard 3·8 to 1 compression ratio. Maximum speed in touring form was about 75 m.p.h. Even so, the "Ghost" was quite a lively car in spite of its high weight. A revealing if obscure success came in 1921 at a Biarritz hill-climb, where one climbed in 24¼ seconds, travelling at over 60 m.p.h. at the finish and beating a 30/98 Vauxhall and two 37·2 Hispano-Suizas.

Despite its early design and against the strong competition of such advanced cars as the Hispano, the 40/50 continued to sell very well and it is thought that some 2500 were produced after the war, a high figure for a car which cost £1850 as a chassis. In 1924 front brakes were added (by no means before they were due), operated by the Rolls-Royce mechanical servo, whose essentials are still used today: these were standard on the last year's production cars. Even up to the end of its career, the "Ghost" had a charming survival in the form of a governor which could be set to any speed, which the governor then maintained more or less regardless of road conditions. Driving on a governor nowadays seems a quite uncanny sensation.

The tremendous character and longevity of this superb motor-car have always caused it to have an immense following among those who can face a fuel consumption of 10–15 m.p.g., and there are still a few in the hands of their original owners, who cherish them as few cars are cherished, performing the endless routine maintenance specified in the instruction book with an almost religious fervour and sending the cars to the factory at Crewe for regular inspection and overhaul. One such owner of a 1921 tourer, a retired doctor living in the north of Scotland, is reputed to have had no less than 15 replacement magnetos (these were, of course, not of Rolls-Royce design) and to have driven the 400 miles to Crewe for the diagnosis of a mysterious noise which turned out to be a maladjustment of the fan belt. All credit must be given to the makers who are prepared to honour their original contract with such service, and who so truly stated that their interest in the car never waned.

The "Ghost" is not a particularly easy car to drive well, though it will stand mishandling in an uncomplaining manner. The gearbox, with the long, slender lever located positively in a notch at the end of its travel in the gate, requires very precise handling if inappropriate noises are to be avoided. The steering too is rather heavy and not helped by the thick and small steering wheel with its central mass of controls; but once the driver is accustomed to the layout there are few cars of any age which will respond so exactly to his wishes and give such a feeling of control. Owners were recommended to send their man to Derby for a fortnight's intensive training followed by a written examination, and any minor discomforts of "Ghost" driving are probably due to its conception as a chauffeur's car.

Shortly after the war Rolls-Royce established a factory in Springfield, Massachusetts, in which "Ghosts" and "Phantoms" I and II were made in some quantities. These differed from the English models only in their equipment, which comprised Bosch electrical gear and native instruments. Although the Springfield Rolls was built to the same exacting standards and even incorporated British parts from time to time, the venture was not a great success, as the American Rolls-buying public insisted on the English-made article. There are a few Springfield Rolls-Royces in this country and they are only with detailed knowledge distinguishable from the native product.

By 1925 the "Ghost" had finally become outclassed and was superseded by the "New Phantom", or "Phantom" I (although it was still available to special order). The "Phantom" had a smaller bore and longer stroke, giving a capacity of 7668 c.c. Overhead valves in a detachable head were operated by pushrods. The manifolding was entirely changed and the flywheel, now enclosed in the crankcase, incorporated a single-plate clutch. This engine, which in some respects is like a giant version of the 1922 "Twenty", was the only new feature of the car, which retained the separate gearbox and chassis layout of the "Ghost". Rolls-Royce have never divulged the horsepower of their cars, but the "Phantom" I probably gave slightly less than 100 b.h.p.

at the maximum permitted engine speed of 2750 r.p.m. It would pass the 3000 r.p.m. mark in complete silence and tick over at less than 150. With its high bonnet line and shuttered radiator it is of more imposing appearance than the "Ghost", and touring versions were capable of about 80 m.p.h. with considerable liveliness and all the refinement of the earlier cars. Somehow the "Phantom" is not such an appealing car as the immortal "Ghost", and the fuel consumption is inferior, due to the enhanced performance. Also, the later twenties was an uncertain period for formal coachwork, having neither the upright elegance of the past, nor the lower and sleeker lines which were to follow. None the less, sales continued at much the same level and about 2000 were made in the four years of its production.

The "Phantom" I and "Silver Ghost" are admitted by Messrs. Rolls-Royce to be obsolete, but the "Phantom" II, which appeared in 1929 and survived for six years, is still entirely current from the servicing and spares viewpoint. This, the last of the Vintage Rolls-Royces, was the first entirely new design in the large-car range since 1906. The manifolding was changed but otherwise the "Phantom" I engine layout and dimensions were retained. The compression ratio became 5·25 to 1, and about 120 b.h.p. was developed at the maximum engine speed of 3500 r.p.m. The very silent gearbox was now in unit with the engine and operated by the short and rigid lever working in a narrow gate such as is still used in these cars. The chassis no long erretained the Edwardian cantilevers but used semi-elliptics all round. The "Phantom" II, although on the heavy side, was a car of considerable performance with a maximum of well over 80 m.p.h. None the less it is not so perpetually agreeable a car to drive as the "Ghost", feeling, as it does, rather heavy and ponderous. During the early thirties it was often fitted with supremely elegant close-coupled coupé or sedanca bodies, and these, particularly on the short-chassis "Continental" version, must be among the most handsome large cars ever made. These were also appreciably faster than normal, with a maximum of well over 90 m.p.h. Even these were rendered obsolete in 1935 with the introduction of the superb V-twelve "Phantom" III, with its three-figure maximum and effortless 90-m.p.h. cruising speed.

Rumours of a small Rolls had been current from 1919, but it was not until October 1922 that the celebrated "Twenty" appeared. It instantly created a tremendous following for itself, which has been maintained by its lineal successors to this day. It had a 3-litre six-cylinder engine with pushrod-operated overhead valves, in unit with a three-speed gearbox controlled by a central lever working in an invisible gate. This arrangement, known as a "ball-change", had hitherto been regarded as a very cheap American practice. Springing was semi-elliptic all round, and brakes operated on the rear wheels only. Although several of these features were strongly criticised at the time, as unworthy of the firm, the exceptional refinement and sweet running of the miniature Royce caused it to become highly popular. It was never a particularly cheap car, the chassic price remaining at 1000 guineas from its inception. The engine, although capable of 3000 r.p.m., produced extremely modest power (probably only about 50 b.h.p.) and with the low compression ratio and low top gear fitted (4·8 to 1) to the early cars the maximum was well under 60 m.p.h. None the less, more than 20 m.p.g. was normal: the makers recommended that the total weight of the car should not exceed two tons.

The "Twenty" underwent continuous development through the period. The greatest change came in 1925, when the three-speed gearbox was replaced by one of four speeds with right-hand visible gate control, and at the same time effective four-wheel brakes were fitted. Maximum speed was about 60 m.p.h. in this form, but the car would cruise silently at 50 m.p.h. The extremely moderate performance does not render these cars nearly so tedious to drive as might be supposed, for the excellent balance and the light and accurate steering are sufficiently enjoyable in themselves to render driving a considerable pleasure. Since they are also entirely reliable and durable to a degree there are few more practical Vintage cars for daily use.

The "Twenty" grew up in 1929 into the "20/25", which had a higher compression ratio and was larger by some 500 c.c. This was a faster car and a few hundred were built before December 1930. This same engine suitably modified formed the basis of the Derby-built Bentleys of 1934 onwards.

8

Motoring Competition in the Twenties

GRAND PRIX racing must always rank as the premier form of motoring competition, although there have been many times when the 24-hour race for sports cars at Le Mans has run it close in popular interest. The English Tourist Trophy race has never aroused anything approaching the interest, or entry, of Le Mans. The story of Grand Prix racing in the Vintage years has already been told from the mechanical point of view, and not very much more needs to be said here. Le Mans, however, calls for somewhat fuller treatment.

In England, Brooklands provided a perpetual interest, and perhaps its greatest charm lay in the infinite variety of cars and drivers which it always attracted. This was made possible by the general use of individual handicapping, so dear to the English, and so deeply incomprehensible to everyone else.

Reliability trials are another largely British sport – at any rate so far as four-wheelers are concerned – and during the twenties they reached their highest level. Normal sports cars were capable of winning any of the classic events, and Frazer-Nashes were generally the most successful. In the thirties the whole business of trials became increasingly specialised and professional. Various types of car gained and lost the ascendancy, but always departing further and further from anything which could be the slightest use for any other purpose. Since the war, trials have sunk to a very low ebb and attract machines quite unsuited to any other use.

GRAND PRIX RACING

Although Grand Prix racing produced machines of great mechanical interest during the twenties, it failed, on the whole, to produce very exciting racing. At different times one make or another had an almost complete ascendancy, while in transition periods two apparently equal teams (such as Alfa Romeo and Delage in 1925) persistently failed to meet.

Before the 1914 war a Grand Prix meant the French Grand Prix. After the war manufacturers agreed not to participate in racing until 1921, when the Grand Prix was first revived. In this year there were two *Grandes Epreuves*, the French and Italian. By 1930 other nationalities were organising Grand Prix races and there were no less than seven during this last Vintage season. Certain other classics, such as the Targa Florio, also enjoyed Grand Prix status.

The Grand Prix has only thrived when it has been run under a formula fairly closely controlling what type of car is eligible, whether by weight or engine capacity. The two periods of free-for-all, or *formule libre* (1902–12 and 1928–33), were relatively uninteresting and even the two years when a fuel consumption limit was applied (1907 and 1913) were not popular with manufacturers (although it is difficult to see why).

1914 was the first year when a capacity limit (4½ litres) was used, and for 1921 the size selected was 3 litres. Although this formula was only used for one season of Grand Prix racing, it actually lasted for three, since the Indianapolis races of 1920 and 1922 and the Tourist Trophy race of 1922 also complied with it. The results were inconclusive, since although the Ballot was the fastest machine, it very rarely won a race. This was partly due to sheer bad luck and partly to their defective system of lubrication, leading to bearing and connecting-rod failures. On balance, therefore, the American Duesenberg was probably the most successful car of the 3-litre formula.

The formula current from 1922 to 1925 inclusive laid down a maximum engine size of 2 litres, and produced both the slowest and fastest cars of the decade, for the drab machines of 1922 could barely exceed 100 m.p.h., while by 1925, equipped with superchargers, they could surpass 140 m.p.h.

In 1922 and 1923 the honours fell mostly to F.I.A.T., who ran a six-cylinder car in 1922 and a supercharged straight-eight in 1923. Only during the French Grand Prix of Tours, while the new blown eight was suffering from teething troubles (rather literally, as they consumed the vanes of their vane-type superchargers), did Sunbeam snatch a victory. This race also saw the first appearance of the remarkable V-twelve Delage, which did not come into its own until 1925. By the time of the Italian Grand Prix, the F.I.A.T. had been equipped with a Roots-type supercharger and proved invincible. This was the first Grand Prix to be won by a supercharged car, although Mercedes had been using superchargers in racing since 1921.

1924 should have been a Sunbeam benefit, but owing to fitting new, defective, Bosch magnetos on the eve of the French Grand Prix, they lost it to the new P.2 Alfa Romeos, which were unbeatable for the rest of this year, and Sunbeam could only collect the Spanish Grand Prix, where the P.2 did not run.

By 1925 the V-twelve Delage had been supercharged, and it and the P.2 Alfa Romeo were extremely closely matched in performance so that some stirring racing seemed likely. Both cars developed about 190 b.h.p. and could exceed 140 m.p.h. But when they first met in the European Grand Prix at Spa, the Delage was not yet *au point*; in the French Grand Prix at Montlhéry the Alfa Romeo team was withdrawn when their driver Ascari was killed in an accident (although Campari's P.2 was leading at the time), leaving the Delage to win; in the Italian Grand Prix Delage did not enter, so that Alfa Romeo had a virtual walk-over; and the opposite happened in the Spanish Grand Prix (one cannot help wondering if these two races were not the subject of an amicable arrangement!). F.I.A.T. did not race in 1925 and Sunbeam, with basically 1923 cars, was outclassed. The Targa Florio was won by Bugatti, being the last occasion (until the post-war period) on which a race of Grand Prix status was won by an unsupercharged car.

For 1926 Bugatti at last forwent his self-denying ordinance and fitted his cars with superchargers, whereupon he had a most successful season. This was the first of the 1½-litre formula, which lasted for two years and was mainly notable for producing the astonishing straight-eight Delages. After teething troubles they came into their own in 1927, when they were unbeatable wherever they ran.

1927 was the last year of formula racing, and the last three years of the decade were run as *formule libre*. This should have produced some very interesting results, since it enabled cars of the various past formulae to compete on equal terms with each other, and also with all-comers of assorted sizes. In actual fact this keen competition failed to materialise, and had it not been for the number of type 35 Bugattis run by the works and private owners very little sport would have been seen. During these three years, out of thirty races in all, half were won by Bugattis. Alfa Romeo came next with seven wins, with their P.2 cars, which thus established their superiority over the V-twelve Delages. For some reason the 1½-litre Delages did not appear, and if they had, the result might possibly have been different, since when they were ten years old they proved to be invincible in 1½-litre racing, against the best that anyone could then produce.

The low ebb to which Grand Prix cars had sunk was shown in the German Grand Prix of 1928 and the Pau Grand Prix of 1929. In the first a team of 7-litre Mercedes, basically production sports cars, showed such speed that they took the first three places; while at Pau, Sir Henry Birkin, on a supercharged 4½-litre Bentley (again based closely upon the production model), ran second only to a type 35c Bugatti.

Only in 1930 did the old-stagers begin to lose ground, when Maserati took the field with a completely new straight-eight 2½-litre, which had five wins and dominated the season. This convinced the other manufacturers that their five year-old machines would no longer serve, and for 1931 they mostly produced something new. Therefore, although the *formule libre* continued for another three years, 1930, the data arbitrarily chosen as the end of the Vintage era, happened also to mark a real turning point in Grand Prix racing.

LE MANS

Few motoring events have ever captured the public imagination to the same extent as "Les Vingt-Quatre Heures du Mans". For one thing, there is something particularly appealing about a night-and-day contest on a road circuit between the cream of the world's sports cars; and again, it has from time to time been something of a British benefit. This has never been so marked as during the late Vintage period, when the Bentleys scored their very remarkable series of success. It is appropriate that an account of the decade should include a sketch of British entries in the Le Mans races and notice the development of these races from a rather gentle tour into an extremely arduous and hard-fought contest. Indeed, in 1927–30, when Grand Prix racing was on a *formule libre* basis, there is no doubt that they produced a far more impressive spectacle.

The event was conceived in 1923, it is said by Charles Faroux, and received the full backing of the French branch of Rudge-Whitworth Ltd. Two contests were to be run simultaneously. The Grand Prix d'Endurance was a straightforward long-distance affair, which obviously favoured the larger cars. Current with it was to be a Triennial Cup for the smaller cars on a handicap basis, coupled with two years' qualifying runs for which minimum distances were imposed. This was very soon abandoned in favour of a Biennial Cup, such as is still competed for today; but it has always been the Grand Prix d'Endurance which has taken the public fancy. Louis Coatalen once said that the only thing that the public remembers about a race is the name on the radiator of the winning car; and certainly a Le Mans win means one thing only. Competing cars were to be strictly catalogue models, with fully equipped four-seater coachwork, except in the 1100-c.c. class; hoods and sidescreens were essential. Two drivers were permissible, but the first twenty laps (about 215 miles) had to be covered with no replenishment whatsoever. Use of the starting handle was forbidden. There is no doubt that these rules were carefully considered with a view to the genuine advancement of touring-car practice, with their insistence on the dependability of electrical systems, which were indeed not a particularly strong point at the time. As a prolonged reliability trial for completely standard models, the event was something entirely new, and came at an appropriate time in the history of the motor-car.

The first Le Mans of all took place late in May 1923. Being the first, it was a rather tentative affair, and some of the rules seem excessively pessimistic. The qualifying mileage varied from 503 (or an average speed of 21·9 m.p.h.) in the 1100-c.c. class to 968 (or 40 m.p.h.) for the 4-litre cars. The entry list was of the greatest interest, the event having support from many of the big French firms who did not subsequently show themselves at the Circuit de la Sarthe, such as Vinot, Voisin, and Berliet. As time went on, the event became increasingly the province of the optimistic French constructor who had a name to make for his cars, and fewer of the *grandes marques* appeared there. A single British entry came in the form of a 3-litre Bentley entered by Duff, to be driven by himself and Clement; it was the actual four-seater in which he had taken the Double Twelve record at Brooklands the previous September at 86·79 m.p.h. It was almost alone among the starters in having no front-wheel brakes, which were, of course, not thought to be essential on Brooklands. Its qualifying average for the race was 35 m.p.h.

The event passed off in a very gentlemanly fashion, and owing to the low averages imposed there was a minimum of mechanical failure. The record proportion of 29 cars finished out of 32 starters, despite the appalling surface of the narrow roads employed. It seems a strange touch to read that one-third of the cars lost time by failure of their electric or acetylene sets, and contemporary accounts state that any car with effective head-lamps was inevitably followed by two or three unlit hangers-on. The Grand Prix d'Endurance was won by a Chenard-Walcker driven by Lagache and Leonard, who averaged just over 57 m.p.h., covering 1372 miles. They were followed into second place by a sister car, and this distinguished pioneer *marque* was to have several more successes on the circuit. In this race they gave considerable opposition to the Bentley, which was noticeably handicapped by its lack of front-wheel brakes. Duff and Clement drove bareheaded, to the alarm of the spectators, who feared that they might catch cold. The lap record was set up early by the 3-litre at 64 m.p.h., and at one stage it seemed that a British victory was possible. Due to a fuel leak, however, the car lost $2\frac{1}{2}$ hours and despite the fastest lap at 67 m.p.h. could manage no better than equal fourth place with a 2-litre Bignan. The least significant performance of all time was made by an 1100-c.c. S.A.R.A., which covered 609 miles at 25·4 m.p.h.

The regulations were considerably tightened for 1924, and many now familiar provisions began to be made. After five laps, hoods had to be raised and two laps covered with them erect.

More care was taken to see that cars complied with the touring specification, with running boards, wings, and windscreens as catalogued. The qualifying distances were also increased. The 3-litre cars had to maintain an average of 51·5 m.p.h., and even the 1100s were required to manage 38 m.p.h. The entry list this time was less interesting, and although the prototype twin-cam Sunbeam was entered, it was withdrawn on the eve of the race. The sole British entry was therefore again that of Duff and Clement in the 3-litre, now equipped with front brakes. Chenard-Walcker entered a very advanced team of overhead-camshaft 4-litre straight-eights, which were much fancied; but their opposition was negligible. For the first time the Bentley was victorious, covering 50 miles more than its qualifying distance to win at the extremely modest average speed of 53·75 m.p.h., the lowest ever recorded. It was closely followed into second and third places by two 3½-litre Lorraine-Dietrich cars. These, in spite of their rather homely pushrod engines, were seen to be a very close match for the British car, and were chiefly handicapped by the stud fixing of their steel artillery wheels. Out of 41 starters this year, only 14 cars qualified.

For 1925 the event began to arouse slightly more British interest, though an A.C. failed to reach the line and an Austin Seven retired with radiator trouble before completing the statutory mileage without replenishment. Once more Clement and Duff competed, joined by Moir and Benjafield in another 3-litre. It was in this race, too, that the twin-cam Sunbeams made their début, one driven by Chassagne and Davis and the other by Duller and Segrave. Public attention was really aroused this time, and the event was enormously successful, with very large crowds in attendance. For the first time the now famous Le Mans start was used, and twenty laps had to be covered with hoods erect, though a French observer remarked sourly that a twenty-first would have caused the majority of these to collapse of their own accord. Ballast equivalent to a full load of passengers was carried. The British showing was not especially impressive; both Bentleys retired for trivial reasons, Moir's due to a simple lack of petrol and Duff's with a broken carburettor lug. The Sunbeams were greatly admired for their complete equipment and comfort, but Segrave was forced to retire with a broken clutch. The Grand Prix d'Endurance was won by a Lorraine at 57·83 m.p.h., with the Chassagne/Davis Sunbeam second at 55·8. This was probably the most notable success of these not very fortunate cars. Another Lorraine followed and fourth and fifth places were taken by 2-litre O.M.s, which had run with the greatest consistency. An excellent showing was put up the very peculiar little beetle-shaped Chenards, which ran this time in the 1100-c.c. class. One of the first Chryslers ran this year but failed to cover the qualifying distance.

1926 saw the circuit reduced to 10·5 miles and also saw the first lap speeds of over 70 m.p.h., but the entries were not of the greatest variety. British interest had waned and three Bentleys were once more the sole representatives. Two normal "Speed Model" 3-litres were to be driven by Davis and Benjafield, and Duller and Clement; the third one was one of the rare short-chassis "100-m.p.h." cars, with tapering radiator. It had been converted for the occasion into a rather improbable-looking four-seater and was to be driven by Clive Gallop and Thistle-thwayte. Peugeot had entered two large sleeve-valve tourers to be driven by Wagner and Boillot, and there was a scattering of American entries, including two Overlands and a Willys-Knight. Bentleys were dogged on this occasion by extremely bad luck. Duller took over Clement's car, which was lying third, and forced it into the lead, only to retire with a broken valve stem; he was shortly followed by Gallop in the "100-m.p.h." car, who suffered a broken rocker arm. These retirements left only Davis in Number Seven, and he indulged in a tremendous struggle with the now extremely purposeful team of Lorraine-Dietrichs. He suffered, however, from a progressive weakening of the brakes and, with only half an hour to go, had the misfortune to enter a corner too fast, in company with a Lorraine, and embed the car firmly in a deep bank. He was unable to extricate the car and as a result Lorraines scored a most remarkable hat-trick, taking first, second, and third places, the leader at 66·08 m.p.h. Fourth and fifth places were once more taken by O.M.s and in spite of his retirement Davis managed sixth greatest distance with 1284 miles. The pace this year was extremely hot and only 14 cars finished. The American showing was negligible and both Peugeots, though much fancied, retired for trivial reasons.

1927 saw the least interesting competition in any Le Mans race and the smallest entry yet received, only 22 cars starting. The race itself would not be of much consequence but for its incorporation of the astonishing White House Corner incident which led to one of the greatest drives in motoring history. Once more three Bentleys were entered, two 3-litres driven by Davis and Benjafield, and Duller and D'Erlanger. The Davis car was that in which he had completed 23½ hours the previous year. The 4½-litre Bentley had just been announced and one of the very first was to be driven here by Clement and Callingham. The team, having the largest engines of any competing cars, and numbered 1, 2, and 3, set off and drove with great regularity, Clement quickly breaking the lap record at 73 m.p.h. All seemed et for a Bentley victory when in the dusk of Saturday evening an obscure French entry (Tabourin on a Th. Schneider) crashed at the spot known as White House Corner, set in a particularly, narrow and curving section of the course. Callingham, driving the 4½, crashed into him and was quickly followed by Thelusson on a Fasto. The remaining Bentleys rapidly joined the accident; Duller crashed irreparably into the wreckage, but Davis, who was close behind him, luckily noticed some fragments of wood lying in this path and was able to brake before reaching the spot. None the less he became considerably entangled and Old Number Seven was only extricated with difficulty. Nobody was injured, but the race was not yet six hours old and it seemed highly unlikely that the damaged Bentley could continue until four o'clock the next afternoon. None the less it was found to be in running order and set out again despite a bent front axle, poor lights, and erratic brakes. As is well known, the car went on to win at 61·36 m.p.h., covering 1472 miles in the 24 hours; a noble performance and a fitting end to the 3-litre Bentley era at Le Mans.

1928 saw a great revival of interest in the event and a first-class entry. English contestants included three Bentleys, Lagondas, front-wheel-drive Alvis, and Aston Martins. American entries included two Chryslers, and Bloch and Brisson driving a 4·9-litre Stutz. Barnato and Rubin drove the same 4½-Bentley which had been involved at White House Corner and did so with great spirit, breaking the lap record again and again and finally winning at 68·5 m.p.h. The Stutz, which had shown a great deal of fight, followed them into second place, and third and fourth places were taken by Chryslers. Although these were not at first considered to be in the running at all, they ran very silently and reliably and finished at 64·56 and 62·45 m.p.h. respectively. Birkin and Chassagne on another 4½ were hampered by tyre trouble and finished fifth. Alvis finished sixth and seventh, scoring a class win.

1929 saw the track altered to exclude the very narrow hairpin at Pontlieue and its length now became 10·1 miles. This year Birkin and Barnato drove the first of the "Speed Six" Bentleys and there were three other Bentley entries, all 4½-litre cars. Encouraged by the previous year's result, there were three Stutz and three Chrysler entries, while Britain was represented by straight-eight front-wheel-drive Alvis and Lagondas. The "Speed Six" showed its paces in no mean fashion, Birkin breaking the lap record at 81 m.p.h. This year was the real pinnacle of Bentley achievement abroad, for the car won at 73·62 m.p.h., followed closely by the remaining three cars into second, third, and fourth places. Fifth and sixth places were taken once more by Chryslers, one of them at the considerable average of 64 m.p.h. A privately entered Lea-Francis was seventh. Only 10 cars finished this year out of 25 starters.

1930, the last race of the Vintage period, saw the first entry of a supercharged 4½-litre Bentley, driven by Birkin, two 6½-litre cars and an unblown 4½. Other British entries included two M.G. Midgets and two Talbot 90s, and this year saw the entry of some really heavy metal in the shape of a 38/250 Mercedes driven by Caracciola. The epic struggle between this car and Birkin, culminating in the retirement of the Mercedes with incurable electrical troubles, has often been told. It permitted first and second places to be taken by 6½-litre Bentleys at 75·8 and 73·33 m.p.h. respectively, a successful last appearance for the *marque* and its fourth successive win. Third and fourth places were taken by the Talbots at 68 and 67 m.p.h. after an impressively silent run, a very good showing for engines of only $2\frac{1}{4}$ litres. Only nine cars survived the 24 hours.

British prestige abroad was enormously enhanced by these successes in an otherwise drab period; and to see British cars in the first four places of the premier sports car race of the world is a fitting end to the Vintage period.

BROOKLANDS

In England, Brooklands was the main centre of racing interest. Indeed, so far as racing went it was the sole centre, since the only other form of speed event possible was a sprint. The track was constructed as a private venture by Mr. H. F. Locke King, primarily with the view of encouraging the sport and providing a proper testing ground for the industry. It consisted of a roughly egg-shaped circuit, $2\frac{3}{4}$ miles long and 100 feet wide. Two short straights of unequal length were connected by steeply banked bends which could be negotiated at speeds in the neighbourhood of 120 m.p.h. In addition, a short straight, intended as the finishing straight, cut across the sharp end of the "egg".

Apart from a few long-distance races, the average meeting consisted by fairly short handicap races, thus establishing the almost exclusively English partiality for handicap racing. Indeed, with the very mixed fields which faced the starter, scratch racing would have been impracticable.

After the war, racing re-started in 1920 and the first race was won by Malcolm Campbell on a 1914 2·6-litre Talbot. The cars, of course, were almost all pre-war and included some which still exist, including H.O.D. Segrave's 1914 Grand Prix Opel (now being superbly restored) and the 1912 Grand Prix Lorraine-Dietrich "Vieux Charles Trois", the last of the Grand Prix giants which survives, although in a sadly neglected condition.

Lap speeds were largely in the neighbourhood of 100 m.p.h. and the fastest lap of the year was recorded by J. Chassagne's 1919 Indianapolis Ballot, at 112·17 m.p.h. The largest car on the track was the 18-litre V-twelve Sunbeam, reputed to develop 335 b.h.p. at 2000 r.p.m. and pulling a top gear ratio of $1\frac{1}{2}$ to 1. At the other end of the scale was "Kim", the extremely fast

V-twin G.N., driven with vivid enthusiasm by its constructor, A. Frazer-Nash, or occasionally by his partner, H. R. Godfrey, who still owns this historic machine.

The 1921 season was much enlivened by the appearance at the track of Count Louis Zborowski, who had a passion for extremely large motor-cars, which he caused to be run together in an apparently extremely light-hearted way. The recipe was the quite simple one of an aero-engine in a very skimpy chassis. Zborowski had four of these in all, of which the first three were called "Chitty-Bang-Bang" I, II, and III. For some mysterious reason the fourth, last, and largest was called the Higham Special. Even if they never attained exceptionally high speeds such cars were extremely colourful and much beloved by the public. In the late twenties the giants were gradually edged out by the timid management and Brooklands, as a spectacle, became very much the poorer. As other people besides Zborowski had similar ideas of building a racing car, there are quite a number of more or less improbable hybrids containing aero-engines and these are invariably said to be the veritable "Chitty-Bang-Bang". Probably no one but W. Boddy, the Editor of *Motor Sport*, knows the truth of the matter. He, too, has recorded the full and detailed history of Brooklands in a fascinating three-volume study, supplemented by a further book on the 200-mile races organised there by the Junior Car Club, and to these the reader is most cordially recommended for a full account of this remarkable chapter in the history of motor racing.

As a foil to Zborowski's monsters and the V-twelve Sunbeam were ex-Grand Prix cars, and again, very ordinary touring cars, stripped of removable equipment and very slightly tuned. Among these, in 1921, was the Austin heavy twenty of F. Scriven. Yet this leisurely car with its very ordinary 3·6-litre side-valve engine used to lap at nearly 85 m.p.h., and a works car with a single-seater body could lap at 94½ m.p.h. Frazer-Nash's V-twin G.N. was going round at 85 m.p.h., while apparently fairly standard A.C. and Hillman chassis with very narrow bodies could manage 89 m.p.h. This year also saw the first appearance in competition of a 3-litre Bentley, lapping at 87 m.p.h., while the fastest lap of the year was put up by K. Lee Guinness, on the V-twelve

Sunbeam, at 120 m.p.h. In this year, too, the Junior Car Club organised the first of its famous series of 2000-mile races, which was won by Segrave on a 1½-litre Talbot-Darracq at 88·8 m.p.h.

Record-breaking also got into its swing again and thereafter it was difficult to visit the track without finding some record-breaking attempt or other in progress. Among others, a special 1½-litre A.C. traversed a flying-start half-mile at 105·14 m.p.h. and covered 94·7 miles in one hour.

1922 saw the arrival of Parry Thomas, who was to become the outstanding personality at Brooklands during the middle twenties, and whose intimate knowledge of the track was perhaps equalled only, a decade later, by John Cobb's. He had designed a super-luxury car for the Leyland company, which is described in the appropriate chapter, but which proved, in his hands, to be also one of the most successful cars ever run at Brooklands (they were still competing successfully until 1936, when the last of them blew up in a tremendously dramatic style). The standard cars would do 90 m.p.h. but Thomas soon had his circulating at 115 m.p.h. Again, at the opposite end of the scale came the Summers brothers, running a bull-nosed Morris "Cowley" and a "Silver Ghost" Rolls-Royce.

An important event on the social side was the presence of the Duke of York (later George VI) at the May meeting. At other times the track was honoured by the Prince of Wales and his younger brother Prince George, so regrettably killed during the war in a flying accident, who was a most enthusiastic motorist and who owned a superb "Speed Six" Bentley.

Much excitement and consternation were caused when "Chitty" and the Count got out of control and passed through the timing hut, at high speed, going backwards. John Duff's 1908 F.I.A.T. also exploded in quite the grand manner when one of the two enormous cylinder blocks parted company with the rest of the engine and departed with dramatic suddenness, taking the bonnet with it.

J. A. Joyce's A.C. was the first 1½-litre car to lap at over 100 m.p.h., its best speed being 103·54 m.p.h. S. F. Edge, who had first used the track for record-breaking in 1907 for his remarkable 24-hour single-handed drive on the Napier, broke his own record driving a 5·7 litre Mercedes-engined Spyker. His average for the 24 hours was 74·27 m.p.h. K. Lee Guinness established a world speed record on the big Sunbeam, this being the last occasion on which Brooklands was used for this purpose. Indeed such records involved some fairly hazardous motoring, since the longest straight was in fact only so for half a mile, so that the driver had to start negotiating the banking immediately after the end of the timed section. This was particularly unpleasant on the reverse run, when lapping anticlockwise. The mean speeds recorded by Lee Guinness were 137·15 m.p.h. for the kilometre and 130·48 m.p.h. for the mile, showing that he actually had to slow up at the end of the mile. The fastest kilometre run was 140 m.p.h. A standing-start mile was also covered at 98·54 m.p.h. and the fastest lap of the year at 123·39 m.p.h. It was this car which Campbell afterwards bought and which, in 1925, took the world speed record at Pendine at 150·86 m.p.h.

1923 saw the appearance of Zborowski's Higham Special, which had a V-twelve Liberty engine with a capacity of 27 litres and was thus the largest car even to be raced at Brooklands, although never with much success. It was geared to do 100 m.p.h. at only 1200 r.p.m. Giant hybrids were now on the track in considerable numbers and another newcomer was the 1908 F.I.A.T., resurrected after its disastrous disintegration, by E. A. D. Eldridge. Suitably lengthened (it was said, with part of the chassis of a London omnibus), he put in it a 21·7-litre F.I.A.T. six-cylinder engine and in this form it still exists, in running order, but its present owner does not apparently care to drive it. In its new guise the F.I.A.T. got the name "Mephistopheles".

Thomas had streamlined the Leyland and carried out the fastest lap of the year at 120 m.p.h.; a 3-litre Bentley lapped at 103 m.p.h.; and Gordon England, in an Austin Seven, covered 100 miles at 64·79 m.p.h. and completed an hour at 73·9 m.p.h.

In 1924 the local residents brought an action against the track authorities on account of noise, and thereafter the well-known "Brooklands Silencer" had to be worn, which undoubtedly caused a certain amount of back-pressure and so handicapped performance. On the racing side, Thomas had made further improvements to the Leyland and again recorded the fastest lap of the year and established a new lap record at 127·7 m.p.h. Joyce, continuing his efforts with the Special A.C., made it the first 1½-litre car to over 100 miles in an hour, the actual distance being 104.19 miles. An impressive newcomer was a Lanchester "40" with a long, high, flat-sided, narrow single-seater body. This was used by the Rapson Company for testing their tyres, which then had a very good reputation. The engine was almost standard, but with a 3·3 to 1 final drive it once covered 400 miles at 99 m.p.h.

This year saw the last appearance of Count Zborowski, for he was killed driving a Mercedes in the Monza Grand Prix.

1924 was the last year of outer circuit racing, which was beginning somewhat to lose its appeal. Once again the Junior Car Club took the initiative and introduced artifical "chicanes" in the course of its 200-mile race for 1925 and also for the first of its exciting one-hour high-speed trials, always known as the "Hour Blind".

Undoubtedly the most exciting event of 1925 was a 10-lap match between Thomas on the Leyland and Eldridge on "Mephistopheles". Both cars were driven to the limit and almost exactly matched in performance. Swaying and snaking as they came off the bankings, *The Autocar* wrote "a more horrid spectacle to sit and watch has probably never been seen in motor racing". Both cars lost a tread on the last lap, and Thomas won by a narrow margin. He had now further improved the streamlining of the Leyland and finally set the lap record at 129·36 m.p.h., which was to stand for two years. In this form so efficient was the streamlining that the Leyland gave a fuel consumption of 15 m.p.g. at 110 m.p.h. Its maximum engine speed was still no more than 3000 r.p.m. The Rapson Lanchester was also active and driven by Thomas made a lap at 109½ m.p.h.

On the record-breaking side, attacks on the test hill (a short, very sharp gradient, not forming part of the circuit) became a popular sport and Frazer-Nash and the G.N. were constant contestants for the record. As previously stated, in this year Campbell took the world speed record at Pendine on the V-twelve Sunbeam at 150·86 m.p.h., and it is remarkable to consider that the ultimate in land speed should stand at a bare 25 m.p.h. above the maximum of the 2-litre formula Grand Prix cars of the time, whereas now, despite the great advance in the performance of modern Grand Prix cars, the world speed record stands at least at twice their maximum.

In 1926 Thomas bought the Higham Special and prepared it for an attempt on the world speed record, after which it was said to develop about 550 b.h.p. at 2000 r.p.m., and duly captured the record at Pendine, the kilometre at 171·01 m.p.h. and the mile at 170·624 m.p.h. In its new hands the Higham was renamed "Babs".

At Brooklands Thomas produced his "flat-iron" special with a 1½-litre straight-eight engine conforming to the current Grand Prix formula and it performed fairly well in his hands, although subsequently it was always most temperamental. When he entered "Babs" at Brooklands, after his success at Pendine, there was tremendous excitement, but although the car was spectacular enough, it could never lap as fast as the more manageable Leyland.

The Junior Car Club ran a production car race with capacity classes for 750 c.c., and 1500 c.c. A. Frazer-Nash won the 1½-litre, but the Salmson which won the middle class was actually faster. Needless to say, an Austin Seven won the 750-c.c. class. But the event of the year was the running at Brooklands of a full international Grand Prix, which was won by the wonderful new Delages which had such a distinguished career over a full decade. In this their first serious outing the exhaust manifold and pipe came so close to the drivers' feet that they suffered untold discomfort and could only endure a short spell at the wheel. In the following year the cylinder-head design was altered so that the exhaust and inlet manifolds changed sides.

In 1927 Thomas was again out early with "Babs" at Pendine to beat his own world speed record, but on March 3rd a driving chain broke and killed him instantly, so that the season's racing at Brooklands was very much the poorer by the loss of this great driver. Indeed, the giant cars were now gradually disappearing, while lap speeds in general were not appreciably higher than they had been just after the war. At such speeds outer circuit racing was an unimpressive spectacle. However, John Cobb now took over the Leyland, and another name still seen in Vintage racing at the wheel of his 1914 T.T. Sunbeam was Sir Francis Samuelson, who must have been racing for much longer than any driver still in active competition.

A Grand Prix was again held at Brooklands, and was again won by Delage with their now reorganised exhaust arrangements.

There was no new lap record, but in 1928 a star rose in the shape of Kaye Don, on a supercharged V-twelve 4-litre Sunbeam. This car had for a short time, before Thomas, held the world speed record, being by far the smallest car ever to do so. Don at last beat Thomas's lap record with a magnificent circuit at 130·76 m.p.h. There were also on the track two 5-litre six-cylinder Delages which consistently lapped at about 120 m.p.h., while a new driver at Brooklands, on a 1922 T.T. Vauxhall, was Tim Carson, now the popular and efficient Secretary of the Vintage Sports-Car Club.

1929 saw the first appearance at Brooklands of the V-twelve 10½-litre Delage which had briefly held the world speed record in 1923. John Cobb was at the wheel and in his hands, and subsequently Oliver Bertram's, the car was long one of the highlights of Brooklands. That the giants were not extinct was shown by the appearance of C. D. Wallbank driving a 1913 21½-litre four-cylinder Benz (which still fortunately exists in first-class order).

Another potent newcomer was the special supercharged 4½-litre Bentley of Sir Henry Birkin, which had many a spectacular struggle with Cobb's Delage, the Delage being quicker off the mark, while the Bentley had a higher maximum speed. Undoubtedly the most successful driver of the year was Don on the Grand Prix and 4-litre Sunbeams.

The Junior Car Club had yet another new and bright idea, in the form of a 24-hour race (divided into two daylight sections, the cars being locked away for the night), which was won by a 1½-litre Alfa Romeo. The Brooklands Racing Drivers Club also staged the first of its 500-mile races. It might be thought that so long a race on the outer circuit would be a tedious spectacle,

213

but this was far from being the case, since the race was run on the basis of a capacity handicap, the small cars starting first, and a considerable time elapsing before the largest were away. With the good system in use of indicating race progress, it was fairly easy to follow how the handicap was working and extremely exciting to speculate whether the big cars were going fast enough to overtake their handicap. Also the sight of them constantly sweeping past the small fry, high up on the banking, was always most stirring. Moreover, being always the last event of the year, people drove with considerable abandon, being able to look forward to an uninterrupted winter in which to make good the ravages of this most searching race, which was the fastest in the world, being run at higher speeds even than the American Indianapolis. At different times cars of all sizes won the race, which showed the efficiency of the handicapping system, but on this first occasion the winners were J. D. Barclay and F. C. Clement on an unblown 4½-litre Bentley at 107·32 m.p.h.

1930, the last year of the Vintage decade, saw the innovation of an excellent new sort of race which rapidly eclipsed the outer circuit in popularity. This was known as the "Mountain Circuit", as it encircled a large mound in the spectator's enclosure, up which ran the test hill, and which was known as "the Mountain". Unlike the outer circuit, which was always circulated anticlockwise, the Mountain races were run in a clockwise direction. The old finishing straight was by this time hardly ever used for finishes, since, with the greatly increased speed of the fastest cars and their generally tentative braking arrangements, they tended to be unable to stop, passed rapidly up the banking, and disappeared dramatically over the top – the drop into the surrounding terrain being at least 25 feet. But in the Mountain Circuit the finishing straight quite came into its own. The cars drove up this straight, which being over half a mile long, allowed high speeds to be obtained, at the end of which they joined the Members' Banking and rapidly came into view again on the other side of the "Mountain", at very high speed, soon to brake violently for the acute hairpin which led them back into the finishing straight. The track being so wide, different drivers took the hairpin on a great variety of lines, some wide, some close, and some clearly unrehearsed, so that exciting incidents were plentiful. The first Mountain race was won by that great driver and sportsman Lord Howe, driving a type 43 Bugatti – a *marque* to which he has always been greatly attached – and he set the lap record at 64·4 m.p.h. It is interesting to note that the lap record was ultimately put up to no less than 84·31 m.p.h. by Raymond Mays, in his E.R.A., who thus holds it for all time. The total lap measured only one and one-fifth miles.

It was in 1930 that the organisers began actively to discourage cars more than ten years old, and while metal-fatigue was undoubtedly a serious factor with the concrete as rough as it had by then become, by their action they robbed the outer circuit of its most spectacular features. Among those turned away were the valiant old 1912 "Vieux Charles Trois", which had become an accepted feature of the landscape, but the 1913 21½-litre Benz of Cyril Paul retained its ticket, and put in some useful laps at around 113 m.p.h. Cobb was prominent on the big Delage, while Birkin took the lap record at 135·33 m.p.h. on the blown Bentley, only to have it taken from him by Don on the 4-litre Sunbeam at 137·58 m.p.h. This, incidentally, stood until 1932, when Birkin got it back again with the Bentley at 137·96 m.p.h. The ultimate record was established in 1935 by John Cobb on his 24-litre Napier-Railton at 143·44 m.p.h. just 20 m.p.h. faster than Lee Guinness's record of thirteen years before.

A car lapping at over 120 m.p.h. on the outer circuit was always a most inspiring sight, and demanded a really brave and skilful driver. Both coming off and going on to the bankings required the most accurate placing, and even the slight kink opposite the beginning of the finishing straight, where the Vickers sheds came right up to the edge of the track, became an alarming hazard.

So ended Brooklands racing during the Vintage decade, but of course the track went on, and the only further innovation of note was the laying out of the "Campbell Circuit" for the 1937 season. This was supposed to simulate road-racing conditions, consisting of a twisty course inside the outer circuit, but it was a poor affair and unsatisfactory from the spectators' point of view.

During the last war the track was, of course, under requisition, although cars occasionally appeared on the circuit. Probably the last car to do so was Clutton's 1908 Grand Prix Itala, which he and Laurence Pomeroy took there during June 1940, when the Byfleet Banking had already been broken through, so that the whole circuit was no longer available. It was, too, the only car for many years to have used the circuit without a Brooklands silencer, and the slow beat of its four big cylinders certainly sounded most impressive round the banking – the officials who allowed it on to track were past caring about the long-standing injunction against unsilenced cars!

After the war the question of reopening the track naturally came under discussion. Undoubtedly there were grave difficulties in doing so, but the majority of the shareholders, led by Sir Malcolm Campbell, who decided to sell out, were greatly criticised for thus throwing away Locke King's great bequest to the nation. Not least among those critics was his widow, Dame Ethel Locke King, who, even at her then great age, had no illusions about the seriousness of what was happening. The motor industry, by contrast, who could easily have redeemed the situation, were all apathy. They were still content to suppose that they could go on selling cars at the dreadfully low standard of the thirties. Only under pointed stimulation from the more informed quarters of the motoring press did they realise, all too late, that to compete in the world market their cars must be tested to destruction under all circumstances. After the loss of Brooklands, and until they much later established their own test circuit elsewhere, this was not possible without going abroad.

So, sadly, ended the great venture of Brooklands, after forty years of existence.

SHELSLEY WALSH

"Sprints", whether on the flat or uphill, have always been popular both in England and abroad. Their main characteristic is that only one car runs at a time. In England the oldest and most famous sprint hill-climb was the difficult 1000-yard course at Shelsley Walsh, near Worcester.

The Midland Automobile Club first ran their hill-climb at Shelsley Walsh in 1905, when a chain-driven Daimler made fastest time of the day in 77·6 seconds. From that day onwards Shelsley has been the premier English hill-climb, and the annual event there has always produced extremely skilful and exciting driving. The story during the Vintage period of is the greatest interest, for it saw the ousting of the production fast tourer by the earliest of the amazing breed of "Shelsley Specials", which in their turn were to give way to the out-and-out racing car as contestants for the "fastest time of day" honours. It is also arguable that it produced the best spectacles, for cars were not yet so fast that they could not be driven flat out all the way; certainly high and heavy cars entered in the early period required a considerable amount of brute force on the corners, as may be confirmed by contemporary photographs. None the less, only 12·8 seconds was taken off the record between June 1913 and 1930, a great tribute to Higginson's celebrated ascent in his primeval 30/98 Vauxhall. It is worth considering in outline the Shelsley history of our period, for the competing cars are not only interesting in themselves, but represent the entry in many lesser hill-climbs.

1920 saw a miscellaneous collection of fast tourers old and new, from Vandervell's very fast 1914 25/50 Talbot to the prototype of the new Straker-Squire Six, driven by Kensington Moir. The venue was always the resort of unsuccessful racing cars, and one of the ill-fated 5-litre Indianapolis Sunbeams made fastest time of day in the hands of Bird, recording 58·6 seconds. The light-car class was dominated, as it was to be for several years, by Frazer-Nash in "Kim II", the extraordinary 1087-c.c. V-twin G.N. This car made the first of several sensational runs to record 60·2 seconds on a damp and loose surface. It was, however, beaten on formula by Ash on a Speed Model Hillman, who took 118·4 seconds. The formula system as then favoured led to considerable ill-feeling until it was modified a few years later; but it did once produce the unparalleled spectacle of Waite winning on formula by a climb in an Austin Twenty tourer with no less than seven up, a dead weight of nearly 2½ tons.

217

1921 saw Higginson's 55·2 seconds broken by Bird in the Sunbeam with 52·2, while two cars also beat record time. These were Park, in the 1914 4½-litre Grand Prix Vauxhall, and Frazer-Nash, who made Kim's best time ever at 54·8 seconds, a really formidable performance. This year, for the first time, one ascent only was permitted.

In 1922 no records fell, but Park, this time in the new 3-litre T.T. Vauxhall, made fastest time of day in 53·8 seconds; Kim made an extremely dangerous run, bursting a tyre and buckling two wheels to continue and record 64·2 seconds! This year also saw one of the rare appearances of a Rolls-Royce "Silver Ghost" tourer, driven by Summers, which recorded a creditable 68 seconds. (At this time the criterion of a really snappy sporting outfit was an ascent in standard trim under 60 seconds.) The first Austin Seven also sped up the hill "like a little thoroughbred", to quote a contemporary, recording 89·8 seconds and receiving tremendous applause. Shelsley was always a playground of the 30/98, which it suited very well, and standard touring models were much in evidence; and this year their fastest run was by Humphrey Cook in 56·8 seconds.

In 1923 fastest time was put up by Raymond Mays, a young man from Lincolnshire driving his "Cordon Bleu" Brescia Bugatti specially tuned for the occasion. He was prevented from taking the record for technical reasons, but was subsequently to hold it on no less than five occasions. His time, in a characteristically polished drive, was 51·9 seconds, while Park in the T.T. Vauxhall could do no better than 52·7.

1924 was an extremely interesting year, the record barely falling to Cyril Paul in a 2-litre twin-camshaft Beardmore, a highly advanced Scottish sporting machine of which too little was heard. He recorded 50·5 seconds against Mays at 50·82. "Bunny", the old Aston Martin, excelled herself in the hand of E. R. Hall, producing 52·6 seconds, while Park took a standard four-seater Vauxhall up in 53·6. This quite staggering time was exactly one second slower than Cook on one of the Tourist Trophy cars from the same factory. Shelsley was never really the *forte* of the Bentley, though a 3-litre two-seater climbed in 59·4 seconds, and Moir put up 56 seconds in one of the Tourist Trophy cars.

1925, a wet day, saw no records but the unusual sight of Segrave, new to the hill, making fastest time of day in one of the 1924 Grand Prix Sunbeams, in 53·8 seconds.

In 1926 the record fell for the first time to B. H. Davenport on the G.N.-based "Spider". This extraordinary car, almost the first of a long line of Shelsley specials, was basically the engine from the 1920 racing G.N. "Mowgli" built into a lightened G.N. chassis. An observer described it as "an engine with four wheels attached by a few connecting shafts and drilled girders"; but nevertheless it began its domination of the hill by an ascent in 48·8 seconds. Mays, this time driving the Tourist Trophy Vauxhall, also ran within the record in 49·4 seconds. Another noteworthy climb was that of Mucklow in a Frazer-Nash in 55 seconds, while a Renault 45 saloon made 69 seconds. Most of the Austin Sevens beat a four-seater Clyno (79·6 seconds).

For 1927 Mays drove one of the supercharged 2-litre Mercedes, but this time of 48·2 seconds was not enought to beat Davenport's second record of 47·8 seconds; while in 1928 this unbelievable two-cylinder machine took its third record at 46·28. A 33/180 Mercedes driven by Clay produced 53·6 seconds, beating Hall's elderly 30/98 four-seater by only a very narrow margin.

For 1929 there was the largest Shelsley entry ever, with 190 competitors, and Mays at last regained the honours driving the 1922 Vauxhall Tourist Trophy car. This had undergone tremendous modifications, having twin rear wheels, Dewandre servo brakes, and a supercharger; although barely recognisable as a Vauxhall it was beautifully turned out in cream and black and renamed the Vauxhall Villiers. It took the record at 45·6 seconds. Lord Howe made an impressive ascent in his newly acquired 38/250 Mercedes, which had recently won the Ulster T.T., in 47·6 seconds, a very fast time for so unsuitable a car.

In 1930 Shelsley was included in ten contests for the European hill-climb championship. This accounted for the presence of Hans Stuck, whose Austro-Daimler reduced the record considerably to 42·8 seconds; this was only improved by a further 6·2 seconds in the ensuing quarter-century. Striking though it was, it was overshadowed by the final Vintage climb of Davenport – still, be it remembered, with no front-wheel brakes – in 44·6 seconds; well within the record. This was surely a fitting end to a fascinating decade. Davenport and the "Spider" are still active at sprint events.

Shelsley Walsh is still held, but is rivalled in popularity and importance by the Bugatti Owners Club hill at Prescott, near Cheltenham. But it is still a much-coveted honour to hold the Shelsley record.

LONG-DISTANCE RELIABILITY TRIALS

A peculiarly British habit was the organisation of long-distance reliability trials open to all comers. Although by the Vintage period these really proved very little about the motor-car and could not include any tremendously difficult sections, they were always extremely well supported. They deserve mention as the mildest and one of the most popular forms of motoring competition in the 1920s. The three classics, all organised by the M.C.C. and all legacies from before the first war, were the London–Exeter, the London–Land's End, and the London–Edinburgh.

These were run at Christmas, Easter, and Whitsun respectively and attracted a wide variety of car entries, from teams unofficially sponsored by manufacturers with works drivers, to private entries of the most diverse and sometimes quite unsuitable machines, such as Bugattis or Rolls-Royces. It was almost obligatory for the aspiring light-car maker to sponsor a team, and many of their best drivers appeared with great consistency, such as Hill (Rhode), Tatlow (Lea-Francis), Chinery (Gwyne), and Cocker (Clyno). The contemporary pictures of these little cars valiantly struggling up Beggar's Roost have a tremendous period charm and all credit is due to their intrepid conductors. It should be remembered that until the very end of our period a speed limit of 20 m.p.h. was universally applied by law (though it was, of course, universally neglected in common usage), so that any machine, however slow, had an equal chance of success. None the less, awards were frequently lost for early arrivals at controls.

In the early period the G.N. was perhaps the most popular

entry for these trials. With the advent of the Austin Seven, cheap, light, and low-geared, the performance of the heavier small cars was made to look a little inadequate and the emphasis shifted to light sporting machines such as the Riley Nine and Frazer-Nash. Indeed, with its solid axle, easily altered ratios, and low unsprung weight, the Nash was very much at home in contests of this sort. Also, where speed was of little consequence the Trojan could safely be entered and towards the late Vintage period it was by no means uncommonly found among the winners of "Golds", the best awards. The low-speed torque of its curious engine rendered it a sure if slow climber and Trojan drivers were frequently to be seen anxiously watching a hand-kerchief dropped outside the car to satisfy themselves that forward motion was in fact being maintained.

All three of the classic trials had their own character. The Exeter, which took place on Boxing Day, was perhaps the least interesting, with no real problems *en route*. The Edinburgh, a 24-hour contest, was by far the most popular and usually attracted some four hundred entries, although of course a high proportion of these consisted of motor-cycles (in 1920, for instance, there were no less than 320 of these to 63 cars). In view of the extremely mixed field no particularly revealing or insurmountable sections were included and the event was really more a test of the drivers than their cars. From time to time the event included a few observed sections on steep and narrow tracks and watersplashes in Yorkshire, and in the early years an ascent of Kirkstone was required. In general, however, the severest problem was for the one driver to keep awake while maintaining the stipulated 20-m.p.h. average. It was not custom-ary to go to sleep at the wheel much before Carlisle, but by Gretna Green it was accepted that many drivers would lose their awards by so doing.

The Land's End was in many ways the most diverting of these trials, as indeed it still is. It was certainly the toughest, for it included the dreaded climbs of Porlock and Lynton, which were by no means as well surfaced as they are today. Although charabancs now roar up them daily and even the family motorist takes them in bottom gear with but a slight moistening of the lips, they were by no means easy meat to the underpowered small cars of the Vintage period. It was always problematical, for instance, whether a standing start could be effected on the steep part of Porlock as demanded. The unsurfaced hills such as Bluehills Mine presented even more formidable problems, with the spectators crowding on to the loose surface and the ambulance waiting expectantly below. None the less, the proportion of failures was surprisingly low, which was appropriate enough for such essentially amateur entertainments.

Postscript

LOOKING back over this book, it emerges that the Vintage decade of automobile design was one of great beginnings and achievements, consolidation, and gradual decline.

What distinguishes all worthwhile Vintage cars is their pronounced personality. Sometimes it is not a very good personality, and sometimes it is distinctly eccentric; but even a bad personality is better than no personality at all. Among their many and grievous faults, it was their utter lack of personality which so dismally characterised most cars of the thirties.

This was due to two things. Firstly, the designer gave way to the committee; and secondly, hand finish and fitting gave way to mass production. Both of these estranged the designer from the driver. In a Bugatti the car itself is a constant bond between them. Bugatti had an overwhelming conviction of how a car should behave and of what it should look like, and through his largely hand-made and hand-fitted products he was able to cause these ideals to be materialised most exactly. A mass-produced Bugatti might have roughly the same handling qualities, but it would certainly not radiate Ettore's very personality as does the actual hand-finished article.

Even when a designer such as Pomeroy had strictly utilitarian views about external finish of the mechanical parts, he still impressed his personality very strongly on his products by their handling qualities. It is because of this that a 30/98 Vauxhall is so attractive; the general appearance of the car is a contributing factor, but under the bonnet there is little visual appeal to the connoisseur.

Thus the spread of mass-production methods in the thirties not only made it almost impossible for the designer to impress his personality upon his cars, but he had not yet discovered the art of making them fulfil his ideals of how a car ought to behave. Moreover, the ascendancy of the salesman over the designer generally precluded him from even trying to secure the fulfilment of those ideals. So it was that a generation grew up who had no proper standards of criticism as to what a car should be and how

223

it should behave, and it seemed likely that the car of real quality (as opposed to superficial ostentation) was a thing of the past.

It was under such conditions that the Vintage Sports-Car Club was founded and the highest standards of automobile criticism were kept alive. It is due to the few people, both within and without the Club, who retained a clear picture of what a motor-car should be and do that we are once more witnessing a general and increasing improvement. Not only is the designer getting the upper hand in the more far-seeing concerns, but he has so far mastered the technique of mass production that he can, once more, fairly closely impress his personality and ideals upon the finished product.

In this trend we believe that the Vintage movement has played an important part. But however good the mass-produced car may become, and however completely it may out-perform the Vintage car, the materialisation of the personalities of such great men as Royce, Bugatti, Pomeroy, Bentley, Morris, Roesch, Lancia, Delage, Coatalen, and a host of others, coupled with the aesthetic pleasure of the hand-finished instrument, will inevitably hold an undying appeal to the true connoisseur, be he rich or poor.

Index

225